The Descendants of John Muss & Elizabeth Ceise

Exploring Four Generations

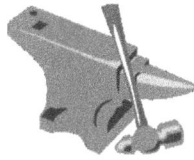

1824 to Present

Bullitt County, Kentucky and Beyond

by
Mark Douglas Browning

Prussian Coat of Arms

This book and others written by this author are available for purchase from Lulu Enterprises, Inc. at http://www.lulu.com, or directly from the author at mark@myfamilypedigree.com.

Proofing and Family Information
Patricia "Pat" Ann East Carby
Sandra Rae Coyle Browning

Bullitt County Genealogical Society Research Assistance
Robert Cline
Martha Lynn "Lynn" Eddington
Wilma Jean Lemons

My Family Pedigree, Book One.
First Edition.
Printed in the United States of America

ISBN: 978-0-9851755-0-4
Library of Congress Control Number: 2012933208

Dedication

This book is dedicated to my wife, Jessica Tyler Frohme Browning. Without her desire to get into genealogical research and start me down the path of investigating my ancestors, I would not have been able to create this book. Additionally, her unfaltering support of my work as I spent late nights researching and writing did not go unnoticed. Thank you my love.

Foreword

The author descends from John Muss, and compiled this information through years of research on his own family history. The author's lineage is as follows:

1. John Muss & Elizabeth "Eliza" M Ceise/Cleise/Ceith/Seice
2. Son, John Carroll Muss & Anna "Annie" Eliza Hopewell
3. Daughter, Anna "Annie" Adress Muss & Orville Emmitt Carby, Sr.
4. Son, Orville Emmitt "J. R." Carby, Jr. & Georgia Lee Griffith
5. Daughter, Sandra Rae Carby Coyle & Haburn/Hayburn Rube Browning, Jr.
6. Son, Mark Douglas Browning & Jessica Tyler Frohme

Book Cover:
The picture, taken by Mark Douglas Browning, that serves as the background on the front and back covers of this book is the Knob Creek Union Church that is located on Kentucky Highway 44 in Cupio, Bullitt County, Kentucky. This was the church that was attended by the first generation, second generation, and some of the third generation Muss family members. Many of the Muss family members are buried in the cemetery that is located beside and behind this church. The oldest section of the cemetery is located at the far back of the property. Most of the burials in that old section date back to the 1800s.

The pictures of John Muss and Elizabeth Ceise shown on the back cover of the book were provided by Lyle Raymond Cook and to Karla Denise Ezell Cook.

Descendants of William "Willie" J. Cook:
Special thanks to Karla Denise Ezell Cook for supplying information regarding the descendants of William "Willie" J. Cook

Introduction

I had been interested in pursuing genealogical research for several years prior to my wife getting a subscription to ancestry.com. Once she got a subscription and I started my research, it was extremely difficult to put my research down. I have always enjoyed working on jigsaw puzzles, Sudoku, and other brain teaser type activities so I guess that my fascination with genealogical research should have come as no surprise. I take a great amount of pleasure in solving the puzzles of my ancestors' relationships. It seems that the more difficult that the puzzle is, the more interested I am in it. I always enjoy coming across new finds that no other researchers seem to have found out about yet. Most importantly, I am thrilled to share the results of my research with others. This book is intended to share those results in a public forum, with the hope that my investigation findings will help someone else with their own research.

After several years of researching, I decided that it was time to write a book about one of my ancestral lines. The problem that I was having was deciding upon which ancestral line to write my first book about. That decision became easy when I was approached by Robert Cline with the Bullitt County Genealogical Society in the Fall of 2011 about my Muss family. He was in the process of a multi-year project that encompassed writing about the residents that could be found in the 1860 Bullitt County, Kentucky census. His next project was a 5 page section in the society newsletter that would describe the descendants of John Muss. John Muss was my great-great-great grandfather.

Robert had found my postings on Find a Grave and Ancestry.com and wrote to ask me for input to the Bullitt County Genealogical Society newsletter. I took this as my starting point for writing the book that follows. I would like to extend a special thanks to Robert Cline for getting me started down the path and encouraging the authoring of my own book. Once started on my path to publication, Wilma Jean Lemons and Martha Lynn "Lynn" Eddington from the Bullitt County Genealogical Society helped me significantly with numerous research requests from the newspapers local to the Louisville, Kentucky area. I would like to extend a very special thanks to Wilma and Lynn for their unwavering support for this project.

It is also important to note the photographic contributions that were made by Karla Cook. I connected with Karla late in the book writing process, and greatly appreciate her giving nature. One thing that had always bothered me as I wrote this book was that no pictures of this side of my family had been passed down to me. While I was certain that there were pictures of the Muss family out there, it was apparent that none of those rare old pictures had been passed down my branch of the family. Karla Cook had those very important missing pictures that made this book complete. Thank you so very much Karla. Your contributions will always be remembered.

Mark Douglas Browning

Table of Contents

Generation No. 1: The Immigrants

1. JOHN[1] MUSS was born September 1824 in Schuschkehmen, East Prussia (GPS Coordinates: 54.489598, 22.106209) and died March 23, 1904 in Dayton, Montgomery County, Ohio. He was the son of unknown parents at this time; however, it is possible that his mother was named Caroline since Carroll and Caroline were the names used for his second and third child. JOHN MUSS married ELIZABETH "ELIZA" M. CEISE/CLEISE/CEITH/SEICE about 1850 (possibly in Saint Louis, Missouri), daughter of unknown parents. ELIZABETH "ELIZA" M. CEISE/CLEISE/CEITH/SEICE was born April 28, 1828 in the Freistaat Bayern (Free State of Bavaria) and died March 07, 1891 in Bullitt County, Kentucky.

Notes for ELIZABETH "ELIZA" M. CEISE/CLEISE/CEITH/SEICE:
    Birth and death dates for Elizabeth Muss are based upon a headstone reading at Pauley Cemetery that was conducted on November 05, 2000 by Linda Blue.
    The death certificate for John Carroll Muss indicates that his mother was Elizabeth Ceith.
    The death certificate for George W. Muss indicates that his mother was Elizabeth Seice.
    The marriage license for Charles Muss and Lida Flanigan indicates that Charles' mother was Elizabeth Clase/Cleise.
    The Kingdom of Bavaria existed from 1806 to 1918, which is when ELIZABETH "ELIZA" M. CEISE/CLEISE/CEITH/SEICE lived there. During this time, the European state was ruled by a constitution that established a bicameral parliament with a House of Lords and a House of Commons. Today, Bavaria is a state of Germany and is located in the southwest of Germany. It is the largest Bundesland (Federal State) within the Federal Republic of Germany, and shares international borders with Austria, the Czech Republic, and Switzerland (across Lake of Constance). Bavaria is divided into 7 Regierungsbezirke (Districts).

Picture of Elizabeth M. Ceise in her 40s
(Lyle Raymond Cook & Karla Denise Ezell Cook)

The above photo of Elizabeth Muss was most likely taken in the early to mid-1870s.

More about ELIZABETH "ELIZA" M. CEISE/CLEISE/CEITH/SEICE:
Burial: Pauley Cemetery which is located just inside the Bullitt County, Kentucky county line from Jefferson County, Kentucky at GPS Coordinates: 38.03560, -85.87610.
Death certificates were not required by the state of Kentucky when Elizabeth died and no death record can be found for her. It is

possible that a death record may exist in the archives at Knob Creek Church in Cupio, Bullitt County, Kentucky since this appears to be where the family regularly attended church.

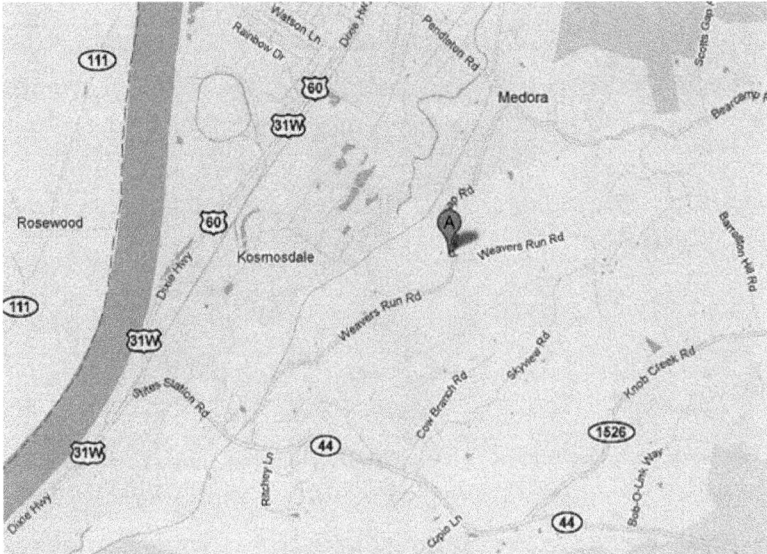

Location of Pauley Cemetery: Burial Place for Elizabeth Ceith Muss
(Google)

Notes for JOHN MUSS:

The town that John Muss was born in; Schuschkehmen, East Prussia; was part of the northern portion of East Prussia that is now located in the jurisdiction of Kaliningrad Oblast, Russia. This area was a Regierungsbezirk (government region) of the Prussian/German Empire and known as East Prussia from 1815 to 1945. The area of Kaliningrad Oblast is currently a federal subject of Russia (an oblast). The small town of Schuschkehmen is located southeast of Insterburg, East Prussia (modern day Chernyakhovsk, Kaliningrad Oblast, Russia); south of Gumbinnen, East Prussia (modern day Gusev, Kaliningrad Oblast, Russia); just south of Nemmersdorf, East Prussia (modern day Mayakovskoye, Kaliningrad Oblast, Russia); and north of Darkehen, East Prussia (modern day Ozyorsk, Kaliningrad Oblast, Russia).

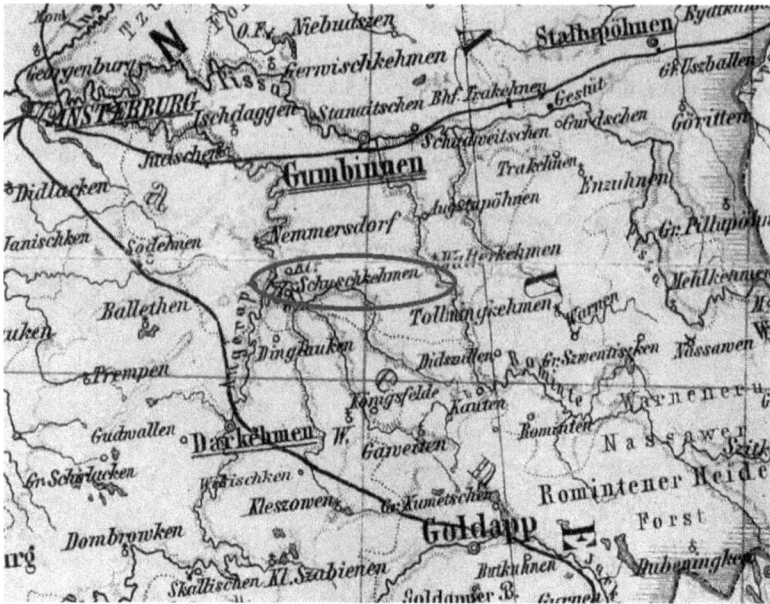

Schuschkehmen, East Prussia: Birth Place for John Muss (Ravenstein)

John Muss immigrated to the United States from his home in East Prussia around 1847 according to the 1900 census. The most likely record for his immigration is a passenger ship list record for J. B. Muss, a Blacksmith from Prussia. J. B. Muss can be found immigrating in to the United States on May 29, 1848 through New Orleans, Orleans Parish, Louisiana. J. B. Muss traveled on board the ship named Louisiana. The port of departure was Bremen, Germany and the port of arrival was New Orleans, Louisiana. J. B. Muss is listed as 22 years old at the time of his arrival in New Orleans. Unfortunatley, no concrete evidence can be found at this time to substantiate that this is the same John Muss who eventually settled in Bullitt County, Kentucky. If immigrant J. B. Muss is the patriarch of the Bullitt County, Kentucky Muss family, then he most likely traveled up the Mississippi River to first settle in Saint Louis, Missouri. Later John Muss and his wife must have traveled down the Mississippi River and then up the Ohio River to settle in Bullitt County, Kentucky. At the time of their travel, the bustling town of West Point, Kentucky (located on the Ohio River) would have been an ideal stopping point for them.

Immigration Record for J B Muss – Entry marked by arrow on right (National Archives and Records Administration, Passenger Lists of Vessels Arriving at New Orleans, Louisiana, 1820-1902)

The Bremen ship Louisiana was a 3-masted, square-rigged ship. Weighing 245 Commerzlasten/645 tons; size 37 x 9.9 x 5.8 meters (length x beam x depth of hold) that sailed from the Weser River (where the towns of Bremen, Bremerhaven, Vegesack, Elsfleth, and Brake are located) to the United States. She was built by H[ermann] F[riedrich] Ulrichs, of Vegesack/F"ahr, for the Bremen firm of D. H. Watjen & Co, for the New Orleans trade, and launched on August 26, 1846. Because of the poor navigation conditions between Vegesack and Bremerhaven, the vessel was not delivered to her owners in Bremerhaven until March 7, 1847 (apparently the vessel had been mired in a shallow place in the Weser, until the spring floods raised the water level high enough to float her). On April 12, 1847, Hermann Batjer, Master or Commander of the Ship Louisiana, made the maiden voyage to New Orleans. Until 1853, the ship served in the packet trade between Bremerhaven and New Orleans, carrying immigrants to the latter port and returning to Europe with cargos of cotton and tobacco. Even after 1853, the ship continued to carry immigrants to the United States, as the following voyages indicate:

1. July 23, 1853 - from Bremerhaven to New York with 237 passengers;
   November 02, 1853 - to London with wheat and flour;
2. December 06, 1853 - from Le Havre to Baltimore with 249 passengers;
   April 21, 1854 - to London with oilcake and flour;
3. May 06, 1854 - from Bremerhaven to New York with 245 passengers;
   November 27, 1854 - to Venice with tobacco;
4. March 12, 1855 - from Marseilles to Richmond, Virginia;
   September 09, 1855 - to Bremerhaven with tobacco

Batjer was succeeded as master by N. Ostermann, H. Deicke, and finally D. Muller, who commanded the Louisiana until she was "sold Norwegian", to Peter Lund, of Arendal, for 16,000 Taler, in 1860. She sailed under the Norwegian flag for only a short time, being lost in 1863; the particulars of her loss, however, are not known. (Pawlik)

The Bremen Ship Louisiana, 1862 (Sörvig)

Many immigrants from Prussia who came through New Orleans ended up in Missouri. The voyage across the Atlantic Ocean at this time took five to eight weeks depending upon the departure and arrival locations. It took longer to immigrate to the United States from the European region at this time because sailing ships were in predominant use. Steam ships, which reduced the travel time to about two or three weeks, were not in regular use until the late 1850s and early 1860s. It is likely that John was a part of the wave of Prussian political refugees that fled to the United States during 1848. This group became known as the "Forty-Eighters", and they were escaping the "Revolutions of 1848 in the German" also called the "March Revolution". It is very likely that John Muss started his journey from Prussia to the United States around March 13, 1848 during the height of the revolution and arrived in the United States on May 29, 1848.

John Muss can possibly be found in the 1850 Saint Louis, Saint Louis County, Missouri census boarding in a house full of German immigrants, and listed as a locksmith or blacksmith.

On May 09, 1950 a John Muss is found seeking allegiance to the United States at the Saint Louis Court of Common Pleas of Saint Louis City, Missouri in the naturalization records that can be found at the Missouri State Archives.

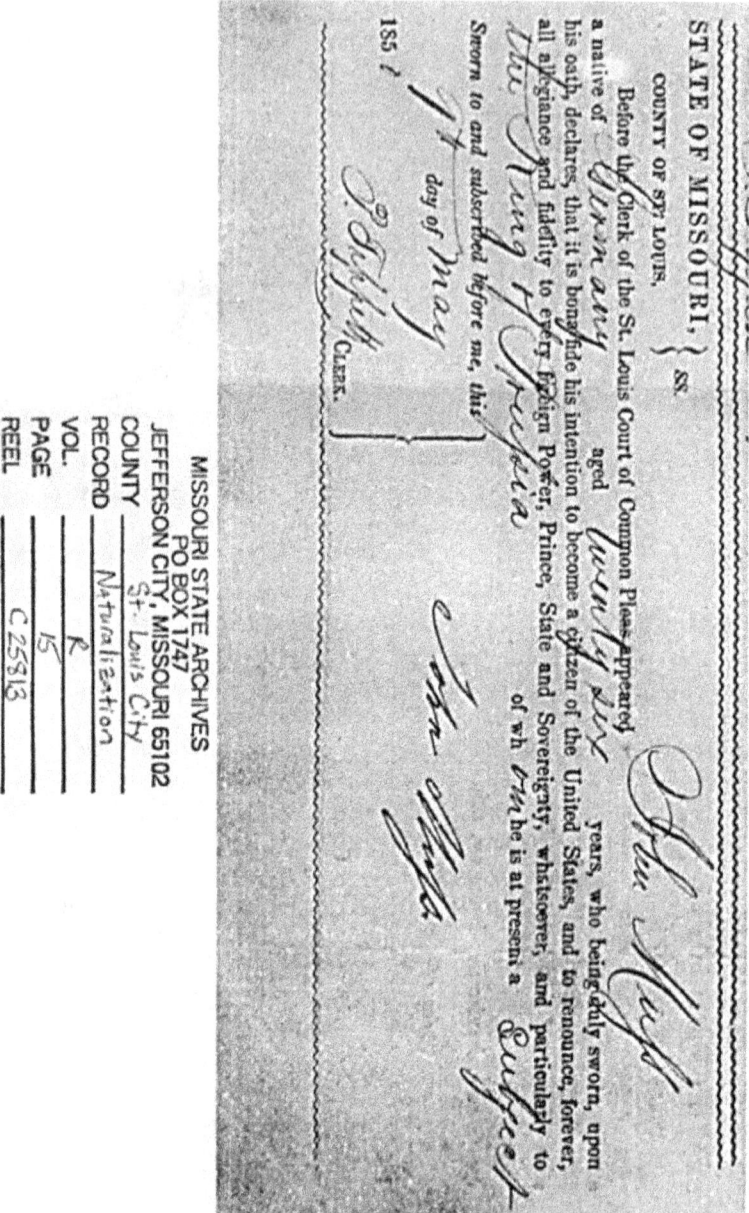

Naturalization Record for John Muss (Missouri State Archives)

In the 1860 Shepherdsville, Bullitt County, Kentucky census (conducted on June 01, 1860) John Muss, 35, is head of the household with Eliza, 30, Kate, 9, John, 7, Caroline, 5, George, 3 and Charles, 8/12.

John Muss enrolled in the Union Army as a Farrier or Blacksmith for three years on September 16, 1861, at Camp Anderson, Jefferson County, Kentucky and was mustered in at Camp Anderson on December 24, 1861. Military records give his age at the time of enlistment as 36 years. John first served in the Kentucky Blue Lick Infantry Company from September 18, 1861 to September 24, 1861 and was later assigned to the 4th Kentucky Cavalry, Company G, Union.

Civil War Enlistment Record for John Muss - 4th Kentucky Cavalry,
Company G
(National Archives and Records Administration, Compiled Service
Records of Volunteer Union Soldiers)

According to the Adjutant General's Report, from September 18,
1861 to September 24, 1861 John Muss was assigned to guarding the
bridge over the Salt River on the Louisville and Nashville Railroad

line. The Salt River is a 150 mile river in Kentucky that drains 2,920 square miles. The river runs east to west just south of Louisville, Kentucky. It begins near Danville, Kentucky, rising from the north slope of Persimmon Knob south of Kentucky 300 (Alum Springs Road) between Alum Springs and Wilsonville, and ends at the Ohio River near West Point, Kentucky.

842   ADJUTANT GENERAL'S REPORT.

ROLL OF CAPTAIN TRISLER'S COMPANY OF HOME GUARDS.
(Guarding Wilson Creek Bridge.)

No. of each grade.	NAME.	RANK.	From	To	No. of each grade.	NAME.	RANK.	From	To
1	A. J. Trisler	Captain	Nov. 14, '61	Dec. 16, '61	10	Gregg, Marshall	Private	Nov. 14, '61	Dec. 16, '61
1	Allen, James	Private	Nov. 31, '61	Nov. 26, '61	11	Hamilton, David	Private	Nov. 14, '61	Dec. 16, '61
2	Butt, Thomas	Private	Nov. 14, '61	Dec. 16, '61	12	Marlow, Thomas	Private	Nov. 14, '61	Nov. 23, '61
3	Burton, Newton	Private	Nov. 14, '61	Dec. 10, '61	13	Rummson, Chas.	Private	Nov. 14, '61	Dec. 16, '61
4	Buckley, Jerry	Private	Nov. 14, '61	Dec. 16, '61	14	Samuels, W., jr.	Private	Nov. 14, '61	Dec. 16, '61
5	Brown, Bernice	Private	Nov. 14, '61	Dec. 16, '61	15	Samuels, John	Private	Nov. 29, '61	Dec. 6, '61
6	Conklin, Owen	Private	Nov. 14, '61	Dec. 16, '61	16	Samuels, W., sr.	Private	Nov. 14, '61	Dec. 16, '61
7	Cope, Jerry	Private	Nov. 14, '61	Nov. 16, '61	17	Trisler, R. M.	Private	Nov. 14, '61	Dec. 16, '61
8	Degum, Henry	Private	Nov. 14, '61	Nov. 20, '61	18	Watson, Perry	Private	Nov. 14, '61	Nov. 27, '61
9	Essex, Stephen	Private	Nov. 14, '61	Nov. 19, '61					

ROLL OF BLUE LICK UNION BAND.
(Guarding Bridge over Salt River on Louisville and Nashville Railroad.)

No.	NAME.	RANK.	From	To	No.	NAME.	RANK.	From	To
1	Thomas L. Hogland	Captain	Sep. 18, '61	Sep. 24, '61	13	Foster, Wm. B.	Private	Sep. 18, '61	Sep. 20, '61
1	John L. Foster	1st Lieutenant	Sep. 18, '61	Sep. 20, '61	14	Foster, Harrison	Private	Sep. 18, '61	Sep. 20, '61
1	John S. Shoplaw	2d Lieutenant	Sep. 18, '61	Sep. 24, '61	15	Foster, F. M.	Private	Sep. 18, '61	Sep. 20, '61
1	Baxter, Wm.	Private	Sep. 18, '61	Sep. 23, '61	16	Hamilton, Richard	Private	Sep. 18, '61	Sep. 20, '61
2	Baxter, Jesse	Private	Sep. 18, '61	Sep. 33, '61	17	Hurling, N. K.	Private	Sep. 18, '61	Sep. 20, '61
3	Bryant, Wm.	Private	Sep. 18, '61	Sep. 22, '61	18	Muss, John	Private	Sep. 18, '61	Sep. 24, '61
4	Bolton, John	Private	Sep. 18, '61	Sep. 24, '61	19	Nettler, Joe	Private	Sep. 18, '61	Sep. 24, '61
5	Chaddic, John, jr	Private	Sep. 18, '61	Sep. 24, '61	20	Newton, Benj.	Private	Sep. 18, '61	Sep. 24, '61
6	Chaddic, Joseph	Private	Sep. 18, '61	Sep. 24, '61	21	Quick, Samuel	Private	Sep. 18, '61	Sep. 24, '61
7	Connell, James L.	Private	Sep. 18, '61	Sep. 24, '61	22	Quick, Richard	Private	Sep. 18, '61	Sep. 20, '61
8	Chaddic, John R.	Private	Sep. 18, '61	Sep. 23, '61	23	Quick, Jackson	Private	Sep. 18, '61	Sep. 20, '61
9	Chaddic, Wm.	Private	Sep. 18, '61	Sep. 24, '61	24	Stire, Henry	Private	Sep. 18, '61	Sep. 24, '61
10	Clark, Zed.	Private	Sep. 18, '61	Sep. 22, '61	25	Troutman, H	Private	Sep. 18, '61	Sep. 22, '61
11	Collier, Joseph	Private	Sep. 18, '61	Sep. 24, '61	26	Troutman, R	Private	Sep. 18, '61	Sep. 24, '61
12	Eckart, Wm.	Private	Sep. 18, '61	Sep. 24, '61					

ROLL OF FIELD AND STAFF.
(Police Guard Kentucky Central Railroad.)

No.	NAME.	RANK.	From	To	No.	NAME.	RANK.	From	To
1	R. W. Foley	Colonel	Sep. 17, '61	Dec. 10, '61	1	F. A. Blackburn	Commissary	Sep. 22, '61	Dec. 2, '61
1	John Marshall	Major	Sep. 17, '61	Dec. 4, '61	1	James E. Simpson	Q. M. Sergeant	Sep. 24, '61	Dec. 2, '61
1	Jo. P. Hunt	Adjutant	Sep. 18, '61	Dec. 2, '61	1	John Flynn	Hosp. Steward	Oct. 29, '61	Dec. 2, '61
1	C. F. Thomas	Surgeon	Sep. 17, '61	Dec. 2, '61					

ROLL OF CAPTAIN M'CLINTOCK'S COMPANY.
(Police Guard Kentucky Central Railroad.)

No.	NAME.	RANK.	From	To	No.	NAME.	RANK.	From	To
1	J. B. McClintock	Captain	Oct. 26, '61	Dec. 2, '61	14	Moffett, J. W.	Private	Oct. 26, '61	Dec. 2, '61
1	A. Casner	1st Lieutenant	Oct. 26, '61	Dec. 2, '61	15	Masoner, J. O.	Private	Oct. 26, '61	Dec. 2, '61
1	J. H. Howard	2d Lieutenant	Oct. 26, '61	Dec. 2, '61	16	Myer, F.	Private	Oct. 30, '61	Dec. 2, '61
1	T. N. Moore	1st Sergeant	Oct. 26, '61	Dec. 2, '61	17	McMillen, C. N.	Private	Oct. 30, '61	Dec. 2, '61
2	O. N. Marston	Sergeant	Oct. 30, '61	Dec. 2, '61	18	Morris, H.	Private	Nov. 1, '61	Dec. 2, '61
3	J. N. Munson	Sergeant	Oct. 26, '61	Dec. 2, '61	19	Magee, H. M.	Private	Oct. 26, '61	Dec. 2, '61
4	G. Sparks	Sergeant	Oct. 30, '61	Dec. 2, '61	20	Rankin, W. W.	Private	Oct. 28, '61	Dec. 2, '61
1	Anderson, W	Private	Oct. 30, '61	Dec. 2, '61	21	Ralson, J. W.	Private	Oct. 26, '61	Dec. 2, '61
2	Bishop, J.	Private	Nov. 6, '61	Dec. 2, '61	22	Raper, A. O.	Private	Oct. 26, '61	Dec. 2, '61
3	Buckley, J. W.	Private	Oct. 30, '61	Dec. 2, '61	23	Renkle, C.	Private	Oct. 26, '61	Dec. 2, '61
4	Burns, T.	Private	Oct. 26, '61	Dec. 2, '61	24	Stephen, J. T.	Private	Oct. 26, '61	Dec. 2, '61
5	Boone, J.	Private	Nov. 6, '61	Dec. 2, '61	25	Smith, A.	Private	Oct. 30, '61	Dec. 2, '61
6	Boone, J. W.	Private	Oct. 30, '61	Dec. 2, '61	26	Smith, G. M.	Private	Oct. 30, '61	Dec. 2, '61
7	Cummins, G. W.	Private	Oct. 30, '61	Dec. 2, '61	27	Teny, J.	Private	Oct. 28, '61	Dec. 2, '61
8	Oxeada, J.	Private	Oct. 30, '61	Dec. 2, '61	28	Trabue, J.	Private	Oct. 26, '61	Dec. 2, '61
9	Collins, B.	Private	Nov. 11, '61	Dec. 2, '61	29	Whoby, B. F.	Private	Oct. 26, '61	Dec. 2, '61
10	Grey, W. C.	Private	Dec. 26, '61	Dec. 2, '61	30	Wilson, M. L.	Private	Nov. 15, '61	Dec. 2, '61
11	Hyatt, H. C.	Private	Oct. 30, '61	Dec. 2, '61	31	Walden, A. H.	Private	Nov. 6, '61	Dec. 2, '61
12	Long, J. W.	Private	Oct. 26, '61	Dec. 2, '61	32	Walden, J.	Private	Nov. 6, '61	Dec. 2, '61
13	McCamey, J. W.	Private	Oct. 26, '61	Dec. 2, '61	33	Zoller, J.	Private	Oct. 26, '61	Dec. 2, '61

Adjutant General's Location Report for John Muss – Entry circled
(Kentucky Yeoman Office)

About March 1863 John is listed as absent on the roll call and has been detached from the company and appointed Regimental Farrier. About October 1863 he was detached from the company and appointed as Brigade Farrier for headquarters and served in this role until January 1864.

On January 11, 1864 John Muss was transferred to the 2nd Kentucky Cavalry, Company B although no order of transfer was received by the 2nd Kentucky Cavalry from the 4th Kentucky Calvary. At the time of his transfer, the 2nd Kentucky Cavalry was stationed at Lookout Valley near Chattanooga, Hamilton County, Tennessee. On February 07, 1864 John was detached from the 2nd Kentucky Cavalry to fetch some horses in Nashville, Davidson County, Tennessee. On March 29, 1864 John was re-transferred to the 4th Kentucky Cavalry from the 2nd Kentucky Cavalry. He arrived back at the 4th Cavalry, Company G on April 02, 1864.

Civil War Service Record for John Muss - 2nd Kentucky Cavalry,
Company B
(National Archives and Records Administration, Compiled Service
Records of Volunteer Union Soldiers)

On December 09, 1864 John Muss was sent from Nashville,
Tennessee (where he was stationed) to Louisville, Kentucky to be

mustered out by order of General Wilson. On December 24, 1864 John was discharged for expiration of service and on January 27, 1865, he was mustered out at Louisville, Kentucky. Military records give his age at that time as 39 years.

Final Civil War Service Record for John Muss - 4th Kentucky Cavalry, Company G
(National Archives and Records Administration, Compiled Service Records of Volunteer Union Soldiers)

In the 1870 Pitts Point, Bullitt County, Kentucky census (conducted on July 20, 1870) John Muss, 45, is head of the household with Elizabeth, 42, John, 16, Caroline, 14, George, 12, Charles, 10, Mary, 4, Elizabeth, 2 and Joseph, 8/12.

Picture of John Muss in his late 40s
(Lyle Raymond Cook & Karla Denise Ezell Cook)

The above photo of John Muss was most likely taken in the early to mid-1870s at the same time that the photo of his wife, Elizabeth Muss, was taken.

In the 1880 Shepherdsville, Bullitt County, Kentucky census (conducted on March 07, 1880) John Muss, 55, is head of the household with Eliza, 52, John C., 26, George, 23, Charles, 20, Mary, 14, Bettie, 12 and Joseph, 9. John is living near the family of Valentine Snellen and William Vaughn. He is also living between JOE H. VAUGHN and CHARLES FOSTER. All of these families later married into the Muss family.

According to National Home for Disabled Volunteers in Dayton, Montgomery County, Ohio, John Muss arrived at their facility on May 28, 1892. He was most likely placed there by his daughter, Elizabeth "Bettie" Muss Applegate, about a year after his wife, Elizabeth M Ceith/Siece/Ceise Muss, passed away.

Picture of John Muss in his 70s
(Lyle Raymond Cook & Karla Denise Ezell Cook)

The above photo of John Muss was taken by the M. Wolfe Photography Company located at 18 East 4th Street in Dayton, Ohio. Therefore, the photo must have been taken after 1892 and when John was living in the Veterans Home located there.

According to the 1892-1893 city directory for Dayton, Ohio, the offices of M. Wolfe were located at 106 South Main Street. For this reason, it is most likely that this photograph was taken in the mid to late 1890s. Milton Wolfe was a photographer, photograph retoucher, maker of half-tone screens, and teacher for three-colour processes who died on July 31, 1903. Della Wolfe, widow of Milton, can be found living at 154 W. Mape Street in the 1911-1912 Dayton, Ohio city directory.

In the 1900 Jefferson, Montgomery County, Ohio census (conducted on June 15, 1900) John Muss, 75, is living in the Central Branch of the National Home for Disabled Volunteers. The Central Branch of the National Home for Disabled Volunteers was a state of the art facility at the time which offered its occupants a lush campus with an abundance of leisure activities.

On March 23, 1904 John died while in the National Home for Disabled Volunteers located in Dayton, Montgomery County, Ohio from Chronic Dementia, Organic Brain Disorder, and Senectus (old age). His daughter, Elizabeth Muss Applegate of Cupio, Bullitt County, Kentucky was notified of his death by mail since there was no telegraph station in Cupio, Bullitt County, Kentucky. John was listed as a Catholic who was widowed at the time of his death.

Death Certificate for John Muss - 3rd entry from the bottom
(Montgomery County Records Center and Archives)

DIED.

MUSS—At the Central Branch, National Military Home for D. V. S., March 23, 1904, John Muss, late of Co. G, 4th Ky. Cav., aged 70. Cause of death, chronic, dementia, with organic brain disease and senectus.

Obituary for John Muss - March 26, 1904 (Dayton Daily Journal)

More about JOHN MUSS:
   Burial: On March 23, 1904. Interred at Dayton National
Cemetery, Montgomery County, Ohio, Section N, Row 17, Site 17.

Headstone for John Muss (Sorah)

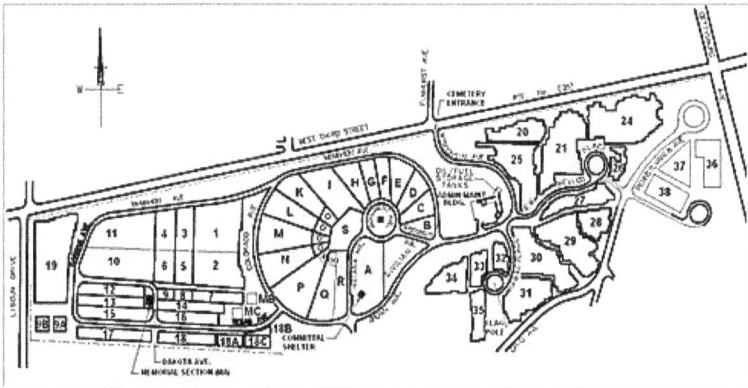

Cemetery Map for John Muss (U.S. Department of Veterans Affairs)

Children of JOHN MUSS and ELIZABETH M. CEISE/CLEISE/CEITH/SEICE are:
   i.   KATE[2] MUSS, b. About 1851 in Kentucky.
   ii.   JOHN CARROLL[2] MUSS, b. July 27, 1853 in Louisville, Jefferson
         County, Kentucky; d. August 07, 1927 in Louisville, Jefferson
         County, Kentucky; m. ANNA "ANNIE" ELIZA HOPEWELL on
         September 20, 1883 in Bullitt County, Kentucky.

iii. CAROLINE "CARRIE" F.[2] MUSS, b. August 14, 1855 in Kentucky; d. January 05, 1937 in Terre Haute, Vigo County, Indiana; m1. SAMUEL JOSEPH BRYANT on August 20, 1878 in Bullitt County, Kentucky; m2. WILLIAM MALCOLM COOK on April 21, 1881 in Bullitt County, Kentucky.

iv. GEORGE W.[2] MUSS b. September 17, 1858 in Bullitt County, Kentucky; d. May 03, 1921 in Louisville, Jefferson County, Kentucky; m. ELLEN "ELLA" W. HANNEPHIN.

v. CHARLES[2] MUSS, b. October 27, 1859 in Bullitt County, Kentucky; d. August 31, 1931 in Frankfort, Franklin County, Kentucky; m1. REBECCA JANE MOORE on April 08, 1886 in Bullitt County, Kentucky; m2. LIDA C. FLANIGAN on April 06, 1913 in Clark County, Indiana.

vi. MARY EMMA[2] MUSS, b. August 04, 1865 in Bullitt County, Kentucky; d. October 30, 1932 in Meadow Lawn, Jefferson County, Kentucky; m. JAMES H. DORIOT on December 12, 1889 in Jefferson County, Kentucky.

vii. ELIZABETH "BETTIE"[2] MUSS, b. July 28, 1867 in Bullitt County, Kentucky; d. January 09, 1945 in Louisville, Jefferson County, Kentucky; m. CHARLES L. APPLEGATE on June 24, 1889 in Jefferson County, Kentucky.

viii. JOSEPH P.[2] MUSS, b. November 1869 in Bullitt County, Kentucky; d. July 08, 1924 in Riley, Vigo County, Indiana; m. FLORENCE CASEY on October 03, 1916 in Bullitt County, Kentucky.

Generation No. 2: The First U. S. Born Descendants

2. KATE[2] MUSS (*JOHN[1] MUSS*) was born about 1851 in Kentucky. Prior to the 1870 census she must have married or died since she is no longer living with her parents when the 1870 census is conducted. No additional information can be found on her at this time. It is believed that Kate Muss died shortly after the 1860 census since there is no mention of her after this, and Elizabeth indicates that she had only 7 children instead of 8.

3. JOHN CARROLL[2] MUSS (*JOHN[1] MUSS*) was born July 27, 1853 in Louisville, Jefferson County, Kentucky (according to his marriage license) and died August 07, 1927 in Louisville, Jefferson County, Kentucky. JOHN married ANNA "ANNIE" ELIZA HOPEWELL on September 20, 1883 in Bullitt County, Kentucky, daughter of MATTHEW HOPEWELL and SARAH A. FOSTER. ANNIE was born December 12, 1858 in Knob Creek, Bullitt County, Kentucky and died January 15, 1927 in Bullitt County, Kentucky. An obituary could not be found for John Carroll Muss or Anna "Annie" Eliza Hopewell Muss in the Louisville Times, Louisville Courier-Journal, or the Bullitt County Pioneer News.

Marriage License for John Carroll Muss and Anna "Annie" Eliza
Hopewell - 1st Entry at top
(Family History Center, Kentucky Marriages, 1785-1979)

Notes for JOHN CARROLL MUSS:

In 1883 John was a Blacksmith, like his father, when he was
married. John and Annie were married in Knob Creek Church, Cupio,
Bullitt County, Kentucky by T. J. Ramsey, Minister. The marriage

license was issued on September 19, 1883, and W. M. C.? (illegible) and Dr. B. H. Blain attended the ceremony. It is possible that the W. M. C.? who is listed on the marriage license (but hard to read) was Annie's only sibling, an older brother, William M Hopewell. B. H. Blain also attended the marriage between Charles Muss and Rebecca Jane Moore. Thomas J. Ramsey also performed the marriage between William Joseph Muss and Martha "Mattie" Roberts Vaughn.

In the 1900 Shepherdsville, Bullitt County, Kentucky census (conducted on June 01, 1900) John C. Muss, 47, is head of the household with Annie W., 41, Wm. J., 15, Margaret R., 13, John E., 10, Roy, 6, Annie A., 5, Claude L., 2 and Sallie E., 1. John is listed as a Blacksmith.

In the 1910 Bullitt County, Kentucky census (conducted on April 21, 1910) J. C. Muss, 55, is head of the household with Annie E., 50, Margaret, 23, Roy, 16, Adris, 14, Claude, 12, Sallie, 11, Naomi, 9 and John, 20. Both John C Muss and Annie Muss are listed as being in their first marriage. John is listed as a Farmer.

In the 1920 Shepherdsville, Bullitt County, Kentucky census (conducted on January 16, 1920) John C. Muss, 66, is head of the household with Annie, 61, John Jr., 30, Roy, 26 and Naomi, 19. John is listed as a Farmer.

More about JOHN CARROLL MUSS:

All of the children for John Carroll Muss and Anna "Annie" Eliza Hopewell, including the girls, were rumored to have been able to shoe a horse since their father and grandfather were both blacksmiths.

The John Carroll Muss family lived south of Hwy 44 in Cupio, Kentucky on land that today is part of the Fort Knox U.S. Army base.

His Kentucky death certificate is #27-18447. John is listed as widowed and a retired blacksmith at the time of his death. He died at 8:45pm.

Informant: C. O. Carby of 621 West 6th Street in Louisville, Jefferson County, Kentucky. This is most likely Orville Emmitt Carby, Sr. who married John's daughter, Anna "Annie" Adress Muss.

Parents: John Muss of Germany and Elizabeth Ceith of Germany.

Cause of death: Lobar pneumonia for 5 days. Lobar pneumonia is a form of pneumonia that affects a large and continuous area of the lobe of a lung.

Funeral Services: W. G. Hardy of West Point, Kentucky.

Burial: August 9, 1927 at Knob Creek Union Church Cemetery in Cupio, Bullitt County, Kentucky.

The residence at 621 West 6th Street is most likely 621 South 6th Street, and that residence no longer exists.

Headstone for John Carroll Muss & Anna "Annie" Eliza Hopewell Muss (Browning, Headstone for John Carroll Muss & Anna "Annie" Eliza Hopewell)

Notes for ANNA "ANNIE" ELIZA HOPEWELL:

In the 1900 census it states that Annie Hopewell Muss had 7 children with 7 living and in 1910 she also indicated that she had 7 children with 7 living. In actuality, she had 8 children based upon our research.

Annie is listed on two of the T.C. Carroll land plats that are stored at the Bullitt County Clerk's office in large plastic envelopes. The listings can be found on Slide # 186, Map # 259 (along with Mr. Ferguson, James Foster, Mr. McNutt, Mr. Merker, and Chester L. Muss) and Slide # 311, Map # 100c (along with James Foster and Mary Ann Samuels). The address for the Bullitt County Clerk's Office is: 149 N. Walnut, Shepherdsville, KY, 40165.

More about ANNA "ANNIE" ELIZA HOPEWELL:

Her Kentucky death certificate is #27-00242. Annie is listed as married and a house wife at the time of her death. She died at 4:25am.

Informant: John Muss of West Point, Kentucky.

Parents: Massie Hopewell of Kentucky and Sarah Foster of New Orleans, Louisiana.

Cause of death: Chronic Myocarditis for 8 months due to senility. Myocarditis is an inflammation of the myocardium (heart muscle) that persists after an acute bacterial infection. Senility is the physical and mental infirmity of old age.

Funeral Services: W. G. Hardy & Brothers of West Point, Kentucky.

Burial: January 17, 1927 at Knob Creek Union Church Cemetery in Cupio, Bullitt County, Kentucky.

Notes for MATTHEW HOPEWELL (Father of ANNIE ELIZA HOPEWELL):

According to census records, Matthew was born in Indiana. It is believed that his parents were THOMAS HOPEWELL (b. about 1790) and ELIZABETH ROBERTS. Possible siblings for Matthew are as follows: WILLIAM J. HOPEWELL (b. November 1825 in Kentucky; m. LUCY ANN PARRIS on October 08, 1849 in Bullitt County, Kentucky), MARRITA HOPEWELL (b. 1829; m. NAPOLEON B. SMALL), HARRISON BERNIS HOPEWELL (b. February 06, 1831 in Kentucky; d. March 22, 1922 in Jefferson County, Kentucky; m1. SARAH C. SPARKS on December 14, 1854 in Bullitt County, Kentucky; m2. MARY F. JONES on December 23, 1903 in Bullitt County, Kentucky), DAVID W. HOPEWELL (b. 1837; m. CHRISTINA JOHNSON on July 06, 1856 in Bullitt County, Kentucky), and JAMES C. HOPEWELL (b. Jan 1838 in Kentucky; m. FLORENCE GOOCH about 1869). None of these relationships have been confirmed at this time.

The deaths of both MATTHEW HOPEWELL and SARAH A. FOSTER may be attributed to the measles outbreak that occurred in the Bullitt County, Kentucky area between 1850 and 1860.

Notes for SARAH A. FOSTER (Mother of ANNIE ELIZA HOPEWELL):

According to census records, Sarah was born in New Orleans, Orleans Parish, Louisiana. Her parents were JAMES FOSTER, SR. (b. 1811 in New York; d. March 12, 1851 in Bullitt County, Kentucky; buried. Knob Creek Union Church Cemetery in Cupio, Bullitt County, Kentucky m. April 28, 1843 in Bullitt County, Kentucky) and MARY ANN WRIGHT (b. October 1815 in Brooklyn, Kings County, New York).

It is likely that SARAH A. FOSTER and MATTHEW HOPEWELL are both buried in the old section of Knob Creek Union Church Cemetery at Cupio, Bullitt County, Kentucky. There are numerous unmarked graves and graves with illegible headstones in this section of the cemetery.

Sarah was the sister of JAMES FOSTER, JR.. JAMES FOSTER, JR. was the father of DAISY E. FOSTER, and DAISY E. FOSTER married JAMES ROY "ROY" TYLINGS MUSS.

The siblings for Sarah were as follows: JAMES FOSTER, JR. (b. Jul 28, 1843 in Bullitt County, Kentucky; d. April 09, 1932 in Cupio, Bullitt County, Kentucky; buried in Knob Creek Union Church Cemetery in Cupio, Bullitt County, Kentucky; m. MARTHA "MARTHY" C. WALLS on June 15, 1898 in Bullitt County, Kentucky), CHARLES "CHARLEY" FOSTER (b. February 1845 in Bullitt County, Kentucky; d. January 30, 1846 in Bullitt County, Kentucky; buried. Knob Creek Union Church Cemetery in Cupio, Bullitt County, Kentucky), and WILLIAM THEODORE FOSTER (b.

November 08, 1851 in Bullitt County, Kentucky; d. January 27, 1896 in Bullitt County, Kentucky; buried in Knob Creek Union Church Cemetery in Cupio, Bullitt County, Kentucky; m1. JEANETTE SAMUELS on May 30, 1878 in Bullitt County, Kentucky; m2. MARTHA "MARTHY" C. WALLS on May 03, 1883 in Bullitt County, Kentucky). MARTHA "MARTHY" C. WALLS first married WILLIAM THEODORE FOSTER, and later married JAMES FOSTER, JR. after William died.

Marriage License for Matthew Hopewell and Sarah A. Foster - 1st
entry at top
(Family History Center, Kentucky Marriages, 1785-1979)

Children of JOHN CARROLL[2] MUSS and ANNA "ANNIE" ELIZA HOPEWELL are:

i.   WILLIAM JOSEPH[3] "JOE" MUSS, b. August 19, 1884 in Kentucky; d. August 11, 1974 in Jefferson County, Kentucky; m. MARTHA "MATTIE" ROBERTS VAUGHN on December 24, 1905 in Bullitt County, Kentucky.

ii. MARGARET P.[3] MUSS, b. July 1886 in Kentucky.

iii. JOHN EARL[3] MUSS, b. September 22, 1889 in West Point, Hardin County, Kentucky; d. July 08, 1956 in Jefferson County, Kentucky; m1. SALLY ANNIS "ANNIS" CRABTREE about 1921 in Kentucky; m2. SUDIE M. VIERS on May 05, 1950 in Clark County, Indiana.

iv. JAMES ROY "ROY" TYLINGS[3] MUSS, b. October 09, 1893 in Cupio, Bullitt County, Kentucky; d. December 29, 1961 in Jefferson County, Kentucky; m1. MAUDE A. MITCHELL on November 26, 1920 in Kentucky; m2. DAISY E. FOSTER about 1932.

v.   ANNA "ANNIE" ADRESS[3] MUSS, b. February 24, 1895 in Bullitt County, Kentucky; d. June 15, 1976 in Montclair, San Bernardino County, California; m. ORVILLE EMMITT "SLIM" CARBY SR. on November 25, 1914 in Valley Station, Jefferson County, Kentucky.

vi. CLAUDE LEE[3] MUSS, b. July 05, 1897 in Bullitt County, Kentucky; d. May 23, 1970 in Louisville, Jefferson County, Kentucky; m. MARY NELLIE MONTGOMERY on July 20, 1920, Bullitt County, Kentucky.

vii. SARAH "SALLIE" ELIZABETH[3] MUSS, b. February 26, 1899 in Bullitt County, Kentucky; d. May 06, 1984 in Louisville, Jefferson County, Kentucky; m. WILLIAM M. SNELLEN on December 24, 1918 in Clark County, Indiana.

viii. GOLDA "GOLDIE" NAOMI "NAOMI"[3] MUSS, b. January 16, 1901 in Bullitt County, Kentucky; d. March 06, 1973 in Louisville, Jefferson County, Kentucky; m. WILLIAM HENRY ARMES, SR. on June 02, 1928 in Clark County, Indiana.

Picture of John Carroll Muss, Anna "Annie" Eliza Hopewell Muss, and
Family
(Lyle Raymond Cook & Karla Denise Ezell Cook)

Back row from left to right: Margaret P. Muss, John Carroll Muss
(with hat), Annie Eliza Hopewell Muss, and Annie Adress Muss
(with hat)
Middle row from left to right: James Roy Tylings Muss (with hat),
Sallie Elizabeth Muss Snellen, and Goldie Naomi Muss Armes
Front row: Claude Lee Muss (seated with hat)

The back of the above photo is a post card addressed to Mrs. W.M.
Cook, Lewis, Ind. The post card is postmarked Feb. 6, 1912,
Westpoint, KY. The note is written in pencil: "This is all the family but
the two oldest boys, Joe and John. From Annie." Over the top of this,
written in a different handwriting in ink is: "Uncle John and Aunt
Annia Muss and family, Feb. 6, 1912."

4. CAROLINE "CARRIE" F. ² MUSS (JOHN¹ MUSS) was born August 14,
1855 in Kentucky and died January 05, 1937 in Terre Haute, Vigo
County, Indiana. She first married SAMUEL JOSEPH BRYANT on August
20, 1878 in Bullitt County, Kentucky, son of ROBERT BRYANT and
ELIZABETH "ELIZA" EWING. He was born July 25, 1846 in Coatesville,
Chester County, Pennsylvania and died May 21, 1879 in Bullitt
County, Kentucky. Caroline next married WILLIAM MALCOLM COOK on
April 21, 1881 in Bullitt County, Kentucky, son of JAMES COOK and
ELIZABETH "ELIZA" STILWELL. He was born September 21, 1847 in

Spencer County, Kentucky and died November 10, 1940 in Terre Haute, Vigo County, Indiana.

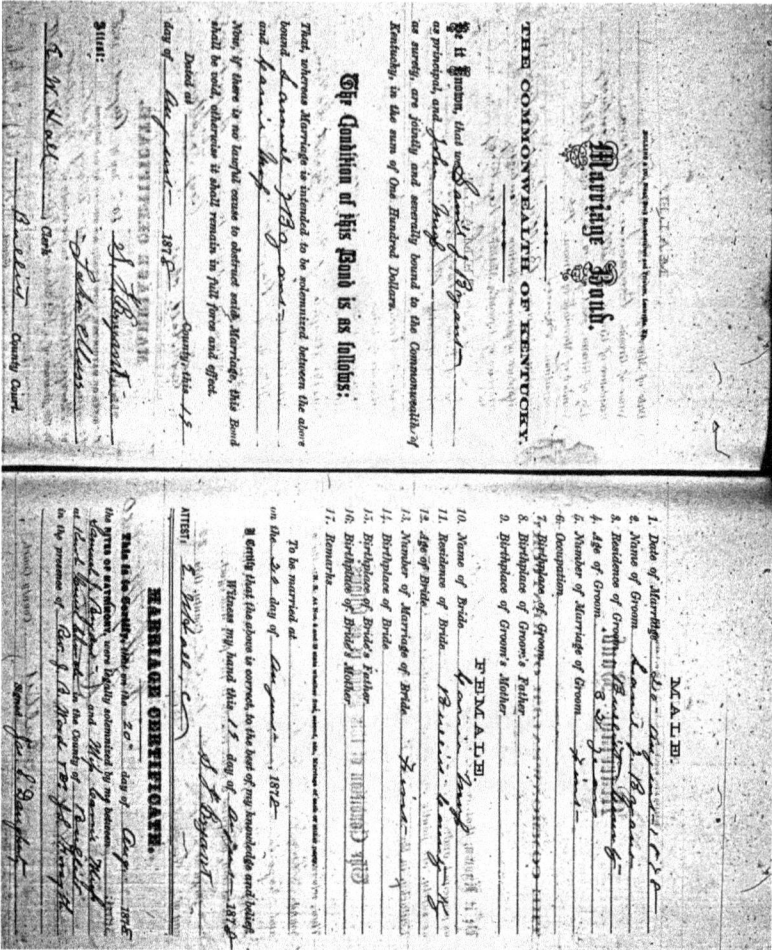

Marriage License for Samuel Joseph Bryant and Caroline "Carrie" F. Muss
(Family History Center, Bullitt County, Kentucky Marriages)

Notes for SAMUEL JOSEPH BRYANT:
Burial: Knob Creek Union Church Cemetery in Cupio, Bullitt County, Kentucky.

His headstone inscription reads: "He being dead, yet Speaketh. Born in Chester Co, Penn. Brother thou art gone to rest. Thine is an early tomb But Jesus summoned thee away. Thy Savior Called thee Home."

Headstone for Samuel Joseph Bryant
(Daniels, Headstone for Samuel Joseph Bryant)

MALE.

1. Date of Marriage *21 April 1881*
2. Name of Groom *W. M. Cook*
3. Residence of Groom *Jefferson county Kentucky*
4. Age of Groom *35 years*
5. Number of Marriage of Groom *2 ⁿᵈ*
6. Occupation *Farmer*
7. Birthplace of Groom *Spencer county Kentucky*
8. Birthplace of Groom's Father *Spencer County Kentucky*
9. Birthplace of Groom's Mother *Kentucky*

FEMALE.

10. Name of Bride *Mrs. Carrie Bryant*
11. Residence of Bride *Bullitt County Kentucky*
12. Age of Bride *25 years*
13. Number of Marriage of Bride *2 ⁿᵈ*
14. Birthplace of Bride *Jefferson county Kentucky*
15. Birthplace of Bride's Father *Germany*
16. Birthplace of Bride's Mother *Germany*
17. Remarks *daughter of John Muss*

N. B.—At Nos. 5 and 13 state whether first, second, etc., Marriage of each or either party.

To be married at _____

on the *21st* day of *April* 18*81*.

I Certify that the above is correct, to the best of my knowledge and belief.

Witness my hand, this *19*" day of *April* 18*81*,

W. M. Cook

Attest: *E. M. Hall clk*

Marriage License for William Malcolm Cook and Caroline "Carrie" F.
Muss
(Family History Center, Bullitt County, Kentucky Marriages)

Notes for CAROLINE "CARRIE" F. MUSS:
   In 1878, Samuel J Bryant and John Muss signed the $100
marriage bond for the marriage between Samuel J. Bryant and Carrie
Muss. Samuel and Carrie were married at Knob Creek Church of

Bullitt County, Kentucky in the presence of Reverend J. B. Wood and Dr. J. S. Forsyth.

In the 1880 Shepherdsville, Bullitt County, Kentucky census (conducted on June 01, 1880) Caroline Bryant, 25, servant, widow, is listed in the household of Joseph Meyers.

In 1881, William Malcolm Cook and Mrs. Carrie Bryant were attested to be married by E. W. Hall. On the marriage license, W. M. Cook is indicated as being born in Spencer County, Kentucky. Mrs. Carrie Bryant is indicated as being born in Jefferson County, Kentucky and the daughter of John Muss. This was the second marriage for William Cook and also the second marriage for Carrie Muss Bryant.

In the 1900 census it states that Caroline Muss Cook had 6 children with 4 living and in 1910 she had 6 children with 4 living.

Picture of William Malcolm Cook and Caroline "Carrie" F. Muss Cook
(Lyle Raymond Cook & Karla Denise Ezell Cook)

More about CAROLINE "CARRIE" F. MUSS:

She died at 9:55am in her residence on 2006 Seventh Avenue in Terre Haute, Indiana.

Funeral Services: Gillis Funeral Home (now Callahan Funeral Home) of Terre Haute, Indiana. Services were first held at 12:30pm on Thursday, January 07, 1937 in the home of George W. Cook (2003 Eighth Avenue in Terre Haute, Indiana) and then continued at 2:00pm in Riley Chapel of Lewis, Indiana.

Burial: Thursday, January 07, 1937 at Maple Grove Cemetery in Clay City, Clay County, Indiana.

The residence at 2006 7th Avenue is a 1,780 square foot, single family home with 3 bedrooms and 2 bathrooms that was built in 1890.

CARRIE COOK.

Carrie Cook, 81 years old, died at the residence, 2006 Seventh avenue, Tuesday morning at 9:55 o'clock. She is survived by the husband, William M. Cook; three sons, George W. and William J., of Terre Haute, and Henry A. Cook, of Danville, Ill.; a daughter, Mrs. Betty M. Brily, of West Frankfort, Ill.; a sister, Mrs. Betty Applegate, and nine grandchildren. The body was taken to the Gillis funeral home and later to the home of the son, George W. Cook, at 2003 Eighth avenue, where funeral services will be held Thursday afternoon at 12:30 o'clock with continued services at Riley chapel at Lewis at 2 o'clock. Burial will be in Maple Grove cemetery at Clay City.

Obituary for Caroline "Carrie" F. Muss Cook – January 05, 1937
(Terre Haute Tribune, Obituary for Caroline "Carrie" F. Muss Cook)

Notes for WILLIAM MALCOLM COOK:

In the 1880 Shepherdsville, Bullitt County, Kentucky census (conducted on June 01, 1880) Malcolm Cook is listed as a widower and is living with his parents. James Cook, 64, is head of the household with Mary, 48, Malcolm, 32, Lillie M., 14, Ada E., 11, Charles, 7, and Abel, 4. William is listed as a Laborer.

In the 1900 Pierson, Vigo County, Indiana census (conducted on June 14, 1900) William M. Cook, 52, is head of the household with Carrie, 44, George W., 14, Bettie M., 11, Henry W., 9, William J., 9/12 and Joseph Muss, 27, brother-in-law. William is listed as a Salesman at a Grocery.

In the 1910 Pierson, Vigo County, Indiana census (conducted on April 27, 1910) William M. Cook, 62, is head of the household with Carrie, 54, George W., 24, Henry W., 19, and William J., 10. William is listed as a Telephone Operator at a Telephone company.

In the 1920 Lewis, Clay County, Indiana census (conducted on January 02, 1920) William M. Cook, 73, is head of the household with Carrie, 66 and Willie J., 20. William is listed as a Farmer.

In the 1930 Lewis, Clay County, Indiana census (conducted on April, 1930) William M. Cook, 82, is head of the household with Carrie, 74. William is listed as a Farmer of Poultry and Garden.

Picture of William Malcolm Cook
(Lyle Raymond Cook & Karla Denise Ezell Cook)

More about WILLIAM MALCOLM COOK:

William's mother, ELIZABETH "ELIZA" STILWELL, died about 1849 when William was only 2 years old. It is possible that she died in child birth while giving birth to William's sister, MARY E. COOK.

According to his marriage license with Carrie, this was his second marriage. It is believed that William first married MATILDA COCHRAN on January 01, 1879 in Bullitt County, Kentucky. Since William is listed as widowed in the 1880 census, Matilda must have died between January 01, 1879 and June 01, 1880.

William was the half-brother of ROBERT F. COOK. Robert's daughter, ZULA COOK, married ROY WALKER APPLEGATE.

William was a member of the Vigo Lodge Number 29, Free and Accepted Mason (F&AM) of Lewis, Indiana.

The obituary for William Malcolm Cook was incorrectly headlined as "WILLIAM A. COOK" in the Terre Haute Tribune.

He died at 7:15pm in the residence of his son, George W. Cook, at 2003 Eighth Avenue in Terre Haute, Indiana.

Funeral Services: Gillis Funeral Home (now Callahan Funeral Home) of Terre Haute, Indiana. Services were first held at 1:00pm on Tuesday, November 12, 1940 in the home of George W. Cook (2003 Eighth Avenue in Terre Haute, Indiana) and then continued at 2:00pm in Briley Chapel of Lewis, Indiana.

Burial: Tuesday, November 12, 1940 at Maple Grove Cemetery in Clay City, Clay County, Indiana.

The residence at 2003 8th Avenue is a 1,052 square foot, single family home with 2 bedrooms and 1 bathroom that was built in 1910.

WILLIAM A. COOK.

William M. Cook, 93 years old, died at 7:15 o'clock Sunday evening at the residence, 2003 Eighth avenue. Surviving are three sons, George and Willie Cook, both of Terre Haute, and Henry Cook, of Danville, Ill.; one daughter, Mrs. Betty Briley, of Centralia, Ill.; one half brother, Abel Cook, of Evans Landing, Ind.; eight grandchildren and several nieces and nephews. He was a member of Vigo Lodge No. 29, F. and A. M. of Lewis, Ind. The body was taken to the Gillis Memory Chapel.

Obituary for William Malcolm Cook - November 11, 1940
(Terre Haute Tribune, Obituary for William Malcolm Cook)

Notes for JAMES COOK (Father of WILLIAM MALCOLM COOK):

James was born about 1817 in Spencer County, Kentucky and is most likely the son of THOMAS COOK and SARAH "SARY" YOUNG.

James first married ELIZABETH "ELIZA" STILWELL on January 06, 1847 in Spencer County, Kentucky. Together they had 3 children as follows: WILLIAM MALCOLM COOK, SARAH C. COOK (b. 1848 in Kentucky), and MARY E. COOK (1849 in Bullitt County, Kentucky; m. BLUFORD "BLUE" L. GOLDSMITH on December 21, 1870 in Bullitt County, Kentucky). Elizabeth Stilwell Cook died about 1849, possibly while giving birth to Mary E. Cook.

After Elizabeth died, James married MARY JANE CONGROVE on December 31, 1850 in Bullitt County, Kentucky, the daughter of unknown parents. Mary was born about 1832 in Kentucky. Together they had 7 children as follows: ROBERT T. COOK (b. October 15, 1851 in Bullitt County, Kentucky; d. March 03, 1924 in Cupio, Bullitt County, Kentucky; m. ROXANA FUNK on October 22, 1873 in Bullitt County, Kentucky), MARTHA A. COOK (b. 1854 in Kentucky), MARY C. COOK (b. March 1860 in Kentucky), LILLIE M. COOK (1866 in Kentucky), ADA E. COOK (1869 in Shepherdsville, Bullitt County, Kentucky), CHARLES "CHARLEY" C. COOK (b. July 19, 1872 in Shepherdsville, Bullitt County, Kentucky; d. January 22, 1938 in West Point, Hardin County, Kentucky; m. CLARA STIVERS about 1898 in Kentucky), and ABEL L. COOK (b. February 28, 1876 in Bullitt County, Kentucky; m. NELLIE G. McKNIGHT on March 07, 1906 in Jefferson County, Kentucky).

There was an empty location in the photo album owned by Lyle Raymond Cook and Karla Denise Ezell Cook for a picture of James Cook. Unfortunately, the photo had been removed at some point in the past and never returned to the album.

Notes for ELIZABETH "ELIZA" STILWELL (Mother of WILLIAM MALCOLM COOK):

Elizabeth was born about 1822 in Kentucky and died about 1849 in Bullitt County, Kentucky. She is the daughter of JOHN STILWELL and ELIZA BOWMAN.

Elizabeth's siblings were CHARLES B. STILWELL (b. 1824 in Kentucky; m. MARTHA "MARTHY" J. MNU about 1856), SAVANNAH PATIENCE STILWELL (b. January 23, 1825 in Spencer County, Kentucky; d. July 03, 1856 in Minnesota; m. JAMES MADISON LACKEY on September 07, 1843 in Taylorsville, Spencer County, Kentucky), JOSEPH STILWELL (b. 1828 in Spencer County, Kentucky), JOHN B. STILWELL (b. 1831 in Kentucky; m1. SARAH AGNES VANAISDAL on December 01, 1855; m2. ELIZABETH "BETTIE" COOK on February 28, 1866 in Spencer County, Kentucky), THOMAS B. STILWELL (b. May 1834 in Spencer County, Kentucky; m. DARTHULA HEADY on August 19, 1856 in Spencer County, Kentucky), ISAAC STILWELL (b. 1836 in Spencer county, Kentucky), and BENJAMIN "BEN" STILWELL (b. November 28, 1840 in Spencer County,

Kentucky; d. October 15, 1933 in Spencer County, Kentucky; m. ELIZABETH "LIZZIE" A. TURNER on August 27, 1864 in Spencer County, Kentucky).

Children of CAROLINE "CARRIE" F.[2] MUSS and WILLIAM MALCOLM COOK are:

i. GEORGE W.[3] COOK, b. August 14, 1885 in Bullitt County, Kentucky; d. September 11, 1965 in Terre Haute, Vigo County, Indiana; m. MYRTLE RUTH COREY on February 05, 1916 in Vigo County, Indiana.

ii. BETTY MAE[3] COOK, b. November 11, 1888 in Bullitt County, Kentucky; d. August 18, 1968 in Vincennes, Knox County, Indiana; m. EMORY ELLIS BRILEY on September 11, 1909 in Vigo County, Indiana.

iii. HENRY WAYNE[3] COOK, b. January 24, 1891, Sullivan County, Indiana; d. September 08, 1954 in Danville, Vermillion County, Illinois; m. BEULAH MAY WITHEM on November 29, 1911 in Vigo County, Indiana.

iv. WILLIAM "WILLIE" J.[3] COOK, b. August 30, 1899, Lewis, Vigo County, Indiana; d. October 02, 1991 in Plainfield, Hendricks County, Indiana; m1. NITIS LOUISE FUNK about 1925; m2. IVY MURIAL MCCOY on March 19, 1944 in Lebanon, Boone County, Indiana.

Picture of William Malcolm Cook, Caroline "Carrie" F. Muss Cook, and Family
(Lyle Raymond Cook & Karla Denise Ezell Cook)

From left to right: Betty Mae Cook, William Malcolm Cook (seated), George W. Cook, Carrie F. Muss Cook (seated), and Henry Wayne Cook

5. GEORGE W.[2] **MUSS** *(JOHN[1] MUSS)* was born September 17, 1858 in Bullitt County, Kentucky and died May 03, 1921 in Louisville, Jefferson County, Kentucky. He married ELLEN "ELLA" W. HANNEPHIN on August 03, 1887 in Louisville, Jefferson County, Kentucky, daughter of JAMES F. HANNEPHIN, SR. and REBECCA ANNE CORBLEY. She was born January 1862 in Louisville, Jefferson County, Kentucky and died March 26, 1959 in Jefferson County, Kentucky.

Marriage License for George W. Muss & Ellen "Ella" W. Hannephin
(Family History Center, Jefferson County, Kentucky Marriages)

Notes for GEORGE W. MUSS:

In 1887, George Muss and James Hannephin, SR., Ella's father, signed the $100 marriage bond for the marriage between George Muss and Ella W. Hannephin.

In the 1900 Louisville, Jefferson County, Kentucky census (conducted on June 09, 1900) George Muss, 42, is head of the household with Ella, 38 and Clyde, 9. George is listed as a "Paperman (tinner)".

In the 1910 Louisville, Jefferson County, Kentucky census (conducted on April 16, 1910) George W. Muss, 50, is head of the household with Ella W., 48 and Clyde, 19. George is listed as a Steam Fitter for the Steam Railroad.

In the 1920 East Oakdale, Jefferson County, Kentucky census (conducted on January 02, 1920) George W. Muss, 61, is head of the household with Ellen, 58 and Clyde M., 26. George is listed as a Steamfitter for the Railroad Shops.

Picture of George W. Muss
(Lyle Raymond Cook & Karla Denise Ezell Cook)

It is estimated that the above photograph was taken between 1872 and 1896. According to the city directories for Louisville, Kentucky, the Bergman & Flexner partnership first opened their doors in 1868 at 94 Main Street. Louis Bergman opened his own, independent Louisville photo studio in 1872 at 38 Market Street. In 1873 he moved his operation to 58 Market Street. In 1880 his studio is listed at 58 Market near 2nd. After 1885, however, Caroline

Bergman (wife of Louise Bergman) is listed as the proprietor and photographer and Louis Bergman is listed only as "manager". This very successful studio was in operation until 1896. Louis Bergman was born in Hanover, Germany to Prussian parents. His wife, Carrie, was born in Louisiana to German parents. Some of this information was obtained from The Encyclopedia of Louisville by John E. Kleber that was published by University Press of Kentucky on December 28, 2000.

More about GEORGE W. MUSS:

His Kentucky death certificate is #21-10455. George is listed as married and a metal worker at the time of his death. He died at 1pm.

Informant: Mrs. George W. Muss.

Parents: John Muss of Germany and Elizabeth Seice of Germany.

Cause of death: Cerebral hemorrhage due to arteriosclerosis. Cerebral hemorrhage is a medical term that describes a stroke. A stroke happens when blood flow to a part of the brain stops. Arteriosclerosis is a hardening of the arteries that occurs when fat, cholesterol and other substances build up in the walls of arteries.

Funeral Services: Schoppenhorst Funeral Home. George lived at 4609 West Broadway in Louisville, Kentucky at the time of his death. The funeral started from his residence at 2:30pm on Thursday, May 05, 1921. The residence at 4609 West Broadway does not exist today. The home has been replaced by Shawnee Park and the home stood where the south entrance to the park is today.

Burial: Thursday, May 05, 1921 at Cave Hill Cemetery in Louisville, Jefferson County, Kentucky, Section 27, Lot Range, 315. No headstone was placed in Cave Hill Cemetery for George.

The Schoppenhorst Funeral Home was founded in 1892 and is still in operation today. They are currently known as the Neurath-Schoppenhorst Funeral Home and Schoppenhorst Brothers Funeral Home. The funeral home is located at 1832 W Market Street in Louisville, Kentucky.

MUSS — Tuesday, May 3, at 10:10 a.m. George W. Muss, beloved husband of Ella Muss (nee Hannephin), in his sixty-third year. Funeral from the family residence, 4609 West Broadway, Thursday, May 5, at 2:30 o'clock. Interment in Cave Hill Cemetery.

Obituary for George W. Muss – May 04, 1921
(Louisville Times, Obituary for George W. Muss)

Notes for ELLEN "ELLA" W. HANNEPHIN:

In the 1900 census it states that Ella Hannaphen Muss had 2 children with 1 living.

Her father, JAMES F. HANNEPHIN SR., worked as a Tinner and was born in Ireland on March 20, 1835 then immigrated to the United States as a child about 1840.

Her younger brother, CHARLES VICTOR HANNEPHIN, worked as a plumber on the L&N Railroad and was run over by a train on November 24, 1907 in Louisville, Jefferson County, Kentucky when he slipped and fell underneath the train. His legs were severed from his body. Charles was buried in Section Y, Lot 14 East Half at Saint Louis Cemetery of Louisville, Jefferson County, Kentucky.

Ella lived at 3840 Southern Parkway for most of her life and up to the time of her death. This was the Hannephin family home where many of her siblings lived.

More about ELLEN "ELLA" W. HANNEPHIN:

Ella died at 11:20am in her home located at 3840 Southern Parkway.

Funeral Services: Blanford-Rattermans of 2815 S 4th Street in Louisville, Kentucky. Services were held at 1:30pm on Saturday, March 28, 1959. Today, Blanford-Rattermans is known as Ratterman Funeral Home. They have been family owned and operated since 1864. Two of the Ratterman brothers, George and Herman, first opened their business at 11th and Market Streets in Louisville, Kentucky and called it G. & H. Ratterman; Carpenters and Makers of Fine Coffins.

Burial: Saturday, March 28, 1959 in Section Y, Lot 14 East Half at Saint Louis Cemetery of Louisville, Jefferson County, Kentucky.

MUSS, Mrs. Ella Hannephin, 98 years, Thursday, March 26, 1959, 11:20 a.m. at her residence, 3840 Southern Pkwy. Beloved sister of Miss Blanche Hannephin, Mrs. Jessie Edginton, Mr. Steve Hannephin and Mr. Clarence Hannephin. Mrs. Muss is at Blanford-Rattermans, 2815 S. 4th, where services will be held Saturday at 1:30 p.m. Interment St. Louis Cemetery.

Obituary for Ellen "Ella" W. Hannephin Muss – March 27, 1959
(Louisville Times, Obituary for Ellen "Ella" W. Hannephin Muss)

Notes for JAMES F. HANNEPHIN, SR. (Father of ELLEN "ELLA" W. HANNEPHIN):

James was born on March 20, 1835 in Ireland to STEPHEN HANNEPHIN and an unknown mother.

He married REBECCA ANNE CORBLEY on February 14, 1860 in Louisville, Jefferson County, Kentucky. Together they had 7 children as follows: ELLEN "ELLA" W. HANNEPHIN (b. January 1862 in Louisville, Jefferson County, Kentucky; d. March 26, 1959 in Louisville, Jefferson County, Kentucky; m. GEORGE W. MUSS), JOHN L. HANNEPHIN (b. about 1869 in Louisville, Jefferson County, Kentucky), JAMES F. HANNEPHIN, JR. (b. May 16, 1872 in Louisville, Jefferson County, Kentucky; d. January 14, 1956 in Jefferson County, Kentucky; buried at Saint Louis Cemetery in Louisville, Jefferson County, Kentucky; m. KATHERINE "KATIE" MAY WAGNER on October 21, 1921 in Indiana), CHARLES VICTOR HANNEPHIN (b. February 1873 in Louisville, Jefferson County, Kentucky; d. November 24, 1907 in Louisville, Jefferson County, Kentucky), STEPHEN EDWARD HANNEPHIN (b. October 26, 1877 in Louisville, Jefferson County, Kentucky; d. March 19, 1973 in Louisville, Jefferson County, Kentucky; buried at Saint Louis Cemetery in Louisville, Jefferson County, Kentucky), BLANCHE D. HANNEPHIN (b. July 1882 in Kentucky; d. June 14, 1961 in Jefferson County, Kentucky; buried at Saint Louis Cemetery in Louisville, Jefferson County, Kentucky; probably never married), CLARENCE ROCH HANNEPHIN (b. April 05, 1884 in Kentucky; d. August 11, 1979 in Whitley County, Kentucky; m. ESSIE ELLEN QUICK on June 26, 1912 in Louisville, Jefferson County, Kentucky), and JESSIE M. HANNEPHIN (b. May 1889 in Kentucky; d. August 25, 1973 in Jefferson County, Kentucky; m. WILLIAM NATHAN EDGINGTON on June 22, 1915 in Oakdale, Jefferson County, Kentucky).

Informant: Miss Blanche Hannephin of 3840 Southern Parkway in Louisville, Kentucky.

Parents: Stephen Hannephin of Kentucky and Unknown.

Cause of Death: Myocarditis for 1 year.

James was a Tanner by occupation and married.

Funeral Services: J. B. Ratterman of 2114 West Market Street in Louisville, Kentucky.

Burial: Section Y, Lot 14 East Half at Saint Louis Cemetery of Louisville, Jefferson County, Kentucky.

Headstone for James F. Hannephin, SR.
(Ballard)

Headstone for Stephen Edward Hannpehin
(Gregorchik)

Notes for REBECCA ANNE CORBLEY (Mother of ELLEN "ELLA" W.
HANNEPHIN):

Rebecca was born about 1845 in Kentucky to an unknown father
and ELLEN CORBLEY (b. about 1818 in Ireland). It is unknown what
happened to Rebecca's father, but he must have died sometime prior
to the 1850 census since he is not listed in this census record.
Rebecca's family was in the liquor distilling and distributing business
for Louisville, Jefferson County, Kentucky since ELLEN CORBLEY is listed
on two IRS tax lists during 1862 and 1863 as being a retail liquor
dealer.

Rebecca appears to have had 3 siblings as follows: JOHN CORBLEY
(b. Feb 1842 in Kentucky; d. January 14, 1916 in Louisville, Jefferson
County, Kentucky), WILLIAM CORBLEY (b. about 1844 in Kentucky), and
MARY CORBLEY (b. about 1846 in Kentucky). JOHN CORBLEY appears to

have taken over the family liquor business from his mother since he is listed on the 1882-1883 and 1884-1885 Caron's Directory for The City of Louisville and the 1900 census record in Louisville, Jefferson County, Kentucky as being a liquor distiller.

Children of GEORGE W.[2] MUSS and ELLEN "ELLA" W. HANNEPHIN are:
   i. MARTINA CLYDE[3] MUSS, b. January 26, 1891 in Louisville, Jefferson County, Kentucky; d. March 14, 1952 in Lakeland, Jefferson County, Kentucky.

   More about MARTINA CLYDE MUSS:
       In the 1930 census Martina is staying at the Central State Hospital for Insane in Jefferson County, Kentucky.
       Died at Central State Hospital in Lakeland, and lived at 3840 Southern Parkway in Louisville, Jefferson County, Kentucky at the time of her death.
       Burial: Saint Louis Cemetery, Louisville, Jefferson County, Kentucky.

6. CHARLES[2] MUSS (*JOHN[1] MUSS*) was born October 27, 1859 in Bullitt County, Kentucky and died August 3, 1931 in Frankfort, Franklin County, Kentucky. He first married REBECCA JANE MOORE on April 08, 1886 in Bullitt County, Kentucky, daughter of LEVI LERU MOORE and ELIZABETH "ELIZA" J. SKINNER. She was born March 1858 and died December 14, 1910 in Louisville, Jefferson County, Kentucky. After the death of his first wife, Charles married LIDA C. FLANIGAN on April 06, 1913 in Clark County, Indiana, daughter of JOHN FLANIGAN and MARTHA "MATTIE" JANE SHERRON. She was born February 06, 1873 in Harrison County, Indiana and died June 12, 1914 in Louisville, Jefferson County, Kentucky. On the marriage license, Charles is listed as widowed and Lida is listed as divorced.

Marriage License for Charles Muss and Rebecca Jane Moore
(Family History Center, Bullitt County, Kentucky Marriages)

Marriage License for Charles Muss and Lida C. Flanigan
(Family History Center, Clark County, Indiana Marriages)

Notes for CHARLES MUSS:
In the 1880 Shepherdsville, Bullitt County, Kentucky census (conducted on June, 1880) Charles Muss, 21, is listed as a laborer in the household of Wm. F. Samuels in addition to being listed with his parents. Charles is listed as a Laborer.

In 1886, Charles and Rebecca were married at the home of Rebecca's mother in Bullitt County, Kentucky. John T. Key and B. H. Blain were witnesses to the marriage, and F. D. Cantrell, Minister of the Gospel, performed the ceremony. B. H. Blain also attended the marriage between John Carroll Muss and Anna Eliza Hopewell.

In the 1900 Pine Tavern, Bullitt County, Kentucky census (conducted on June 01, 1900) Charles Muss, 40, is head of the household with Rebecca, 42, Nora E., 13, Stella E., 9, Clarence L., 6 and William H., 4. Charles is listed as a Farmer.

In the 1910 Louisville, Jefferson County, Kentucky census (conducted on April 27, 1910) Charles Muss, 50, is head of the household with Rebecca, 52, Nora, 22, Stella E., 19, Clarence, 17, William, 14 and Eliza Moore, 82, mother-in-law. Charles is listed as a Carpenter for a Contractor.

In 1913, Charles and Lida were married by Oscar L. Hay, Justice of the Peace, in Clark County, Indiana. Charles lists his parents as John Muss and Elizabeth Clase/Cleise. Lida lists her parents as John Flanigan and Martha Sherron.

In the 1920 Frankfort, Franklin County, Kentucky census (conducted on January 02, 1920) Charles Muss, 62, is listed as a prisoner in the Kentucky State Reformatory. Charles is listed as a Carpenter for the Reformatory.

In the 1930 Frankfort, Franklin County, Kentucky census (conducted on April 09, 1930) Charles Muss, 70, is listed as a prisoner in the Kentucky State Reformatory. Charles is listed as having no occupation.

More about CHARLES MUSS:
In the 1880 census, WILLIAM F. SAMUELS and BARBARA C. SAMUELS (who are boarding Charles Muss) are the parents of William Theodore Foster's wife, Jeanette Samuels. William T. Foster is living next door. WILLIAM THEODORE FOSTER is the brother of SARAH A. FOSTER. SARAH A. FOSTER is the mother of Anna "Annie" Eliza Hopewell who married John Carroll Muss.

In the 1910 census, Charles is listed as a carpenter that has been married for 23 years. He is renting his house.

On June 12, 1914 Charles Muss killed his wife, LIDA C. FLANIGAN, around 9:30am at their home on 645 South Sixth Street in Louisville, Jefferson County, Kentucky. Charles used a razor to slash her throat and then slashed his own throat. Lida died immediately, but Charles survived. During the investigation, Charles charged that Lida was being unfaithful and going out with other men. Charles also indicated that he did not regret killing his wife.

MUSS ASSERTS HE IS NOT SORRY HE KÍLLED WIFE

MURDER CASE IS CONTINUED IN POLICE COURT UNTIL JUNE 23.

"I killed her, and that is all I have to say."

Charles Muss, who slew his wife at their home, 645 South Sixth street, at 9:30 o'clock Friday morning, and then attempted to end his own life by slashing his throat with a razor, made this statement to a reporter yesterday afternoon. His condition is serious, but physicians at the city hospital believe he will recover.

"Are you sorry for what you have done?" Muss was asked.

"No," he replied.

Although Muss has made several requests to see his daughter, Miss Nora Muss, the young woman has not called at the hospital.

The case of Muss, charged with murder, was called in the Police Court yesterday morning, and was continued until June 23. Coroner Duncan will not hold an inquest until Muss recovers sufficiently to testify.

Sisters of Mrs. Muss accompanied the body to Milltown, Ind., yesterday morning, where the burial will be held.

Murder Case for Charles Muss - June 12, 1914
(The Courier-Journal, Muss Asserts He Is Not Sorry He Killed Wife)

CORONER'S JURY CHARGES MUSS WITH WIFE MURDER

A Coroner's Jury decided yesterday that Mrs. Lida Muss, who was killed at her home, 6C South Sixth street, June 12, came to her death as the result of wounds inflicted by her husband, and charged that her husband, Charles Muss, was guilty of willful murder. Muss killed his wife by cutting her throat with a razor and then tried to end his own life. He charged her with going out with other men.

Murder Charges against Charles Muss - June 26, 1914
(The Courier-Journal, Coroner's Jury Charges Muss With Wife Murder)

Charles died in the Franklin State Reformatory. He is listed as inmate #16074.

Informant: W. B. Fuller of the State Reformatory Transfer.

Parents: John Muss of Germany and Elizabeth Muss.

Cause of death: Apoplexy for 31 days (August 1, 1931 – August 31, 1931). Apoplexy is used to describe the sudden loss of consciousness, often followed by paralysis, caused by the rupture of a blood vessel in the brain due to a stroke.

Funeral Services: R. Rogers Baus? (illegible) of Frankfort, Franklin County, Kentucky with services held at 2:30pm on Wednesday in Seabrook's Chapel located at East Twelfth and Market Streets in New Albany, Indiana.

Burial: August 5, 1931 at Graceland Memorial Park on Charlestown Road (now called Kraft-Graceland Memorial Park) in New Albany, Floyd County, Indiana. His daughter, Stella E. Muss Duesing Hicks, is living in New Albany at this time, and she took responsibility for burying her father.

> **MUSS FUNERAL SET**
> Funeral services for Charles Muss, 72 years old, Franklin Ky., were held at 2:30 o'clock Wednesday at Seabrook's Chapel, East Twelfth and Market Streets, with burial in Graceland Memorial Park on the Charlestown Road. He died Monday at his home. Mrs. Stella E. Hick, 819 West Market Street, his daughter, survives.

Obituary for Charles Muss - August 07, 1931
(New Albany Weekly Ledger, Obituary for Charles Muss)

Notes for REBECCA JANE MOORE:
In the 1900 census it states that Rebecca Moore Muss had 4 children with 4 living and in 1910 she had 4 children with 4 living.

> MUSS—At 12:30 p. m. December 14, residence, 318 E. Ormsby, Mrs. Rebecca Jane, wife of Charles Muss, aged 54 years. Funeral from residence at 2 o'clock, Thursday, December 15. Interment, Cave Hill cemetery.

Obituary for Rebecca Jane Moore Muss – January 06, 1912
(The Courier-Journal, Obituary for Rebecca Jane Moore Muss)

More about REBECCA JANE MOORE:
Rebecca died at 12:30pm on December 14, 1910. She lived at 318 East Ormsby Avenue in Louisville, Kentucky at the time of her death. This home does not exist today, and has been replaced by Interstate 65.

Her death record source is the mortuary record, page 131. Doctor: William Morse. She is listed as married at the time of her death.

Informant: Not listed.

Parents: Not listed.

Cause of death: Cancer of the uterus.

Funeral Services: Lee A. Cralle Funeral Home. The funeral started at her residence on East Ormsby Avenue at 2pm on Thursday, December 15, 1910 and traveled to Cave Hill Cemetery where she was buried.

Burial: Thursday, December 15, 1910 at Cave Hill Cemetery in Louisville, Jefferson County, Kentucky, Section 8, Lot Range, 242. No headstone was placed in Cave Hill Cemetery for Rebecca.

The records for the Lee E. Cralle Funeral Home are now maintained by Highlands Funeral Home of Louisville, Kentucky. The Highlands Funeral Home is located at 3331 Taylorsville Road.

Notes for LEVI LERU MOORE (Father of REBECCA JANE MOORE):

Levi was born on March 22, 1821 in Bullitt County, Kentucky to WILLIAM B. MOORE and DELILAH ALICIA JOYCE. Levi first married SARAH ELLEN CRASK on July 04, 1844 in Jefferson County, Kentucky. Levi next married ELIZABETH "ELIZA" J. SKINNER on December 22, 1850 in Bullitt County, Kentucky. Together Levi and Elizabeth had at least 8 children as follows: WILLIAM PRESTON MOORE (b. January 1852 in Bullitt County, Kentucky; d. 1894 in New Albany, Floyd County, Indiana), MARY ELIZABETH MOORE (b. October 07, 1853 in Skinner Ridge, Bullitt County, Kentucky; d. December 07, 1860 in Bullitt County, Kentucky), RICHARD "DICK" MOORE (b. February 29, 1856 in Bullitt County, Kentucky; d. July 21, 1920 in Bullitt County, Kentucky; m. DORTHEA ELLEN "DORA" STEIN on December 19, 1877 in Louisville, Jefferson County, Kentucky), REBECCA JANE MOORE (b. March 1858 in Kentucky; d. December 14, 1910 in Louisville, Jefferson County, Kentucky; m. CHARLES MUSS), NATHAN MOORE (b. January 11, 1861 in Bullitt County, Kentucky; d. July 15, 1938 in Louisville, Jefferson County, Kentucky; m. ELIZA SANFORD on August 19, 1881 in Jeffersonville, Clark County, Indiana), JOHN DOUGLAS MOORE (b. February 26, 1865 in Kentucky; d. July 27, 1944 in Jefferson County, Kentucky; m. CORA HARSHFIELD on December 20, 1898 in Bullitt County, Kentucky), THOMAS L. MOORE (b. February 1868 in Kentucky; d. August 28, 1910 in Grand Junction, Mesa County, Colorado; m. MARY "MADIE" J. CAMPBELL), and AMANDA P. MOORE (b. 1868 in Kentucky).

Notes for ELIZABETH "ELIZA" J. SKINNER (Mother of REBECCA JANE MOORE):

Elizabeth was born on July 22, 1827 in Kentucky to RICHARD SKINNER (b. 1794 in Bullitt County, Kentucky; d. March 17, 1852 in Bullitt County, Kentucky) and REBECCA CONNOR (b. about 1803 in Kentucky). She died on December 18, 1910 in Bullitt County, Kentucky.

It is possible that Elizabeth first married CHARLES FOSTER on February 10, 1842 in Bullitt County, Kentucky. Charles is the brother of the JAMES FOSTER, SR. who was the father of SARAH A. FOSTER. This may be incorrect since this Elizabeth Skinner most likely was about 10 years older than the ELIZABETH "ELIZA" J. SKINNER that married LEVI LERU MOORE. There also appears to be separate entries in the 1850 Bullit County, Kentucky census for these two different Elizabeth

Skinner. The first 1850 census record is dated August 1, 1850 and has Elizabeth living with Charles. The second census is dated August 2, 1850 and has Elizabeth still living with her parents, Richard and Rebecca.

The residence at 318 East Ormsby Avenue in Louisville, Jefferson County, Kentucky no longer exists. That residence has since been demolished, and Interstate 65 (Dr. Martin Luther King, Jr. Expressway) passes over Ormsby Avenue at that point.

Elizabeth had at least 6 siblings as follows: MARGARET SKINNER (b. about 1826 in Kentucky; m. ROBERT NCNUTT on October 26, 1851 in Bullitt County, Kentucky), ISAAC D. SKINNER (b. about 1830 in Kentucky; m. MARGARET C. RAWLINGS on February 05, 1857 in Bullitt County, Kentucky), JOHN C. SKINNER (b. about 1833 in Kentucky; m. AMELIA S. TYDINGS on May 29, 1862 in Bullitt County, Kentucky), NATHAN B. SKINNER (b. about 1835 in Kentucky; m. MANERVA E. HILTON on December 11, 1866 in Bullitt County, Kentucky), CHARLES D. SKINNER (b. about 1838 in Kentucky; d. October 07, 1854 in Bullitt County, Kentucky), and KORILLA J. SKINNER (b. about 1841 in Kentucky, m. GILBERT GRIFFIN on August 12, 1862 in Bullitt County, Kentucky).

More about ELIZABETH "ELIZA" J. SKINNER (Mother of REBECCA JANE MOORE):

The Pioneer News (Bullitt County, Kentucky) - December 23, 1910 - "Mrs. Eliza Moore was born July 22, 1827 and died December 18, 1910. She was the daughter of Richard and Rebecca Skinner, who were among the first settlers of Bullitt County. She was married to Levi Moore in January 1850. To this union was born two daughters and six sons, only four of whom survive her. One son, Thomas Moore, died August 28, 1910. Her daughter, Mrs. Muss, died December 14, just four days before her death. She lost her husband in 1870. She had united with the Methodist Church south very early in life in the grove where Mt. Eden church now stands under the ministry of Bro. Scoby."

Children of CHARLES[2] MUSS and REBECCA JANE MOORE are:

    i.   NORA E.[3] MUSS, b. December 1886 in Kentucky; d. August 18, 1950 in Cook County, Illinois; m. EDWIN MALLIBIEN STOLL on August 17, 1915 in Louisville, Jefferson County, Kentucky.

    ii.   STELLA E.[3] MUSS, b. July 21, 1890 in Louisville, Jefferson County, Kentucky; m1. DAVID FREDERICK DUESING on June 27, 1910 in Clark County, Indiana; m2. JOSEPH ALEXANDER HICKS on July 10, 1918 in Floyd County, Indiana; m3. JAMES O. MCALLISTER; d. January 06, 1955 in New Albany, Floyd County, Indiana.

    iii.   CLARENCE LEE[3] MUSS, b. October 28, 1892 in Kentucky.

iv. WILLIAM NATHAN[3] MUSS, b. February 14, 1896 in Harrison County, Indiana; d. February 20, 1957 in Virginia; m. MARY KATHERINE LAUGHLIN about 1925.

Notes for LIDA C. FLANIGAN:

She first married DANIEL "DAN" M. HARRIS on August 01, 1895 in Floyd County, Indiana, son of unknown parents. Dan was born in September 1854 in Illinois and died on May 23, 1921 in Madison, Jefferson County, Indiana. Dan was a member of the Central Christian Church in New Albany, Indiana at the time of his death. Together Dan and Lida had 4 children as follows: MATTIE MAY HARRIS (b. Sep 1896 in Floyd County, Indiana; d. August 12, 1910 in New Albany, Floyd County, Indiana from diphtheria in her home at 306 Cherry Street), BLUCHER HARRIS (b. 1902 in New Albany, Floyd County, Indiana), STELLA HARRIS (b. 1903 in New Albany, Floyd County, Indiana and died August 07, 1910 in New Albany, Floyd County, Indiana from diphtheria in her home at 306 Cherry Street), and CHESTER S. HARRIS (b. 1908 in New Albany, Floyd County, Indiana; d. March 10, 1967 in Memphis, Clark County, Indiana).

Lida's first husband, DANIEL "DAN" M. HARRIS, was previously married to FANNIE BECLER on July 16, 1874 in Floyd County, Indiana. She was born about 1858 in Indiana. Together they had 3 children as follows: EDITH MAY HARRIS (b. April 1875 in Floyd County, Indiana; d. November 10, 1959 in New Albany, Floyd County, Indiana; m. DAVID F. ESPIN on January 11, 1893 in Floyd County, Indiana), FLORENCE ISABEL HARRIS (b. November 07, 1877 in New Albany, Floyd County, Indiana; d. September 27, 1941 in Minneola, Clark County, Kansas; m. JOSEPH BEVERLY SCHOONOVER on December 15, 1900 in Floyd County, Indiana), and UNKOWN HARRIS (b. about 1881 in New Albany, Floyd County, Indiana; m. A. S. WILLIAMS). Funeral Services for Daniel M. Harris were handled by George A. Kraft (now known as the Kraft Funeral Home of New Albany, Indiana). Kraft Funeral Home has been in business for six generations and 150 years.

DEATH OF D. H. HARRIS.

The body of Daniel H. Harris, of this city, who died in Madison arrived Tuesday at noon and was taken to the funeral parlors of George A. Kraft pending arrangements for the funeral. Mr. Harris was 81 years old. Surviving are three daughters, Mrs. David S. Espin, of this city, Mrs. Florence Schoonover of Minneola, Kan., and Mrs. A. S. Williams, of Long Beach, Cal. He was a member of Central Christian church.

Obituary for Daniel "Dan" M. Harris - May 24, 1921
(New Albany Daily Ledger, Obituary for Daniel "Dan" M. Harris)

Daniel's daughter from his first marriage, EDITH MAY HARRIS, married DAVID "DAVE" F. ESPIN on January 11, 1893 in Floyd County, Indiana, son of RICHARD ESPIN and MALENA MNU. Dave was born in January 1869 in Taylor, Harrison County, Indiana.

Edith died on Tuesday, November 10, 1959 at 4:10pm at the Floyd County Memorial Hospital in New Albany, Indiana. She lived at 1612 Culbertson in New Albany, Indiana at the time of her death, and was a member of the First Presbyterian Church.

Funeral Services: Mullineaux Funeral Home of New Albany, Floyd County, Indiana. Mullineaux Funeral Home is still in business today as the Pyke-Calloway Funeral Service and Mullineaux Chapel. They operate at 1217 E Spring Street in New Albany, Indiana.

Mrs. Edith Espin

Mrs. Edith Espin, 81, died at 4:10 p.m. Tuesday at Floyd County Memorial Hospital. She was the widow of Dave Espin. She lived at 1612 Culbertson and was a member of the First Presbyterian Church.

Survivors include three sons, Gordon and Melvin Espin, both of New Albany and Vernon Espin, of Cincinnati; three daughters, Mrs. Mildred Kinman and Mrs. Margaret Kepley of New Albany, and Mrs. Alma E. Martin, Georgetown; five grandchildren and eight great-grandchildren.

The body is at the Mullineaux Funeral Home where arrangements are pending. Friends may call after 5 p.m. today.

Obituary for Edith May Harris Espin – November 11, 1959
(New Albany Tribune, Obituary for Edith May Harris Espin)

Lida's son, BLUCHER HARRIS, died at Saint Edward's Hospital at midnight on Saturday, September 23, 1922 after an attack of pleurisy. Blucher had suffered from the illness for three weeks prior to his death. Funeral Services were handled by George A. Kraft (now known as the Kraft Funeral Home of New Albany, Indiana).

DIES OF PLEURISY

Blucher Harris, 20 years old, son of the late Daniel Harris, died at midnight Saturday at St. Edward's Hospital, following an attack of pleurisity from which he had suffered for the past three weeks. He is survived by a brother, Chester Harris, of Louisville, and a sister, Mrs. David Espin, New Albany. The body was removed to the funeral establishment of George A. Kraft.

Obituary for Blucher Harris - September 27, 1922
(New Albany Weekly Ledger, Obituary for Blucher Harris)

Daniel divorced Lida on December 10, 1912 in New Albany, Floyd County, Indiana. The allegations that Daniel made in the divorce decree against Lida were cruel treatment and desertion.

The home at 306 Cherry Street no longer exists. A church has been built where the house once stood at the corner of Cherry Street and Griffin Street.

Mattie Harris, thirteen years of age and a daughter of Mr. and Mrs. Daniel Harris, 306 Cherry street, died this morning of diphtheria and will be buried in Fairview cemetery tomorrow morning. This is the second death from the disease in the family within a week, and two other children are critically ill of the malady.

Obituary for Mattie May Harris - August 12, 1910
(New Albany Daily Ledger, Obituary for Mattie Harris)

Stella, the seven year old daughter of
Mr. and Mrs. Daniel Harris; died Sunday at their home, 306 Cherry street,
after an illness of several weeks of
diphtheria.

Obituary for Stella Harris - August 09, 1910
(Public Press, Obituary for Stella Harris)

Decrees of divorce have been entered
of record in the circuit court in the
suit of Daniel M. Harris against Lida
C. Harris, cruel treatment and desertion being the allegations, and in the
suit of Stella Prince against John T.
Prince, the allegation being desertion
and failure to provide. The evidence
was heard several weeks ago by Judge
W. C. Utz.

Divorce Announcement for Daniel "Dan" M. Harris and Lida C.
Flanigan Harris - December 10, 1912
(New Albany Evening Tribune, Decree of Divorce for Daniel "Dan" M.
Harris and Lida C. Flanigan)

More about for LIDA C. FLANIGAN:
Her Kentucky death certificate is #14-15754. Lida is listed as
married and with no occupation at the time of her death. She died at
10am in her home on 645 South 6th Street.
Informant: L. E. Flanigan (most likely LUTHER EMERY FLANIGAN, a
cousin who is also buried in Milltown Cemetery).
Parents: John Flanigan of Indiana and Martha Sheron of Indiana.
Cause of death: Incised wound of neck, homicide.
Funeral Services: Lee A. Cralle of 600 West Chestnut Street in
Louisville, Jefferson County, Kentucky. This is the same undertaker
that was used for Charles' first wife, Rebecca Jane Moore, and his
address is just down the street from Charles' address.
Burial: June 13, 1914 at Milltown Cemetery in Milltown, Harrison
County, Indiana. She is buried next to her parents and two of her
sisters.
The residence at 645 South 6th Street no longer exists.

Charles Muss Kills Wife at Louis-ville.

Charles Muss, aged forty-five years, of Louisville, cut his wife's throat with a razor last Friday week and then slashed his own throat. The woman died instantly, but Muss was still living at last report. Mrs. Muss was a daughter of Mrs. Ida Flanigan, of Milltown, and the body was shipped to Milltown for burial. She was also a cousin of William Flanigan, of Heth township, this county.

News Story for Charles Muss and Lida C. Flanigan - June 24, 1914
(Corydon Democrat)

Headstone for Lida C. Flanigan Harris Muss (Ransdell)

Notes for JOHN FLANIGAN (Father of LIDA C. FLANIGAN):
　　John was born on August 05, 1833 in Indiana and died on March 05, 1905 in Harrison County, Indiana. He is buried at Milltown Cemetery in Milltown, Harrison County, Indiana. He was the son of WILLIAM FLANIGAN and REBECCA MNU. John married MARTHA "MATTIE"

JANE SHERRON on June 07, 1860 in Crawford County, Indiana. Together John and Mattie had at least 10 children as follows: REBECCA J. FLANIGAN (b. about 1861 in Indiana), SARAH A. FLANIGAN (b. March 1862 in Indiana; m. JOSEPH L. BOLDT on July 09, 1880 in Harrison County, Indiana), JOHN W. FLANIGAN (b. about 1864 in Indiana; m. MARY IDA BABCOCK on March 04, 1894 in Harrison County, Indiana), MARY FLANIGAN (b. about 1867 in Indiana), FRANCES FLANIGAN (b. about 1869 in Indiana), LIDA C. FLANIGAN (b. February 06, 1873 in Harrison County, Indiana; d. June 12, 1914 in Louisville, Jefferson County, Kentucky; m1. DANIEL "DAN" M. HARRIS on August 01, 1895 in Floyd County, Indiana; d1. DANIEL "DAN" M. HARRIS on December 10, 1912; m2. CHARLES MUSS on April 06, 1913 in Clark County, Indiana), MARGARET IDA FLANIGAN (b. January 08, 1875 in Harrison County, Indiana; d. August 25, 1956 in Harrison County, Indiana), ETTA FLANIGAN (b. May 03, 1878 in Harrison County, Indiana; March 29, 1964 in Harrison County, Indiana), CORA FLANIGAN (b. June 1881 in Indiana), and MATTIE FLANIGAN (b. September 1885 in Indiana).

Notes for MARTHA "MATTIE" JANE SHERRON (Mother of LIDA C. FLANIGAN):
    Mattie was born on April 06, 1840 in Indiana to unknown parents. She is buried at Milltown Cemetery in Milltown, Harrison County, Indiana. She shares an obelisk headstone with her husband, but no date of death was engraved for her side of the headstone.

7. MARY EMMA[2] MUSS (JOHN[1] MUSS) was born August 04, 1865 in Bullitt County, Kentucky and died October 30, 1932 in Meadow Lawn, Jefferson County, Kentucky. She married JAMES H. DORIOT on December 12, 1889 in Louisville, Jefferson County, Kentucky, son of CHARLES "CHARLIE" DORIOT, SR. (born in France) and SARAH ZENOR (born about 1827 in Kentucky). He was born December 06, 1857 in Kentucky and died May 31, 1918 in Louisville, Jefferson County, Kentucky.

320

MARRIAGE

DATE OF LICENSE.	PARTIES' NAMES.	BY WHOM MARRIED

Marriage License for James H. Doriot and Mary Emma Muss
(Family History Center, Jefferson County, Kentucky Marriages)

Notes for MARY EMMA MUSS:

In the 1900 census it states that Mary Muss Doriot had 5 children with 3 living and in the 1910 census she had 7 children with 4 living.

In the 1920 Jefferson County, Kentucky census, Mary Doriot, 54, widow, is head of the household with David, 17 and Nannie, 23.

Picture of Mary Emma Muss Doriot
(Lyle Raymond Cook & Karla Denise Ezell Cook)

The above photograph was taken between 1886 and 1892. Charles H. Devenny opened his studio in 1886 at 267 West Jefferson Street and operated his studio there until 1890. In 1893, he reopened his studio as a partnership called Carpenter & Devenny. Devenny apparently merged with Carpenter & Company that was operated by Robert J. Carpenter since 1882, and had previously operated at 846 West Market. The new partnership operated at 846 West Market Street for only one year. Robert J. Carpenter continued sole proprietorship until 1895, and Charles H. Devenny reopened his business for one year in 1897 at 708 East Green.

More about MARY EMMA MUSS:
Mary died at 9am on Sunday, October 30, 1932 at the residence of Mrs. Fred Zoller in Meadow Lawn, Jefferson County, Kentucky.

Her Kentucky death certificate is #32-23815. Mary is listed as widowed, but previously married to James Doriot and a housekeeper at the time of her death. She died at 9am.

Informant: David Doriot of Valley Station, Kentucky.

Parents: Charles Muss (incorrect) and Elizabeth.

Cause of death: Bronchial Pneumonia and myocarditis due to hypertension. Bronchial pneumonia is a respiratory disease characterize by inflammation of the lung parenchyma with congestion caused by viruses or bacteria or irritants. Myocarditis is an inflammation of the myocardium (heart muscle) that persists after an acute bacterial infection. Hypertension describes high blood pressure.

Funeral Services: W. G. Hardy of West Point, Kentucky. Services were held on Tuesday, November 1, 1932 at 2pm in the South Jefferson Baptist Church. Today South Jefferson Baptist Church is located at 6506 Pendleton Road in Louisville, Kentucky near the intersection of Dixie Highway and Pendleton Road.

Burial: Tuesday, November 01, 1932 at Pauley Cemetery in Bullitt County, Kentucky.

DORIOT—Sunday, October 34, 1932, at 9 a.m., Mrs. Mary E. Doriot, in her seventy-first year, at the residence of Mrs. Fred Zoller at Meadowlawn, KY. Funeral Tuesday, November 1, at 2 p.m. at the South Jefferson Baptist Church. Burial in Pauley Cemetery.

Obituary for Mary Emma Muss Doriot – Occtober 31, 1932
(Louisville Times, Obituary for Mary Emma Muss Doriot)

Notes for JAMES H. DORIOT:
In the 1900 Shepherdsville, Bullitt County, Kentucky census (conducted on June 01, 1900) James H. Doriot, 41, is head of the household with Mary, 34, James C., 7, Nannie M., 3 and Morna, 2/12. James is listed as a Farmer.

In the 1910 Bewleyville, Breckinridge County, Kentucky census (conducted on April 15, 1910) James Doriot, 52, is head of the household with Mary, 44, Clyde, 17, Nannie, 13, David, 7 and Lonnie, 4. James is listed as a Carpenter.

More about JAMES H. DORIOT:

His Kentucky death certificate is #18-13618. James is listed as married and without occupation at the time of his death. He died at 11:20pm.

Informant: City Hospital.

Parents: Charles Doriot of Kentucky and Unknown.

Cause of death: Cerebral hemorrhage and chronic interstitial nephritis due to arteriosclerosis. Interstitial nephritis is an inflammation of the kidney tissues. Cerebral hemorrhage is a medical term that describes a stroke. A stroke happens when blood flow to a part of the brain stops. Interstitial nephritis is a kidney disorder in which the spaces between the kidney tubules become swollen and inflamed. Arteriosclerosis is a hardening of the arteries that occurs when fat, cholesterol and other substances build up in the walls of arteries.

Funeral Services: Illegible of Highland Park, Kentucky.

Burial: June 02, 1918 in Medora, Jefferson County, Kentucky. James is most likely buried in Pauley Cemetery which is nearby.

Notes for CHARLES "CHARLIE" DORIOT, SR. (Father of JAMES H. DORIOT):

Charles was born about 1923 in France and died on September 20, 1885 in Daviess County, Kentucky.

Charles first married SARAH ZENOR on November 30, 1848 in Jefferson County, Kentucky. Charles and Sarah had 4 known children as follows: ELIZABETH "LIZZIE" DORIOT (b. about 1850 in Jefferson County, Kentucky), WILLIAM T. DORIOT (b. February 08, 1851 in Jefferson County, Kentucky; d. May 04 1935 in Hopkinsville, Christian County, Kentucky; m. MARY F. CRABTREE on October 23, 1874 in Daviess County, Kentucky), JULIA DORIOT (b. about 1853 in Jefferson County, Kentucky; d. January 13, 1894 in Bullitt County, Kentucky; m. DR RICHARD L. TYDINGS on March 25, 1877 in Bullitt County, Kentucky), and JAMES H. DORIOT (b. December 06, 1857 in Jefferson County, Kentucky; d. May 31, 1918 in Louisville, Jefferson County, Kentucky; m. MARY EMMA MUSS on December 12, 1889 in Jefferson County, Kentucky).

Charles later married NANCY JANE ZENOR on September 01, 1859 in Louisville, Jefferson County, Kentucky. It is unknown at this time whether Sarah and Nancy Jane Zenor were sisters, but it assumed that they were. Together Charles and Nancy had 5 known children as follows: CHARLES DORIOT, JR. (b. July 1860 in Louisville, Jefferson County, Kentucky), THOMAS JACOB DORIOT (b. April 18, 1862 in Jefferson County, Kentucky; d. December 09, 1952 in Daviess County, Kentucky; m. MAY VICTORINE WALKER about 1888), JOHN ZENOR DORIOT (b. January 03, 1864 in Bullitt County, Kentucky; d. October 02, 1935 in Hopkinsville, Christian County, Kentucky; m. his cousin, SARILDA JANE "JENNIE" BURNS on October 18, 1899 in Daviess County,

Kentucky), AGNES S. DORIOT (b. March 06, 1868 in Jefferson County, Kentucky; d. April 03, 1926 in Daviess County, Kentucky; m. JOHN LYONS on January 07, 1903 in Hawesville, Hancock County, Kentucky), and ADALAIDE "ADA" B. DORIOT (b. May 1870 in Kentucky; m. WILLIAM H. POWERS about 1896).

Notes for SARAH ZENOR (Mother of JAMES H. DORIOT):
Sarah was born about 1827 in Kentucky. It is highly likely she is the older sister of NANCY JANE ZENOR.

Notes for NANCY JANE ZENOR (Step Mother of JAMES H. DORIOT):
Nancy was born on June 09, 1829 in Kentucky and died January 02, 1920 in Owensboro, Davies County, Kentucky. She was the daughter of HENRY ZENOR and ELIZA "LUCY" TYLER.
Burial: Elmwood Cemetery (now called Rosehill Elmwood Cemetery) in Owensboro, Daviess County, Kentucky.

Children of MARY EMMA[2] MUSS and JAMES H. DORIOT are:

    i.   JAMES CLYDE[3] DORIOT, b. April 1893 in Bullitt County, Kentucky.

    ii.   NANNIE M.[3] DORIOT, b. August 25, 1895 in Bullitt County, Kentucky; d. May 18, 1970 in Louisville, Jefferson County, Kentucky.

    iii.   MORNA[3] DORIOT, b. March 1900 in Bullitt County, Kentucky; d. Before 1910.

    iv.   DAVID P.[3] DORIOT, b. About 1903 in Kentucky; d. September 17, 1957, Jefferson County, Kentucky.

    v.   LONNIE[3] DORIOT, b. About 1906 in Kentucky; d. February 13, 1919 in Frankfort, Franklin County, Kentucky.

8. ELIZABETH "BETTIE"[2] MUSS (*JOHN[1] MUSS*) was born July 28, 1867 in Bullitt County, Kentucky and died January 09, 1945 in Louisville, Jefferson County, Kentucky. She married CHARLES L. APPLEGATE on June 24, 1889 in Jefferson County, Kentucky, son of JAMES W. APPLEGATE and ELIZABETH JANE CRONE. He was born March 1869 in Kentucky and died 1935 in Jefferson County, Kentucky.

Marriage Bond

THE COMMONWEALTH OF KENTUCKY.

Be it Known, That we *Charles Applegate*

as principal, and *Chas Muss*

as surety, are jointly and severally bound to the Commonwealth of Kentucky in the sum of One Hundred Dollars.

THE CONDITION OF THIS BOND IS AS FOLLOWS:

That, whereas Marriage is intended to be solemnized between the above bound *Charles Applegate*

and *Bettie Muss*

Now, if there is no lawful cause to obstruct said Marriage, this bond shall be void, otherwise it shall remain in full force and effect.

Dated at Louisville, Jefferson County, this _24_ day

of _June_ 188_9_.

Attest:

Chas D Geppert
Clerk Jefferson County Court.

Charles Applegate
Charles Muss

Marriage License for Elizabeth "Bettie" Muss and Charles L. Applegate
(Family History Center, Jefferson County, Kentucky Marriages)

Notes for ELIZABETH "BETTIE" MUSS:

In 1889, Charles Applegate and Charles Muss, Bettie's older brother, signed the $100 marriage bond for the marriage between Charles Applegate and Bettie Muss.

In the 1900 census it states that Bettie Muss Applegate had 3 children with 3 living and in the 1910 census she had 4 children with 4 living.

More about ELIZABETH "BETTIE" MUSS:

Her Kentucky death certificate is #45-00979. Elizabeth is listed as widowed, but previous husband was Charles Applegate at the time of her death. She died at 4:45pm in the Norton Infirmary.

Informant: Mr. Edward Applegate of Shepherdsville, Kentucky.

Parents: John Muss of Germany and Unknown.

Cause of death: Shock for 5.5 hours due to third degree burns over entire body surface caused by an accident in her home.

Funeral Services: W. G. Hardy of Shively, Kentucky. Services were conducted at 2pm on Thursday, January 11, 1945 in her residence on Knob Creek Road.

Burial: Thursday, January 11, 1945 at South Jefferson Cemetery in Jefferson County, Kentucky.

The Norton Infirmary was a hospital located on the northeast corner of Third and Oak Streets in Louisville, Kentucky. The hospital was first opened in 1886 as the John N. Norton Infirmary, and named after a local Episcopal priest and missionary who died in 1881. The house that became the infirmary was purchased by John N. Norton's wife in 1881 with proceeds from the sale of her home on Broadway. This was the city's first protestant hospital.

APPLEGATE, Mrs. Elizabeth (nee Muss), in her 78th year, suddenly, Tuesday, January 9, 1945, at 4:45 p.m. at the Norton Infirmary. Residence on the Knob Creek Road. Beloved mother of Edward, Roy W., Charles E. and J. Wesley Applegate; also survived by 9 grandchildren and 5 great-grandchildren. Notice of funeral services later.

Obituary 1 for Elizabeth "Bettie" Muss Applegate – January 10, 1945 (Louisville Courier-Journal, Obituary 1 for Elizabeth "Bettie" Muss Applegate)

APPLEGATE, . Mrs. Elizabeth (nee Muss), in her 78th year, suddenly, Tuesday, January 9, 1945, at 4:45 p.m. at the Norton Infirmary. Residence on the Knob Creek Road. Beloved mother of Edward, Roy W., Charles E. and J. Wesley Applegate; also survived by 9 grandchildren and 5 great-grandchildren. Funeral services Thursday, January 11, at 2 p.m. at the residence. Interment in South Jefferson Cemetery.

Obituary 2 for Elizabeth "Bettie" Muss Applegate – January 11, 1945
(Louisville Courier-Journal, Obituary 2 for Elizabeth "Bettie" Muss Applegate)

Headstone for Charles L. Applegate & Elizabeth "Bettie" Muss Applegate
(Swelnis, Headstone for Charles L. Applegate & Elizabeth "Bettie" Muss Applegate)

Notes for CHARLES L. APPLEGATE:
In the 1900 Shepherdsville, Bullitt County, Kentucky census (conducted on June 01, 1900) Charley Applegate, 31, is head of the household with Bettie, 32, Lewis E., 10, Roy W., 8 and James W., 1. Charles is listed as a Farmer.

In the 1910 Bullitt County, Kentucky census (conducted on April 21, 1910) Chas. Applegate, 41, is head of the household with Bettie,

42, Edward, 21, Roy, 17, Wesley, 11 and Emory, 2. Charles is listed as a Farmer.

In the 1920 Shepherdsville, Bullitt County, Kentucky census (conducted on January 13, 1920) Chas. Applegate, 50, is head of the household with Bettie, 52, Roy, 27, Wesley, 21 and Emery, 13. Charles is listed as a Farmer.

In the 1930 Shepherdsville, Bullitt County, Kentucky census (conducted on May 01, 1930) Charles Applegate, 62, is head of the household with Bettie, 61 and Charles E., 23. Charles is listed as a Farmer.

More about CHARLES L. APPLEGATE:

A Kentucky death certificate cannot be found for him in 1935 so he may have died in another state.

Burial: 1935 at South Jefferson Cemetery in Jefferson County, Kentucky.

Picture of Charles L. Applegate and Elizabeth "Bettie" Muss Applegate
(Lyle Raymond Cook & Karla Denise Ezell Cook)

The above photograph was taken between 1886 and 1892.
Please refer to the photo of Mary Emma Muss for additional
information regarding the photography company that took this photo.

Notes for JAMES W. APPLEGATE (Father of CHARLES L. APPLEGATE):

James was born about 1833 in Harrison County, Indiana to STACY APPLEGATE (b. October 01, 1810 in Louisville, Jefferson County, Kentucky; d. June 08, 1884 in West Point, Hardin County, Kentucky; buried in Applegate Cemetery in Kosmosdale, Jefferson County, Kentucky; m1. CATHARINE DETRICK on December 29, 1831 in Harrison County, Indiana; m2. REBECCA M. BROWN on September 26, 1836 in Harrison County, Indiana) and CATHERINE DETRICK (b. about 1812; d. about 1834 in Harrison County, Indiana).

James married ELIZABETH JANE CRONE on October 06, 1864 in Bullitt County, Kentucky. James and Elizabeth had 2 known children as follows: ANDREW APPLEGATE (b. about 1866 in Kentucky) and CHARLES "CHARLIE" L. APPLEGATE (b. March 1869 in Kentucky; d. 1935 in Jefferson County, Kentucky; m. ELIZABETH "BETTIE" MUSS on June 24, 1889 in Jefferson County, Kentucky). It is believed that James and Elizabeth both died some time between 1870 and 1880 since both Andrew and Charles can be found living with their grandmother, CHARLOTTE MARTHA MOORE (b. about 1814 in Kentucky; m. JOHN CRONE on November 06, 1934 in Bullitt County, Kentucky), in the 1880 census for Meadow Lawn, Jefferson County, Kentucky.

James was the only known child from STACY APPLEGATE and CATHARINE DETRICK. James had 6 half siblings from the marriage between Stacy and REBECCA M. BROWN as follows: DAVID THOMAS APPLEGATE (b. July 12, 1837 in Harrison County, Indiana; d. June 26, 1904 in Kentucky; m. ANNA MULLIN on November 20, 1875 in Louisville, Jefferson County, Kentucky), ELIZABETH APPLEGATE (b. March 11, 1839 in Harrison County, Indiana; d. August 02, 1864 in Kentucky; m. RAWLEY M. DAVIS on March 17, 1857 in Hardin County, Kentucky), JOHN WESLEY APPLEGATE (b. November 30, 1842 in Kentucky; d. December 06, 1902 in Kentucky; m1. MARY E. MILES on February 03, 1875 in Jefferson County, Kentucky; m2. ANNA E. WITHERS on June 07, 1881 in Hardin County, Kentucky at The Methodist Church), HENRY C. APPLEGATE (b. about 1848 in Kentucky; m. ANNIE MASON on March 18, 1880 in Louisville, Jefferson County, Kentucky), DR. ABEL BROWN APPLEGATE (b. December 25, 1849 in Hardin County, Kentucky; d. April 01, 1914 in Kosmosdale, Jefferson County, Kentucky; m. JOSEPINE "JOSIE" COLVIN on December 30, 1877 in Harrison County, Indiana), WILLIAM C. APPLEGATE (b. about 1853 in Kentucky; m. MARGARET "MAGGIE" R. MILES on December 25, 1879 in Jefferson County, Kentucky).

Notes for ELIZABETH JANE CRONE (Mother of CHARLES L. APPLEGATE):

Elizabeth was born about 1837 in Bullitt County, Kentucky to JOHN CRONE and CHARLOTTE MARTHA MOORE.

Children of ELIZABETH "BETTIE"[2] MUSS and CHARLES L. APPLEGATE are:

    i.   LOUIS EDWARD "ED"[3] APPLEGATE, b. March 15, 1890 in Riverview, Jefferson County, Kentucky; d. October 05, 1969 in Shelby County, Kentucky; m. LILLIAN "LILLIE" MAY MERKER.

    ii.   ROY WALKER[3] APPLEGATE, b. August 31, 1891 in West Point, Bullitt County, Kentucky; d. April 30, 1976 in West Point, Hardin County, Kentucky; m. ZULA COOK on December 25, 1920 in Kentucky.

    iii.   JAMES WESLEY[3] APPLEGATE, SR., b. June 07, 1898 in Bullitt County, Kentucky; d. June 22, 1979 in Louisville, Jefferson County, Kentucky; m. ANNABEL "ANNA" B. STOVALL about 1923.

    iv.   CHARLES EMORY "JACK"[3] APPLEGATE, b. July 22, 1906 in Bullitt County, Kentucky; d. May 18, 1967 in Louisville, Jefferson County, Kentucky.

9. JOSEPH P.[2] MUSS *(JOHN[1] MUSS)* was born November 1869 in Bullitt County, Kentucky and died July 08, 1924 in Riley, Vigo County, Indiana. He married FLORENCE CASEY DUVALL LENDEL GAILBREATH on October 03, 1916 in Bullitt County, Kentucky, daughter of JOSIAH "JOE" CASEY and SUSAN UTTERBACK. She was born February 27, 1875 in Anderson County, Kentucky and died on May 27, 1953 in Louisville, Jefferson County, Kentucky.

Notes for JOSEPH P. MUSS:

In the 1900 Pierson, Vigo County, Indiana census (conducted on June 14, 1900) Joseph Muss, 27, is listed in the household of his brother-in-law, William M. Cook. Joseph is listed without an occupation.

In the 1910 Pierson, Vigo County, Indiana census (conducted in April 1910) Joseph P. Muss, 40, is listed alone. Joseph is listed as a Horseman in the Grooming industry.

In the 1920 Robbs, Jefferson County, Kentucky census (conducted on January 10, 1920) Joseph P. Muss, 50, is head of the household with Florence, 44 and LESLIE COMBS DUVALL, 24 (Joseph's step son and Florence's son from a previous marriage to Charles T. Duvall). Joseph is listed as a Farmer for a Truck Farm.

Picture of Joseph P. Muss
(Lyle Raymond Cook & Karla Denise Ezell Cook)

The above photo was taken around 1900. Photograph by E. Eppert.

More about JOSEPH P. MUSS:
Joseph died Tuesday, July 08, 1924 Riley, Vigo County, Indiana according to his obituary.

Funeral Services: Fox's Chapel in Riley, Indiana (now the Mattox-Fox Funeral Home at 6350 South Canal Street). Services were held at 10:00am.

Burial: Tuesday, July 08, 1924 in Maple Grove Cemetery of Clay City, Clay County, Indiana.

> ## JOSEPH MUSS.
> By Special Correspondent.
>
> RILEY, Ind., July 8.—Joseph Muss, age 53 years, died at 1:30 o'clock Tuesday morning. Funeral services will be held at Fox's chapel at Riley, Thursday at 10:00 a. m. Burial at Maple Grove cemetery near Clay City, Ind.

Obituary for Joseph P. Muss - July 08, 1924
(Terre Haute Tribune, Obituary for Joseph P. Muss)

Marriage Notes for JOSEPH P. MUSS and FLORENCE CASEY:

The Pioneer News (Bullitt County, Kentucky) - October 06, 1916 - "Mrs. Florence Lendall and Mr. J. P. Muss were quietly married at the residence of the Rev. Hardin Tuesday. Mrs. Lendall is one of the best known ladies of near Cupio, while Mr. Muss is a well known man. They will make their home on Mrs. Lendall's farm near Cupio. Their many friends join the Pioneer News in wishing them a long and happy life."

Notes for FLORENCE CASEY:

Florence was born on September 27, 1875 in Anderson County, Kentucky. She was the daughter of JOSIAH "JOE" CASEY and SUSAN UTTERBACK.

In 1894, she first married CHARLES T. DUVALL most likely in Franklin County, Kentucky, son of CHARLES W. DUVALL and MARGARET ANN BRAWNER. Charles was born in December 1866 in Kentucky. Together they had 2 children as follows: LESLIE COMBS DUVALL (b. August 15, 1895 in Franklin County, Kentucky; d. September 06, 1963 in Jefferson County, Kentucky) and BESSIE C. DUVALL (b. November 02, 1897 in Frankfort, Franklin County, Kentucky; m. ALFRED MELROSE PEIFFER; d. May 29, 1897 in Kenton County, Kentucky).

She later married PHILLIP LENDEL, JR. on August 20, 1908 in Jefferson County, Kentucky, son of PHILLIP LENDEL, SR. and SOPHIA TROUT. Phillip was born on October 26, 1855 in Buffalo, Erie County, New York and died on June 02, 1915 in Louisville, Jefferson County, Kentucky.

After the death of her second husband, Phillip, Florence married
JOSEPH P. MUSS on October 03, 1916 in Bullitt County, Kentucky.

After the death of her third husband, Joseph, Florence married
MR. GAILBREATH.

The Kentucky death certificate for Florence is #116 53 10424.
Florence died on Wednesday, May 27, 1953 at 11:15pm in her home
1425 Kentucky Avenue of Louisville, Jefferson County, Kentucky. She
was widowed at the time of her death.

Informant: Leslie Duvall.

Parents: Joseph Casey and Susan Utterback.

Cause of death: Adenocarcinoma of breast bilaterally for 6 years.

Burial: Wednesday, May 27, 1953 Evergreen Cemetery Louisville,
Jefferson County, Kentucky.

Notes for JOSIAH "JOE" CASEY (Father of FLORENCE CASEY):

Joe was born on February 11, 1839 in Kentucky and died October
02, 1887 in Anderson County, Kentucky. He was born to HENRY CASEY
(b. about 1808 in Kentucky) and and JANETTA "JANETTE" ETHINGTON (b.
about 1809 in Kentucky).

Joe married SUSAN UTTERBACK on May 04, 1861 in Anderson
County, Kentucky. Joe and Susan had 8 known children as follows:
THOMAS G. CASEY (b. about 1862 in Kentucky). WILLIAM H. CASEY (b.
August 02, 1864 in Anderson County, Kentucky; d. January 09, 1913
in Frankfort, Franklin County, Kentucky; m. ELIZA C. CROW on April 19,
1882 in Anderson County, Kentucky). CHARLES "CHARLEY" D. CASEY (b.
about 1867 in Kentucky). ELIJAH CASEY (b. about 1869 in
Lawrenceburg, Anderson County, Kentucky). EZRA CASEY (b. January
06, 1872 in Anderson County, Kentucky; d. April 21, 1939 in Shelby
County, Kentucky). FLORENCE CASEY (b. February 27, 1875 in Anderson
County, Kentucky; d. May 24, 1953 in Louisville, Jefferson County,
Kentucky; m1. CHARLES T. DUVALL about 1894; m2. PHILLIP LENDEL on
August 20, 1908 in Jefferson County, Kentucky; m3. JOSEPH P. MUSS on
October 03, 1916 in Bullitt County, Kentucky). NANNIE J. CASEY (b.
about 1878 in Anderson County, Kentucky). STRAWN CASEY (b. May 19,
1880 in Anderson County, Kentucky).

Joe had 6 siblings as follows: EMARINE CASEY (b. about 1831 in
Franklin County, Kentucky; m. SOLOMON KING TEMPLES on April 15,
1852 in Anderson County, Kentucky), MARY E. CASEY (b. about 1841 in
Kentucky; m. MOSES A. BLAKEMAN on August 10, 1861 in Anderson
County, Kentucky), DAVID HADE CASEY (b. about 1844 in Kentucky; m.
AMANDA "MANDA" E. GOWEN on July 23, 1864 in Anderson County,
Kentucky), REUBEN TURNER CASEY (b. July 1846 in Kentucky; m. LUCY
"ALICE" JANE GRUBBS on October 27, 1866 in Anderson County,
Kentucky), WILLIAM H. CASEY (b. about 1847 in Kentucky), and MARTHA
A. CASEY (b. about 1851 in Anderson County, Kentucky; m. ALFRED
BILITER on January 01, 1871 in Anderson County, Kentucky).

Notes for SUSAN UTTERBACK (Mother of FLORENCE CASEY):

Susan was born about 1843 in Anderson County, Kentucky to WILLIAM UTTERBACK and NANCY TINSLEY MCGINNIS.

Susan was the oldest child, and sister to 8 siblings as follows: JOHN W. UTTERBACK (b. about 1844 in Anderson County, Kentucky; m. PERMELIA H. V. WATERFILL on December 05, 1871 in Anderson County, Kentucky), SARAH FRANCES UTTERBACK (b. about 1846 in Anderson County, Kentucky; m. GEORGE JOHN LUCAS on June 06, 1867 in Anderson County, Kentucky), LAURA ANNA UTTERBACK (b. about 1849 in Anderson County, Kentucky; m. JAMES THOMAS PRATHER on September 10, 1868), HEZEKIAH UTTERBACK (b. about 1850 in Anderson County, Kentucky), NIMROD UTTERBACK (b. December 17, 1853 in Anderson County, Kentucky; m. MARY ETTER JOHNSON on August 31, 1881 in Anderson County, Kentucky), JAMES T. UTTERBACK (b. October 1856 in Anderson County, Kentucky; m. JENNIE STRANGE on July 20, 1880 in Anderson County, Kentucky), CORBIN DANIEL UTTERBACK (b. July 1859 in Lawrenceburg, Anderson County, Kentucky; m. JENNIE K. SHOUSE on February 16, 1887 in Anderson County, Kentucky), ELLA UTTERBACK (b. about 1863 in Anderson County, Kentucky).

Generation No. 3: All Known Descendants

10. WILLIAM JOSEPH "JOE"[3] MUSS *(JOHN CARROLL[2] MUSS, JOHN[1] MUSS)* was born August 19, 1884 in Kentucky and died August 11, 1974 in Jefferson County, Kentucky. He married MARTHA "MATTIE" ROBERTS VAUGHN December 24, 1905 in Bullitt County, Kentucky, daughter of JOHN LEWIS VAUGHN and MALISSA "MALISSIE" JANE SANDERS. She was born February 09, 1880 in Bullitt County, Kentucky and died March 25, 1947 in West Point, Bullitt County, Kentucky.

Marriage License for William Joseph "Joe" Muss and Martha "Mattie"
Roberts Vaughn - 2nd entry from top
(Family History Center, Kentucky Marriages, 1785-1979)

Notes for WILLIAM JOSEPH "JOE" MUSS:
    In the September 12, 1918 World War I draft registration,
William Joseph is listed as living in Valley Station, Jefferson County,
Kentucky and is a helper in pipe fitting for Griffith and Son out of New

York, New York. His nearest relative is Mattie Muss living at his address. William is medium height and build with brown eyes and black hair.

In the 1920 Shepherdsville, Bullitt County, Kentucky census (conducted on January 22, 1920) Joe Muss, 35, is head of the household with Mattie, 39, Anna, 11, Charles, 6 and Willie, 7/12. Joe is listed as a Farmer.

In the 1930 Bullitt County, Kentucky census (conducted on April 25, 1930) W. J. Muss, 45, is head of the household with Nettie, 50, Chester L, 16, and Roy, 10. William Joseph's brother, Roy, 36, is also living with them. William Joseph is listed as a Foreman for Portland Cement Plant.

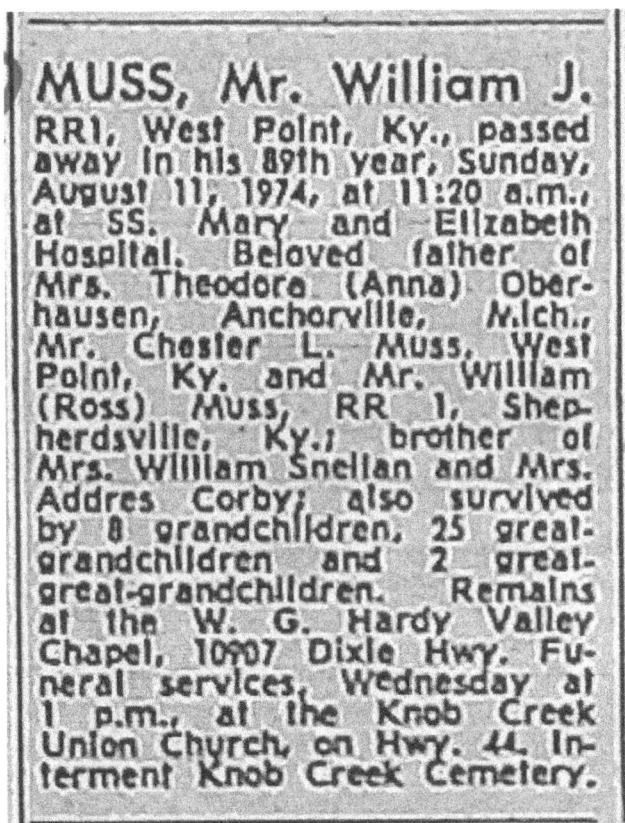

> **MUSS, Mr. William J.**
> RR1, West Point, Ky., passed away in his 89th year, Sunday, August 11, 1974, at 11:20 a.m., at SS. Mary and Elizabeth Hospital. Beloved father of Mrs. Theodore (Anna) Oberhausen, Anchorville, Mich., Mr. Chester L. Muss, West Point, Ky. and Mr. William (Ross) Muss, RR 1, Shepherdsville, Ky.; brother of Mrs. William Snellan and Mrs. Addres Corby; also survived by 8 grandchildren, 25 great-grandchildren and 2 great-great-grandchildren. Remains at the W. G. Hardy Valley Chapel, 10907 Dixie Hwy. Funeral services, Wednesday at 1 p.m., at the Knob Creek Union Church on Hwy. 44. Interment Knob Creek Cemetery.

Obituary for William Joseph "Joe" Muss – August 12, 1974
(Louisville Times, Obituary for William Joseph "Joe" Muss)

More about WILLIAM JOSEPH "JOE" MUSS:
In 1905, William Joseph and Martha were married at Knob Creek Church in Bullitt County, Kentucky. Joe Able and Burk Vaughn were

witnesses to the marriage ceremony that was performed by Thomas J. Ramsey, L.D. Thomas J. Ramsey also performed the marriage between John Carroll Muss and Anna Eliza Hopewell.

Joe died on Sunday, August 11, 1974 at 11:20am in Saints Mary and Elizabeth Hospital in Louisville, Kentucky.

Funeral Services: W. G. Hardy at 10907 Dixie Highway in Valley Station, Kentucky. Funeral services were held at 1pm on Wednesday, August 14, 1974 in the Knob Creek Union Church at Cupio, Kentucky.

Burial: Wednesday, August 14, 1974 at Knob Creek Union Church Cemetery in Cupio, Bullitt County, Kentucky.

Headstone for William Joseph "Joe" Muss and Martha "Mattie" Roberts Vaughn
(Browning, Headstone for William Joseph "Joe" Muss and Martha "Mattie" Roberts Vaughn)

Notes for MARTHA "MATTIE" ROBERTS VAUGHN:

Martha was first married a MR. JEFFERS or JEFFRIES about 1900. No record can be found for their marriage at this time, but Martha was listed with the last name of JEFFERS on the marriage license and the last name of JEFFRIES on the Bullitt County Pioneer News newspaper article.

MUSS, Martha Roberts (nee Vaughn), of West Point, Ky., R. R. 1, passed away in her 68th year, Tuesday, March 25, 1947, at 11:15 p.m., at her residence. Beloved wife of William Joseph Muss; mother of Mrs. Anna V. Obenhausen, Chester L. and William Ray Muss; sister of Mrs. Pearl Sanders, Mrs. Hugh King, Mrs. Carl Greenfield, Charles R. Vaughn and William A. Vaughn. Remains at her residence at West Point, Ky., R. R. 1. Funeral services Friday, March 28, at 2:30 p.m., at the Knob Creek Church. Interment in Knob Creek

Obituary for Martha "Mattie" Roberts Vaughn Jeffers Muss - March 27, 1947
(Louisville Courier-Journal, Obituary for Martha "Mattie" Roberts Vaughn Jeffers Muss)

More about MARTHA "MATTIE" ROBERTS VAUGHN:
Her Kentucky death certificate is #47-04898. Martha is listed as married at the time of her death.

Martha died Tuesday, March 25, 1947 at 11:15pm in her home on Rural Route 1 in West Point, Kentucky

Informant: John W. Muss of West Point, Kentucky.

Parents: John Vaughn of Kentucky and Malessa JANE Snaders of Kentucky.

Cause of death: Myocarditis. Myocarditis is an inflammation of the myocardium (heart muscle) that persists after an acute bacterial infection.

Funeral Services: W. G. Hardy of 4101 Dixie Highway in Shively, Kentucky. Services were held on Friday, March 28, 1947 at 2:30pm in the Knob Creek Church.

Burial: Friday, March 28, 1947 at Knob Creek Union Church Cemetery in Cupio, Bullitt County, Kentucky.

Marriage Notes for WILLIAM JOSEPH "JOE" MUSS and MARTHA "MATTIE" ROBERTS VAUGHN:
The Pioneer News (Bullitt County, Kentucky) - January 05, 1906 - Cupio Section - "A pretty Yule Tide wedding was that of Mrs. Mattie Jeffries and Mr. Joe Muss which was solemnized at the church December 24 with the Rev. T. J. Ramsey officiating. Miss Florence Griffin was the maid of honor and Mr. Edward Smith was the best man. Wedding march played by Mrs. Cleo Vaughn. Reception given at home of bride's aunt, Mrs. George Griffin, of Kosmosdale. Will make home at Cupio."

Children of WILLIAM JOSEPH "JOE"[3] MUSS and MARTHA "MATTIE" ROBERTS VAUGHN are:

    i.   ANNA VAUGHN[4] MUSS, b. March 03, 1908 in Bullitt County, Kentucky; d. September 12, 1985 in Mount Clemens, Macomb County, Michigan; m1. LLOYD NELSON MARTIN on July 29, 1923 in Clark County, Indiana; m2. THEODORE EMMETT OBERHAUSEN about 1927.

    ii.   CHESTER LOUIS[4] MUSS, b. December 04, 1913 in Bullitt County, Kentucky; d. August 04, 1985 in Louisville, Jefferson County, Kentucky.

        More about CHESTER LOUIS MUSS:
            Burial: Knob Creek Union Church Cemetery in Cupio, Bullitt County, Kentucky

    iii.   MARY PEARL[4] MUSS, b. May 09, 1918 in Bullitt County, Kentucky; d. May 09, 1918 in Bullitt County, Kentucky.

        More about MARY PEARL MUSS:
            Burial: Vaughn Burying Grounds in Bullitt County, Kentucky
            Cause of Death: 6 months old when born. Her mother was in her forties.
            Informant: Joseph Muss of Valley Station, Kentucky.

    iv.   WILLIAM "WILLIE" RAY[4] MUSS, b. May 28, 1919 in Bullitt County, Kentucky; d. February 26, 1980 in Bullitt County, Kentucky.

11. MARGARET P.[3] MUSS *(JOHN CARROLL[2] MUSS, JOHN[1] MUSS)* was born July 1886 in Kentucky. No additional information can be found on Margaret P. Muss at this time. Since she is not found in the 1920 census she may have married or died prior to this.

Notes for MARGARET P. MUSS:
    In the 1910 Bullitt County, Kentucky census (conducted on April 21, 1910) Margaret Muss, 23, is single and living with her parents.
    On February 06, 1912 Margaret can be found in the family photo which was taken in Bullitt County, Kentucky.

12. JOHN EARL[3] MUSS *(JOHN CARROLL[2] MUSS, JOHN[1] MUSS)* was born September 1889 in West Point, Hardin County, Kentucky and died July 08, 1956 in Jefferson County, Kentucky. He first married SALLY ANNIS "ANNIS" CRABTREE about 1921 in Kentucky, daughter of JOHN C. CRABTREE and MARTHA E. FISHER. She was born May 08, 1889 in Garfield, Breckinridge County, Kentucky and died September 03, 1944 in West Point, Hardin County, Kentucky. John later married SUDIE M. VIERS on May 05, 1950 in Clark County, Indiana, daughter of WILLIAM "WILL" VIERS and ELIZABETH RAILEY. Sudie was born July 17, 1900 in Elizabethtown, Hardin County, Kentucky and died January 19, 1955 in Jefferson County, Kentucky.

Notes for JOHN EARL MUSS:
In the 1930 Blandville, Hardin County, Kentucky census (conducted on April 03, 1930) John E. Muss, 41, is head of the household with Annie, 41, Nillie J., 21, Raymond W., 18, Francis L., 14, James H., 11, Muss E., 7, Mildred J., 5 and Earl B., 11/12. John is listed as a Factory Laborer.
The children; Nellie J, Raymond W., Francis L., and James H.; found living with John in the 1930 census are not John's children. They are the children of Sally Annis "Annis Crabtree and her first husband, JAMES HENRY DAUGHERTY, SR..

Obituary for John Earl Muss – July 09, 1956
(Louisville Times, Obituary for John Earl Muss)

More about JOHN EARL MUSS:
John died at 6am on Sunday, July 08, 1956 in Saints Mary and Elizabeth Hospital in Louisville, Kentucky. He was living in West Point, Hardin County, Kentucky at the time of his death.
Funeral Services were held at 3pm on Tuesday, July 10, 1956 in the West Point Baptist Church. Today, the West Point Baptist Church is located at 103 North 8th Street in West Point, Kentucky.
Burial: Tuesday, July 10, 1956 at Knob Creek Union Church Cemetery in Cupio, Bullitt County, Kentucky.

Headstone for John Earl Muss & Sally Annis "Annis" Crabtree
(Browning, Headstone for John Earl Muss & Sally Annis "Annis"
Crabtree)

Notes for SALLY ANNIS "ANNIS" CRABTREE:
　　Sally was first married to JAMES HENRY DAUGHERTY, SR. who was
born January 12, 1878 in Kentucky and died about 1918. Sally and
James had 6 children as follows: VIOLA DAUGHERTY (b. 1904 in
Kentucky), JOHN DAUGHERTY (b. 1908 in Kentucky), NELLIE J. DAUGHERTY
(b. 1909 in Kentucky), RAYMOND W. DAUGHERTY (b. May 09, 1912 in
Meade County, Kentucky; d. June 03, 1959 in Jefferson County,
Kentucky), FRANCIS E. DAUGHERTY (b. August 23, 1915 in Hardin
County, Kentucky), and JAMES HENRY DAUGHERTY, JR. (b. June 05, 1919
in Shepherdsville, Bullitt County, Kentucky; d. March 25, 1992 in
Louisville, Jefferson County, Kentucky).

MUSS, Mrs. Annis Crabtree, in her 56th year, Sunday, September 3d, 1944, at 2:10 a.m. at her residence, West Point, Ky. Beloved wife of John Earl Muss, mother of Mrs. Willard King, Mrs. William Cook, Mrs. William Daley, Mrs. Francis Jones, Mrs. Frederick Staley, John Louis, Raymond and James Henry Daugherty and Charles Muss. Funeral services Tuesday, September 5th, at 11 a.m. at the West Point Baptist Church. Interment, Knob Creek Cemetery.

Obituary for Sally Annis "Annis" Crabtree Muss – September 04, 1944 (Louisville Courier-Journal, Obituary for Sally Annis "Annis" Crabtree Muss)

More about SALLY ANNIS "ANNIS" CRABTREE:
Her Kentucky death certificate is #44-20035. Annis is listed as married and a housekeeper at the time of her death.

She died on Sunday, September 03, 1944 at 2:10am in her West Point, Kentucky home.

Informant: John E. Muss of West Point, Kentucky.

Parents: Unknown Crabtree of unknown location and Unknown mother of unknown location.

Cause of death: Carcinomatosis of abdomen found through exploratory operation. Carcinomatosis is a pathological condition characterized by the presence of carcinomas that have metastasized to many parts of the body.

Funeral Services: W. G. Hardy of Shively, Kentucky. Services were held on Tuesday, September 05, 1944 at 11:00am in the West Point Baptist Church.

Burial: Tuesday, September 05, 1944 at Knob Creek Union Church Cemetery in Cupio, Bullitt County, Kentucky.

Children of JOHN EARL[3] MUSS and SALLY ANNIS "ANNIS" CRABTREE are:
 i. EULA ANNA "POLLY"[4] MUSS, b. November 20, 1922 in Kentucky; d. October 01, 1993 in Somerset, Perry County, Ohio; m. WILLIAM "BILL" RAYMOND DALEY SR. about 1938.
 ii. MILDRED J.[4] MUSS, b. September 09, 1925 in Bullitt County, Kentucky, m. FRED STALEY.
 iii. EARL B.[4] MUSS, b. October 09, 1928 in West Point, Hardin County, Kentucky; d. January 06, 1933, Hardin County, Kentucky.

  More about EARL B. MUSS:
  Cause of Death: Acute Nephritis contributed to by Scarlet Fever.

The informant on his death certificate was J. E. Muss (his father).
Burial: Knob Creek Union Church Cemetery in Cupio, Bullitt County, Kentucky.

    iv.   CHARLES E.[4] MUSS, SR., b. June 19, 1931 in Hardin County, Kentucky.

13. JAMES ROY "ROY" TYLINGS[3] MUSS *(JOHN CARROLL[2] MUSS, JOHN[1] MUSS)* was born October 09, 1893 in Cupio, Bullitt County, Kentucky and died December 29, 1961 in Jefferson County, Kentucky. He first married MAUDE A. MITCHELL on November 25, 1920 in Kentucky, daughter of JACOB H. MITCHELL and IDA BELLE MASON. She was born May 28, 1905 in Kentucky and died May 09, 1922 in Fairdale, Jefferson County, Kentucky. There were no known children from this marriage. Roy later married DAISY E. FOSTER about 1932, daughter of JAMES FOSTER, JR. and MARTHA "MARTHY" C. WALLS. She was born December 12, 1903 in Bullitt County, Kentucky and died October 07, 1990 in Bullitt County, Kentucky.

Notes for MAUDE A. MITCHELL:
Her Kentucky death certificate is #22-11349. Maude is listed as married and a houseworker at the time of her death.
Informant: J. H. Mitchel of Shively, Kentucky.
Parents: J. H. Mitchel of Kentucky and Ida Mason of Kentucky.
Cause of death: "Pyelo nephritis". Pyelonephritis is a urinary tract infection that has reached the pelvis of the kidney.
Funeral Services: L. A. Blanford of 2815 South 4th Street in Louisville, Kentucky.
Burial: May 10, 1922 at Mitchell Hill Cemetery in Fairdale, Jefferson County, Kentucky.

Headstone for Maude A. Mitchell (Morris)

Notes for JAMES ROY "ROY" TYLINGS MUSS:

In the June 03, 1917 World War I draft registration, James Roy Tylings is listed as living in Valley Station, Jefferson County, Kentucky and is a farmer working for Thomas McNutt in Cupio, Bullitt County, Kentucky. He is single. Roy is tall and medium build with gray eyes and light colored hair.

In the 1930 Bullitt County, Kentucky census (conducted on April 25, 1930) Roy Muss, 36, is living with his brother William Joseph Muss. Roy served in the military during World War I according to the 1930 census. Roy is listed as a Farmer. Roy is also living next to the family of James Foster and his future wife, Daisy Foster (daughter of James Foster).

> MUSS, Mr. James R. T., of West Point, Ky., R. R. 1, passed away in his 60th year, Friday, December 29, 1961, at 5:20 a.m., at the Veterans Hospital. Beloved husband of Mrs. Daisy Muss; devoted father of Miss Margaret and Mr. Guthrie Muss; brother of Mrs. Address Carby, Mrs. Naomi Armes, Mrs. Sarah Snellen, Mr. Claude and Mr. Joseph Muss. Remains at the W. G. Hardy Valley Chapel, 10907 Dixie Hwy. Funeral services Sunday, December 31, at 2 p.m. at the Hillview Methodist Church. Interment, Knob Creek Cemetery.

Obituary for James Roy "Roy" Tylings Muss – December 30, 1961
(Louisville Times, Obituary for James Roy "Roy" Tylings Muss)

More About JAMES ROY "ROY" TYLINGS MUSS:

James R. T. Muss was living on Rural Route 1 in West Point, Bullitt County, Kentucky at the time of his death. He died at 5:20am in the Veterans Hospital in Louisville, Kentucky. It is not clear whether he died in the nearest Veterans Hospital located at Shively, Kentucky on North Dixie Highway or whether he was at the main facility in downtown Louisville, today known as the Robley Rex VA Medical Center.

Funeral Services: W. G. Hardy at 10907 Dixie Highway in Valley Station, Kentucky. Funeral Services were held at the Hillview Methodist Church on Sunday, December 31 at 2pm.

Burial: Sunday, December 31 at Knob Creek Union Church Cemetery in Cupio, Bullitt County, Kentucky.

Headstone for James Roy "Roy" Tylings Muss and Daisy E. Foster (Browning, Headstone for James Roy "Roy" Tylings Muss and Daisy E. Foster)

Notes for DAISY E. FOSTER:

She was a first cousin of Anna Hopewell who married John Carroll Muss.

Daisy died at her home in West Point, Hardin County, Kentucky.

Funeral Services: W. G. Hardy Valley Funeral Home at 10907 Dixie Highway in Valley Station, Kentucky. Funeral Services were held on Wednesday, October 10, 1990 at 2pm in the funeral home.

Burial: Wednesday, October 10, 1990 at Knob Creek Union Church Cemetery in Cupio, Bullitt County, Kentucky.

Daisy E. Muss, 86, of West Point, died Sunday at her home.

She was the former Daisy Foster, a native of Bullitt County.

Survivors: a daughter, Margaret Muss; a son, Guthrie Muss; a sister, Deany Thompson; and a brother, Dewey Foster — all of West Point.

Funeral: 2 p.m. Wednesday, W. G. Hardy Valley Funeral Home, 10907 Dixie Highway. Burial: Knob Creek Church Cemetery in West Point. Visitation: after 11 a.m. Wednesday.

Obituary for Daisy E. Foster Muss – October 09, 1990
(Louisville Courier-Journal, Obituary for Daisy E. Foster Muss)

Notes for JAMES FOSTER, JR. (Father of DAISY E. FOSTER):
James was the brother of SARAH A. FOSTER. Sarah married MATTHEW HOPEWELL and they had ANNA "ANNIE" ELIZA HOPEWELL. Annie married JOHN CARROLL MUSS.

Burial: Knob Creek Union Church Cemetery in Cupio, Bullitt County, Kentucky.

James is listed on two of the T.C. Carroll land plats that are stored at the Bullitt County Clerk's office in large plastic envelopes. The listings can be found on Slide # 186, Map # 259 (along with Mr. Ferguson, Mr. McNutt, Mr. Merker, Annie E. Muss, and Chester L. Muss) and Slide # 311, Map # 100c (along with Annie E. Muss and Mary Ann Samuels). The address for the Bullitt County Clerk's Office is: 149 N. Walnut, Shepherdsville, KY, 40165.

Notes for MARTHA "MARTHY" C. WALLS (Mother of DAISY E. FOSTER):
Burial: Knob Creek Union Church Cemetery in Cupio, Bullitt County, Kentucky.

Headstone for James Foster, Jr. and Martha "Marthy" C. Walls
(Daniels, Headstone for James Foster, Jr. and Martha "Marthy" C.
Walls)

Children of JAMES ROY "ROY" TYLINGS[3] MUSS and DAISY E. FOSTER are:
- i. ROY F.[4] MUSS, b. May 14, 1933 in Bullitt County, Kentucky; d. May 25, 1933 in Bullitt County, Kentucky.
- ii. EDWARD GUTHRIE "GUTHRIE"[4] MUSS, b. October 30, 1934 in Bullitt County, Kentucky.
- iii. COLA MARGARET[4] MUSS, b. November 13, 1939 in Bullitt County, Kentucky; d. May 27, 2002 in West Point, Hardin County, Kentucky.

    More about COLA MARGARET MUSS:
        Burial: Knob Creek Union Church Cemetery in Cupio, Bullitt County, Kentucky.

14. ANNA "ANNIE" ADRESS[3] MUSS *(JOHN CARROLL[2] MUSS, JOHN[1] MUSS)* was born February 24, 1895 in Bullitt County, Kentucky and died June 15, 1976 in Montclair, San Bernardino County, California. She married ORVILLE EMMITT "SLIM" CARBY, SR. on November 25, 1914 in Valley Station, Jefferson County, Kentucky, son of ALEXANDER FRANCIS CARBY and ELNORA "NORA" BELL HUNT. He was born February 04, 1894 in Millerstown, Grayson County, Kentucky and died January 04, 1970 in Sylmar, Los Angeles County, California.

Marriage License for Anna "Annie" Adress Muss and Orville Emmitt "Slim" Carby, Sr.
(Family History Center, Kentucky Marriages, 1785-1979)

Notes for ANNA "ANNIE" ADRESS MUSS:

Annie and Orville, Sr. divorced about 1940 in Kentucky and they later both moved to California independent of each other.

More about ANNA "ANNIE" ADRESS MUSS:

Her California death certificate is #2744 with a local registration #3600 and state file number 76-079583. Annie is listed as widowed and a housewife at the time of her death. She died at 5:30 am.

Informant: Juanita R. Dixon of Sulphur Springs, Texas.

Parents: John C. Muss of Kentucky and Annie A. Hopewell of Kentucky.

Cause of death: Cardiac arrest due to metastatic carcinoma to peritoneum cavities and uremia. Metastatic carcinoma is a form cancer that typically is found in the bone. The peritoneum is the membrane that forms the lining of the abdominal cavity. Uremia is a term used to loosely describe the illness accompanying kidney failure.

Funeral Services: Draper Mortuary.

Burial: Inglewood Park Cemetery, Plot 368, Lake Section in Inglewood, Los Angeles County, California. She is buried next to her granddaughter, ADRESS ETHEL MAE "SISSY" HARPOOL JOHNSON. Sissy was the daughter of EULA MAY CARBY and WILLIAM "BILL" HOWE HARPOOL.

MRS. CARBY

Adress Carby, 81, of 4514 Bandera Street, Montclair, died June 15 at Doctors' Hospital of Montclair. She was a native of Bullitt County, Kentucky, and a Montclair resident one year. Survived by two sons, Harel Carby, Sylmar, Roy "Pete" Carby, Lexington, Ky.; six daughters, Mrs. Eula Harpool, Montclair, Mrs. Clara Ciresi, Sylmar, Mrs. Violet Flake, Lancaster, Mrs. Dorothy Wilbur, Victorville, Mrs. Glenna Barrett, Buena Park, Mrs. Juanita Dixon, Sulphur Springs, Texas; a sister, Mrs. Sally Snellen, Louisville, Ky. 20 grandchildren and 21 great grandchildren. Services will be held at 10:30 a.m. Friday at Draper Chapel. Interment 1 p.m. Friday at Inglewood Park Cemetery, Inglewood. Draper Mortuary is in charge of arrangements.

Obituary for Anna "Annie" Adress Muss Carby – June 17, 1976
(The Daily Report)

Headstone for Anna "Annie" Adress Muss (Bellows)

Death Certificate for Anna "Annie" Adress Muss Carby
(California Department of Public Health)

Notes for ORVILLE EMMITT "SLIM" CARBY, SR.:

In the June 05, 1917 World War I draft registration, Orville is listed as living in Louisville, Jefferson County, Kentucky and is a carpenter for T. A. Gillespie Co. out of Louisville, Kentucky. He is married and has one child. Orville is tall and slender with brown eyes and brown hair.

In the 1920 Louisville, Jefferson County, Kentucky census (conducted on January 05, 1920) J. C. Carby, 33, is head of the household with Josephine, 28, Estill, 12, Genevra, 10, Norman, 5 along with the following boarders Orville Carby, 25, Address, 24, Ula May, 3

10/12, Clara L, 2 1/12 and Orville, 10/12. Orville is living with his older brother, John Clinton "J. C." "Clint" Carby, at this time. Orville is listed as a House Carpenter.

In the 1930 Jefferson County, Kentucky census (conducted on April 07, 1930) Arville E. Carby, 35, is head of the household with Adres, 34, Eula M., 14, Clara L., 12, Orville E., 11, Violet O., 7, Dorothy V., 5, David C., 2 11/12 and Harold L., 10/12. Orville is listed as a Farm Hand.

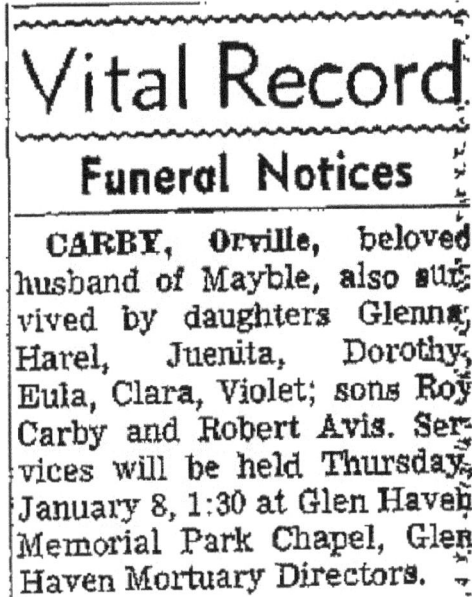

Vital Record

Funeral Notices

CARBY, Orville, beloved husband of Mayble, also survived by daughters Glenna, Harel, Juenita, Dorothy, Eula, Clara, Violet; sons Roy Carby and Robert Avis. Services will be held Thursday, January 8, 1:30 at Glen Haven Memorial Park Chapel, Glen Haven Mortuary Directors.

Obituary for Orville Emmitt "Slim" Carby, Sr. – January 08, 1970
(The Valley News)

More About ORVILLE EMMITT "SLIM" CARBY, SR.:
After his divorce from Annie, Orville married MAYBLE "MAY" J. SHEPHERD about 1950 in Kentucky, daughter of RANSOME ARTHUR SHEPHERD and MAUDE LEE TOLLE. Mayble was born January 11, 1915 in Jefferson County, Kentucky and died November 30, 1981 in Moore, Fergus County, Montana.

Orville was divorced from May Shepherd at the time of his death, however, they were living together.

Cause of death: Emphysema and Cancer. Emphysema is part of a group of diseases collectively known as chronic obstructive pulmonary disease (COPD), and is a long-term, progressive disease of the lungs that primarily causes shortness of breath. Smoking is the leading cause of emphysema. With this disease, the tissues necessary to support the shape and function of the lungs are destroyed.

Burial: Glen Haven Memorial Park & Mortuary in Sylmar, Los Angeles County, California. Orville is buried in the same grave site as his step son, ROBERT J. AVIS, who was the son of MAYBLE "MAY" J. SHEPHERD. For clarification, they are collocated in the same grave site.

Headstone for Orville Emmitt "Slim" Carby, Sr. (Bushman)

Notes for ALEXANDER FRANCIS CARBY (Father of ORVILLE EMMITT "SLIM" CARBY, SR.):

Alexander was born on September 07, 1860 in Millerstown, Grayson County, Kentucky and died April 14, 1937 in Spurrier, Hardin County, Kentucky. He was the son of HENRY CARBY (b. May 28, 1825 in Hardin County, Kentucky) and MARY MARGARET CARBY (b. August 13, 1831 in Hardin County, Kentucky).

HENRY CARBY and his wife, MARY MARGARET CARBY, were first cousins.

Alexander married ELNORA "NORA" BELL HUNT about 1884, most likely in Millerstown, Grayson Conty, Kentucky. Alexander and Nora had 10 known children as follows: JOHN CLINTON "J. C." CARBY (b. December 25, 1886 in Millerstown, Grayson County, Kentucky; d. January 08, 1973 in Louisville, Jefferson County, Kentucky; m. JOSEPHINE "JOSIE" MILLER on June 10, 1906 in Grayson County, Kentucky), DONNIE M. CARBY (b. January 1890 in Kentucky; d. November 02, 1970 in Hardin County, Kentucky; m. JOSEPH "JOE" T. HENDERSON on October 21, 1906 in Grayson County, Kentucky), IDA MAE CARBY (b. October 04, 1891 in Millerstown, Grayson County, Kentucky; d. February 13, 1984 in Louisville, Jefferson County, Kentucky; m. WILLIAM "WILL" ABRAHAM FLUHR on August 16, 1908 in Jefferson County, Kentucky), ORVILLE EMMITT "SLIM" CARBY, SR. (b.

February 04, 1894 in Millerstown, Grayson County, Kentucky; d.
January 04, 1970 in Sylmar, Los Angeles County, California; m. ANNA
"ANNIE" ADRESS MUSS on November 25, 1914 in Valley Station,
Jefferson County, Kentucky), ALVY CARBY (b. June 22, 1895 in Grayson
County, Kentucky), FRED THOMAS CARBY (b. July 31, 1897 in Kentucky;
d. April 08, 1980 in Louisville, Jefferson County, Kentucky; m. LURTER
MAE WITTEN on July 02, 1919 in Jeffersonville, Clark County, Indiana),
CARRIE CARBY (b. about 1901 in Kentucky), MADGIE CARBY (b. April 20,
1903 in Kentucky; m. ROY HENDERSON on Decmebr 22, 1919 in Clark
County, Indiana), STRAUD RAYMOND CARBY (b. June 13, 1906 in
Millerstown, Grayson County, Kentucky; d. August 06, 1996 in
Houston, Harris County, Texas; m. ESTER P. LOGSDON on August 04,
1928 in Jeffersonville, Clark County, Indiana), and GLADYS M. CARBY (b.
March 11, 1909 in Millerstown, Grayson County, Kentucky; m. JOSEPH
"JOE" WILLIAM STEWART on October 27, 1928 in Clark County, Indiana).
    Alexander had 6 siblings as follows: ZARADA CARBY (b. July 1850 in
Grayson County, Kentucky; d. February 08, 1937 in Valley Station,
Jefferson County, Kentucky; m. HENDRICKS HICKS about 1874; buried at
Louisville Memorial Park in Louisville, Jefferson County, Kentucky),
ALMIRA CARBY (b. May 10, 1852 in Grayson County, Kentucky), THOMAS
R. CARBY (b. January 02, 1855 Grayson County, Kentucky; m1. SUSAN
ELIZABETH LAWSON about 1878 in Kentucky; m2. IDA S. MNU about
1908 in Kansas), ZACHARIAH "ZACK" C. CARBY (b. December 11, 1857 in
Grayson County, Kentucky; JUDITH "JUDIE" FANNIE MNU about 1883),
LYLIAN CARBY (b. about 1865 in Hardin County, Kentucky), and
WILLIAM SAMUEL CARBY (b. September 1870 in Kentucky; d. 1949; m.
SARAH KATE MANION about 1892; buried at Old Lone Oak Cemetery in
Lone Oak, Grayson County, Kentucky).
    Burial: White Mills Community Cemetery in White Mills, Hardin
County, Kentucky.

Notes for ELNORA "NORA" BELL HUNT (Mother of ORVILLE EMMITT "SLIM"
CARBY, SR.):
    Nora was born on September 07, 1868 in Millerstown, Grayson
County, Kentucky and died on February 16, 1955 in Hardin County,
Kentucky. She was the daughter of SYLVESTER J. HUNT (b. September
1845 in Missouri) and EVELYN MELISSA NUNN (b. about 1849 in
Kentucky).
    Nora had 2 siblings as follows: JAMES F. W. HUNT (b. about 1866 in
Grayson County, Kentucky), and E. G. HUNT (b. about 1872 in
Kentucky).
    Nora had 2 half siblings as follows: LON ERMINE HUNT (b. May 09,
1880 in Rock Creek, Grayson County, Kentucky; d. August 14, 1926 in
Valley Creek, Hardin County, Kentucky; m. DAVID "DAVIE" HART), and
JOHN A. HUNT (b. August 1887 in Grayson County, Kentucky).

Headstone for Alexander Francis Carby and Elnora "Nora" Bell Hunt (Browning, Headstone for Alexander Francis Carby and Elnora "Nora" Bell Hunt)

Notes for MAYBLE "MAY" J. SHEPHERD:
She was first married to MR. AVIS. ROBERT J. AVIS, who is buried next to ORVILLE EMMITT "SLIM" CARBY SR., is Mayble's son from her first marriage.

Children of ANNA "ANNIE" ADRESS[3] MUSS and ORVILLE EMMITT "SLIM" CARBY, SR. are:

i.   EULA MAY[4] CARBY, b. March 19, 1916 in Jefferson County, Kentucky; d. September 01, 1988 in Buena Park, Orange County, California; m. WILLIAM "BILL" HOWE HARPOOL.

ii. CLARA LEE[4] CARBY, b. December 27, 1917 in Jefferson County, Kentucky; d. September 24, 1994 in Sun Valley, Los Angeles County, California; m1. WILLIAM "BILL" SMITH about 1936; m2. MICHAEL EDWARD CIRESI about 1941.

iii. ORVILLE EMMITT "J.R."[4] CARBY, JR., b. February 28, 1919 in Jefferson County, Kentucky; d. March 17, 1960, Los Angeles, Los Angeles County, California; m1. BETTY HALE on December 20, 1941 in Phenix City, Russell County, Alabama while serving in the U.S. Army at Fort Benning, Georgia; m2. GEORGIA LEE GRIFFITH about 1944 (never formally married); m3. FRANCES COFFEY; m4. RITA BLANCHE MULKINS on October 08, 1949 in Floyd County, Indiana.

iv. VIOLET "VI" OPAL[4] CARBY, b. September 15, 1922 in Jefferson County, Kentucky; m. JAMES EDWARD FLAKE SR. on April 14, 1948.

v. DOROTHY VIRGINIA[4] CARBY, b. August 26, 1924 in Jefferson County, Kentucky; d. November 03, 1998 in Lexington, Fayette County, Kentucky; m1. MR. ARWOOD about 1943; m2. STANLEY DONALD WILBUR on August 03, 1946.

vi. ROBERT EARL[4] CARBY, b. May 14, 1926 in Louisville, Jefferson County, Kentucky; d. May 14, 1926 in Louisville, Jefferson County, Kentucky.

vii. DAVID CALVIN[4] CARBY, b. April 26, 1927 in Louisville, Jefferson County, Kentucky; d. June 18, 1949 in Louisville, Jefferson County, Kentucky.

viii. HAREL LYN[4] CARBY, SR., b. May 07, 1929 in Louisville, Jefferson County, Kentucky; d. March 09, 2011 in McQueeney, Guadalupe County, Texas; m1. ROSEMARY MULKINS on November 23, 1949 in Jeffersonville, Clark County, Indiana; m2. SHIRLEY BURCH on July 17, 1992 in Harris County, Texas (divorced on December 23, 1992 in Harris County, Texas); m3. FLORETTA "FLO" COMLEY on March 17, 1992 in Harris County, Texas.

ix. ROY EDWIN "PETE"[4] CARBY, b. January 21, 1931 in Jefferson County, Kentucky; d. April 13, 2004 in Lexington, Fayette County, Kentucky; m. MARGARET "MARGIE" L. GREGORY.

x. GLENNA IRENE[4] CARBY, b. November 22, 1932 in Louisville, Jefferson County, Kentucky; d. April 15, 1999 in Buena Park, Orange County, California; m. NORMAN LEE BARRETT, JR.

xi. JUANITA ROSE "TINY"[4] CARBY, b. March 15, 1938 in Okolona, Jefferson County, Kentucky; m1. BOYD ALAN ROBERTS on July 10, 1954 in Wichita, Sedgwick County, Kansas; m2. DOYLE LEE "LEE" LYNCH on March 03, 1962 in Sylmar, Los Angeles County, California; m3. L. C. DIXON on October 09, 1970 in Sulphur Springs, Hopkins County, Texas.

15. CLAUDE LEE[3] MUSS *(JOHN CARROLL[2] MUSS, JOHN[1] MUSS)* was born July 05, 1897 in Bullitt County, Kentucky and died May 23, 1970 in Louisville, Jefferson County, Kentucky. He married MARY NELLIE MONTGOMERY on July 20, 1920 in Bullitt County, Kentucky, daughter of JOSEPH P. MONTGOMERY and MAHALA "MAHALIE" HIGDON. She was born April 1892 in Kentucky.

Notes for CLAUDE LEE MUSS:
In the August 24, 1918 World War I draft registration, Claude is listed as working for the Portland Cement Plant in Jefferson County, Kentucky. His nearest relative is Annie E. Muss (mother), who is also living on Route 1 in Valley Station, Kentucky. Claude has gray eyes and light brown hair. The registration was done in Bullitt County, Kentucky.

In the 1930 Louisville, Jefferson County, Kentucky census (conducted on April 04, 1930) Claude L. Muss, 32, is head of the household with Nellie M., 37, Dennis G. Green, 18, Pauline G. Green, 16, James R. Green, 14, Ernest J. Green, 12, Mary L., 8, Katherine V., 6, Agnes J., 4 9/12 and Nancy M., 2 8/12.

The children; Dennis G. Green, 18, Pauline G. Green, 16, James R. Green, 14, Ernest J. Green, 12; found living with Claude in the 1930 census are not Claude's children. They are the children of Mary Nellie Montgomery and her first husband, John T. Green.

Notes for MARY NELLIE MONTGOMERY:

Mary was first married to JOHN T. GREEN on February 21, 1911 in Springfield, Washington County, Kentucky, son of unknown parents. John was born about 1891 in Kentucky and died about 1919 in Kentucky. Together they had 4 children as follows: JOHN DENNIS GREEN (b. December 20, 1911 in Washington County, Kentucky), FRANCIS PAULINE GREEN (b. November 11, 1913 in Kentucky), JAMES RUBIN GREEN (b. November 23, 1915 in Washington County, Kentucky; d. October 06, 1988 in Louisville, Jefferson County, Kentucky), ERNEST J. GREEN (b. November 11, 1917 in Washington County, Kentucky; d. November 09, 1993 in Louisville, Jefferson County, Kentucky).

Children of CLAUDE LEE[3] MUSS and MARY NELLIE MONTGOMERY are:
  i.   MARY L.[4] MUSS, b. May 18, 1921 in Jefferson County, Kentucky.
  ii. CATHERINE V.[4] MUSS, b. March 08, 1923 in Jefferson County, Kentucky.
  iii. AGNES INEZ "INEZ"[4] MUSS, b. June 10, 1925 in Jefferson County, Kentucky.
  iv. NANCY M.[4] MUSS, b. July 13, 1927 in Jefferson County, Kentucky.

16. SARAH "SALLIE" ELIZABETH[3] MUSS *(JOHN CARROLL[2] MUSS, JOHN[1] MUSS)* was born February 26, 1899 in Bullitt County, Kentucky and died May 06, 1984 in Louisville, Jefferson County, Kentucky. She married WILLIAM M. SNELLEN on December 24, 1918 in Clark County, Indiana, son of JEFFERSON MAYNARD "MAYNARD" SNELLEN and MARY BAUMGARDNER. He was born on December 22, 1900 in Kentucky and died April 1987 in Louisville, Jefferson County, Kentucky.

Notes for SARAH "SALLIE" ELIZABETH MUSS:

Sarah lived at 1034 Alder Avenue in Louisville, Kentucky at the time of her death. The home at 1034 Alder Avenue does not exist today, and is an empty lot on a narrow paved road without any shoulder.

Sarah died on Sunday, May 06, 1984 at the home of her son, John W. Snellen.

Funeral Services: Embry-Bosse Funeral Home at 2723 Preston highway in Louisville, Kentucky. Services were held at 11am on

Wednesday, May 09, 1984 at Embry-Bosse Funeral Home. Visitation was from 5-9pm on Monday, May 07, 1984 and from 9am-9pm on Tuesday, May 08, 1984.

Burial: Wednesday, May 09, 1984 in the Mausoleum at Evergreen Cemetery in Louisville, Jefferson County, Kentucky.

> **Mrs. Sarah E. Snellen,** 85, of 1034 Alder Ave., died Sunday at the home of her son, J. W. Snellen.
>
> She was the former Sarah Muss, a native of Bullitt County.
>
> Survivors besides her son include her husband, William M. Snellen; a grandchild; and two great-grandchildren.
>
> The funeral will be at 11 a.m. Wednesday at Embry-Bosse Funeral Home, 2723 Preston Highway, with entombment in Evergreen Mausoleum.
>
> Visitation will be at the funeral home from 5 to 9 p.m. Monday and from 9 a.m. to 9 p.m. Tuesday.

Obituary for Sarah "Sallie" Elizabeth Muss Snellen – May 07, 1984
(Louisville Times, Obituary for Sarah "Sallie" Elizabeth Muss Snellen)

Notes for WILLIAM M. SNELLEN:

In the 1920 South Highland Park, Jefferson County, Kentucky census (conducted on January 13, 1920) William E. Snellen, 19, is head of the household with Sarah Elizabeth, 20. William is listed as an inspector for a Claring? (illegible) Mill.

In the 1930 Camp Taylor, Jefferson County, Kentucky census (conducted on April 09, 1930) William M. Snellen, 29, is head of the household with Sarah E., 31, John W., 9 and Charley M., 26 (half-brother). William is listed as a Collector for a Furniture Company, and Charley is a Block Setter for a Saw Mill.

Children of SARAH "SALLIE" ELIZABETH[3] MUSS and WILLIAM M. SNELLEN are:

    i.   JOHN W.[4] SNELLEN, b. May 31, 1920 in Kentucky; d. June 11, 1995 in Louisville, Jefferson County, Kentucky.

17. GOLDA "GOLDIE" NAOMI "NAOMI"[3] MUSS (*JOHN CARROLL[2] MUSS, JOHN[1] MUSS*) was born January 16, 1901 in Bullitt County, Kentucky and died March 06, 1973 in Louisville, Jefferson County, Kentucky. She married WILLIAM HENRY ARMES, SR. on June 02, 1928 in Clark County, Indiana, son of CLIFFORD "CLIFF" A. ARMES and JULIA ALLEN. He was born on July 14, 1908 in Jefferson County, Kentucky and died on April 14, 1979 in Louisville, Jefferson County, Kentucky.

Notes for GOLDA "GOLDIE" NAOMI "NAOMI" MUSS:

A marriage license for Goldie with another man cannot be found at this time. Goldie had two boys prior to marrying WILLIAM HENRY ARMES, SR. Their names were ARLEY R. MUSS and LINDSEY W. MUSS. It is unclear whether or not these children were born out of wedlock and whether these children have the same father.

More about GOLDA "GOLDIE" NAOMI "NAOMI" MUSS:

Goldie died on Tuesday, March 6, 1973 at 3:15am in Saints Mary and Elizabeth Hospital in Louisville, Kentucky. At the time of her death, she lived at 8007 1/2 Ashbottom Road. This part of Louisville now appears to be encompassed by the Louisville International Airport.

Funeral Services: W. G. Hardy at 10907 Dixie Highway in Valley Station, Kentucky. Services were held at 10:00am on Thursday, March 08, 1973 in the W. G. Hardy Chapel of Valley Station, Kentucky.

Burial: Thursday, March 08, 1973 at Knob Creek Union Church Cemetery in Cupio, Bullitt County, Kentucky.

ARMES, Goldie Naomi

Of 8007½ Ashbotton Rd., passed away in her 73rd year, Tues., Mar. 6th, 1973, at 3:15 a.m., at SS. Mary & Elizabeth Hospital. Beloved wife of Mr. William Henry Armes, Sr. Devoted mother of Mr. Arley R., and Mr. Lindsey W. Muss, William H. Armes, Jr., John C., and James T. Armes, sister of Mrs. Annie A. Carby, Mrs. Sarah E. Snellen, and Mr. William J. Muss, 4 grandchildren and 1 great-grandchild. Remains at the W. G. Hardy Valley Chapel, 10907 Dixie Hwy., where funeral services will be held Thurs., at 10:00 a.m. Interment Knob Creek Cemetery.

Obituary for Golda "Goldie" Naomi "Naomi" Muss Armes – March 07, 1973
(Louisville Times, Obituary for Golda "Goldie" Naomi "Naomi" Muss Armes)

Notes for WILLIAM HENRY ARMES, SR.:

In the 1930 Jefferson County, Kentucky census (conducted on April 7, 1930) William H. Armes, 22, is head of the household with Goldie, 29, Arley R., 7, Lindsey, 2, and William, 11/12. William is listed as a Farm Hand. The family is living next door to the Orville E. Carby, Sr. family.

William Henry Armes Sr., 70, of 534
E. Adair St., died at 11:55 p.m. Saturday
at St. Joseph Infirmary.
He was a retired truck driver.
Survivors include five sons, William
H. Jr., John C., and James T. Armes,
and Arley R. and Lindsey W. Muss;
seven grandchildren; and two great-
grandchildren.
The funeral will be at 1 p.m. Tuesday
at Old Colonial Funeral Home, Sixth
and Ashland avenues, with burial in
Knob Creek Cemetery in Bullitt County.
Visitation is at the funeral home.

Obituary for William Henry Armes, Sr. – April 16, 1979
(Louisville Courier-Journal, Obituary for William Henry Armes, Sr.)

More about WILLIAM HENRY ARMES, SR.:

William was first married to LALLA BARNES and possibly a second
woman.

He was a retired truck driver who lived at 534 E Adair Street.

William died on Saturday, April 14, 1979 at 11:55pm in Saint
Joseph Infirmary of Louisville, Jefferson County, Kentucky. Saint
Joseph Infirmary originally stood at the corner of Eastern Parkway
and Preston Street. The Sisters of Charity of Nazareth operated the
infirmary beginning in the 1830's. In 1926, the infirmary was moved
to a 324 bed hospital that was part of the mid 19th century Samuel
Churchill rural estate on Flat Rock Road, now Preston Highway. In
1970, The Sisters of Charity sold the then aging infirmary to what is
now Humana Inc. The hospital was moved to Poplar Level Road at
that time, and it is now called Norton Audobon Hospital. The original
building, located at the corner of Preston Street and Eastern Parkway,
was razed in 1980.

The home at 534 East Adair Street in Louisville, Kentucky
appears to have been demolished. All of the homes on this street near
the Kentucky Fairgrounds and Exposition Center appear to have been
razed, except the homes at 536, 538, and 521 East Adair Street. All of
the remaining homes on this street were built between 1933 and
1945.

Funeral Services: Old Colonial Funeral Home at Sixth and Ashland
Avenues in Louisville, Kentucky. Services were held at 1:00pm on
Tuesday, April 17, 1979 in the funeral home.

Burial: Tuesday, April 17, 1979 at Knob Creek Union Church
Cemetery in Cupio, Bullitt County, Kentucky.

Headstone for William Henry Armes, Sr. and Golda "Goldie" Naomi Muss (Luitweiler)

Children of GOLDA "GOLDIE" NAOMI "NAOMI"[3] MUSS and UNKOWN are:
  i.   ARLEY R.[4] MUSS, b. August 24, 1922 in Bullitt County, Kentucky; d. March 01, 1987 in Louisville, Jefferson County, Kentucky; m. Leola Downs on June 15, 1941 in Campbell County, Tennessee.
  ii. LINDSEY W.[4] MUSS, b. October 29, 1927 in Jefferson County, Kentucky; d. February 27, 1993 in Louisville, Jefferson County, Kentucky.

Children of GOLDA "GOLDIE" NAOMI "NAOMI"[3] MUSS and WILLIAM HENRY ARMES, SR. are:
  i.   WILLIAM HENRY[4] ARMES, JR., b. May 26, 1929 in Jefferson County, Kentucky.
  ii. JOHN C.[4] ARMES, b. October 24, 1943 in Jefferson County, Kentucky; d. February 27, 1993 in Louisville, Jefferson County, Kentucky.
  iii. JAMES T.[4] ARMES, b. July 22, 1946 in Jefferson County, Kentucky.

18. GEORGE W.[3] COOK *(CAROLINE CARRIE F.[2] MUSS, JOHN[1] MUSS)* was born August 14, 1885 in Bullitt County, Kentucky and died September 11, 1965 in Terre Haute, Vigo County, Indiana. He married MYRTLE RUTH COREY on February 05, 1916 in Vigo County, Indiana, daughter of JOHN WESLEY COREY, SR. and EMILY "EMMA" ELLEN WYETH. She was born January 1895 in Indiana and died June 14, 1967 in Terre Haute, Vigo County, Indiana.

Notes for GEORGE W. COOK:
    In the September 12, 1918 World War I draft registration, George is listed as a farmer for Alfred Slunkley in Clinton, Vermillion County, Indiana, and is married. Myrtle Ruth Cook is listed as his nearest relative. She is living at Rural Route 3 in Clinton along with George. George is of medium height and slender build. His eyes are brown and his hair is black.

In the 1920 Terre Haute, Vigo County, Indiana census (conducted on January 22, 1920) George W. Cook, 34, is head of the household with Myrtle, 25 and James W., 2 6/12. George is listed as a Machinist.

In the 1930 Terre Haute, Vigo County, Indiana census (conducted on April 25, 1930) George W. Cook, 43, is head of the household with Myrtle R., 35, James W., 12 and Ellen R., 8. George is listed as an Inspector for the Railroad.

In the 1942 World War II draft registration, George is living in Terre Haute, Vigo County, Indiana and is listed as working for G. C. Spellman at the N. Y. Central Railroad. His place of birth is listed as Bullet County, Kentucky. The name of the person that will always know his address is Myrtle R. Cook.

P. F. Owen,   MARSHALL. IND.

Picture of George W. Cook
(Lyle Raymond Cook & Karla Denise Ezell Cook)

More about GEORGE W. COOK:
His marriage has been substantiated through the Vigo County Marriage Record Ledger on Page 452.

George died Saturday, September 1, 1965 at Union Hospital in Terre Haute, Indiana. He was a retired railroad car inspector and living at 2003 8th Avenue at the time of his death.

Union Hospital was founded in 1892 at the corner of Seventh Street and Eighth Avenue in Terre Haute, Indiana.

The residence at 2003 8th Avenue in Terre Haute, Vigo County, Indiana is a 1,052 square foot single family home with 2 bedrroms and 1 bathroom that was built in 1910.

Funeral Services: Schoppenhorst Funeral Home of Clay City, Indiana. Services were held at 1:00pm on Tuesday, September 14, 1965 in Bedino Peace Chapel at 228 South Sixth Street of Terre Haute, Indiana with the Reverend Don Edwards officiating. Bedino Peace Chapel was demolished in 2010 to create parking spaces for the adjacent, former YMCA building that was turned into business office space.

Burial: Tuesday, September 14, 1965 at Maple Grove Cemetery in Clay City, Clay County, Indiana.

GEORGE W. COOK

Services for George W. Cook, 80, 2003 8th Ave., who died Saturday, will be at 1 p.m. Tuesday at the Bedino Peace Chapel, with the Rev. Don Edwards officiating. Burial will be in Maple Grove Cemetery, Clay City. Friends may call at the Peace Chapel after 2 p m. Monday.

Obituary for George W. Cook - September 13, 1965
(Terre Haute Tribune, Obituary for George W. Cook)

Notes for MYRTLE RUTH COREY:

Myrtle died Wednesday, June 14, 1967 at 12: 45pm in Meadows Manor of Terre Haute, Indiana. Meadows Manor is a retirement home. Her home residence at the time of her death is 2003 8th Avenue in Terre Haute, Indiana.

Funeral Services: Schoppenhorst Funeral Home of Clay City, Indiana. Visitation was held at 1:00pm on Friday, June 16, 1967 in Bedino Peace Chapel at 228 South Sixth Street of Terre Haute, Indiana. Services were held at 1:00pm on Saturday, June 17, 1967 with the Reverend Don Edwards officiating.

Burial: Saturday, June 17, 1967 at Maple Grove Cemetery in Clay City, Clay County, Indiana.

MRS. MYRTLE COOK

Mrs. Myrtle Corey Cook, 72, 2003 8th Ave., died at 12:45 p.m. Wednesday at Meadows Manor. She is survived by a son, James W. Cook, Terre Haute; one sister, Mrs. Estella Barley, RR 1, Lewis. Ind.; a brother, Harry C. Corey, Terre Haute; two grandchildren and two great-grandchildren. The body was taken to the Schoppenhorst Funeral Home at Clay City, and will be brought Friday to the Bedino Peace Chapel, where friends may call after 1 p.m. Friday. Funeral services will be at 1 p.m. Saturday, with the Rev. Don Edwards officiating. Burial will be in the Maple Grove Cemetery at Clay City.

Obituary for Myrtle Ruth Corey Cook – June 15, 1967
(Terre Haute Tribune, Obituary for Myrtle Ruth Corey Cook)

Children of GEORGE W.[3] COOK and MYRTLE RUTH COREY are:
    i.   JAMES W.[4] COOK, b. Jul 03, 1917 in Indiana; d. February 17, 1998 in Indiana.
    ii. ELLEN R.[4] COOK, b. About 1922 in Indiana.

19. BETTY MAE[3] COOK *(CAROLINE CARRIE F.[2] MUSS, JOHN[1] MUSS)* was born November 11, 1888 in Bullitt County, Kentucky and died August 18, 1968 in Vincennes, Knox County, Indiana. She married EMORY ELLIS BRILEY on September 11, 1909 in Vigo County, Indiana, son of JOSEPH FLAVIUS "THOMAS" BRILEY and ELIZABETH STEWART. He was born January 03, 1887 in Clay County, Indiana and died September 1973 in Bicknell, Knox County, Indiana.

Notes for EMORY ELLIS BRILEY:
    In the 1910 Lewis, Clay County, Indiana census (conducted on April 16, 1910) Emery Briley, 23, is a son living with his parents.

Flavius (his father), 59, is listed as the head of the household with Elizabeth, 58, Emery, 23, Bettie (daughter-in-law), 21 and Fuller, 12.

In the June 05, 1917 World War I draft registration, Emery E. is listed as a bookkeeper for Vandalia Coal in Linton, Greene County, Indiana, and is married. Emory is of tall height and stout build. His eyes are gray and his hair is brown. He is also listed as being born in Lewis, Clay County, Indiana. His registration occurred in the Stockton Township of Greene County.

In the 1920 Linton, Greene County, Indiana census (conducted on January 13 and 14, 1920) Emery E. Briley, 32, is head of the household with Betty, 31. Emory is listed as a Bookkeeper for the Coal Mine.

In the 1930 Washington, Daviess County, Indiana census (conducted on April 15, 1930) Emory Briley, 43, is head of the household with Betty, 41. Emory is listed as an Accountant for the Coal Mine.

More about EMORY ELLIS BRILEY:
Burial: Fairview Cemetery in Linton, Greene County, Indiana.

Picture of Betty Mae Cook Briley
(Lyle Raymond Cook & Karla Denise Ezell Cook)

Notes for BETTY MAE COOK:
    Her marriage has been substantiated through the Vigo County
Marriage Record Ledger on Page 27.

Betty, a resident of Bicknell, Indiana at the time of her death, died Sunday at Good Samaritan Hospital in Vincennes, Indiana. Good Samaritan Hospital first opened its doors on February 08, 1908 as a 25-bed facility. It was the first county hospital in Indiana.

Funeral Services: McClure Funeral Home (now Frederick and Son McClure-Utt Funeral Homes and Cremation) of Bicknell, Indiana. Services were held at 2:00pm on Wednesday, August 21, 1968 in McClure Chapel of Bicknell, Indiana.

Burial: Wednesday, August 21, 1968 at Fairview Cemetery in Linton, Greene County, Indiana.

MRS. BETTY MAE BRILEY

BICKNELL, Ind. (Special) —Mrs. Betty Mae Briley, 79, formerly of Linton, presently residing in Bicknell, died at 5:30 p.m. Sunday at the Good Samaritan Hospital in Vincennes. She is survived by her husband, Emory E. and one brother Willey Cook, of Lebanon. Ind. Services will be held at 2 p.m. Wednesday at the McClure Chapel in Bicknell with burial in the Fairview Cemetery in Linton. Friends may call after 2 p.m. Tuesday.

Obituary for Betty Mae Cook Briley – August 19, 1968
(Terre Haute Tribune, Obituary for Betty Mae Cook Briley)

Headstone for Emory Ellis Briley and Betty Mae Cook
(Heaton, Headstone for Emory Ellis Briely and Betty Mae Cook)

Children of BETTY MAE[3] COOK and EMORY ELLIS BRILEY are:
  i.   JANE ELLEN[4] BRILEY, b. About 1920 in Linton, Greene County, Indiana; d. March 12, 1920 in Linton, Greene County, Indiana.

       More about JANE ELLEN BRILEY:
          Burial: Fairview Cemetery in Linton, Greene County, Indiana

Headstone for Jane Ellen Briley
(Heaton, Headstone for Jane Ellen Briley)

20. HENRY WAYNE[3] COOK *(CAROLINE CARRIE F.[2] MUSS, JOHN[1] MUSS)* was born January 24, 1891 in Sullivan County, Indiana and died September 08, 1954 in Danville, Vermilion County, Illinois. He married BEULAH MAY WITHEM on November 29, 1911 in Vigo County, Indiana, daughter of JOHN W. WITHEM and SARAH FRANCIS WITCRAFT. She was born August 15, 1894 in Spencer County, Indiana and died Jul 05, 1953 in Danville, Vermilion County, Illinois.

Notes for HENRY WAYNE COOK:

In the June 05, 1917 World War I draft registration, Henry is listed as a farmer for Henry Smith in Terre Haute, Vigo County, Indiana, and is married with 3 children. Henry is listed as tall with a medium build. His eyes are blue and his hair color is light. Henry is also listed as being born in Lewis, Vigo County, Indiana.

In the 1920 Terre Haute, Vigo County, Indiana census (conducted on January 06, 1920) Henry W. Cook, 28, is head of the household with Bulah, 25, William M., 7, Mary E., 4 8/12, Frances J., 2 9/12 and Leona M., 4/12. Henry is listed as a Motorman for the Street Car.

Picture of Henry Wayne Cook
(Lyle Raymond Cook & Karla Denise Ezell Cook)

More about HENRY WAYNE COOK:
  His marriage has been substantiated through the Vigo County Marriage Record on Ledger Page 535.
  Henry died Wednesday afternoon on September 08, 1954 at Lake View Hospital in Danville, Illinois. Lake View Hospital was established in 1892, and was housed in the McCrone building on East Fairchild St (just across the street from the present-day Danville High School). Today, Lake View Hospital is known as the Provena United Samaritans Medical Center.

Funeral Services: McClure Funeral Home (now Frederick and Son McClure-Utt Funeral Homes and Cremation) of Bicknell, Indiana. Services were held at 2:00pm on Friday, September 10, 1954 in the Danville Church of Christ of Danville, Illinois.

Burial: Friday, September 10, 1954 at Oak Hill Cemetery in Danville, Vermilion County, Illinois.

Obituary Notes for HENRY WAYNE COOK:

Published in The Commercial-News in Danville, Illinois on Saturday, September 11, 1954

"Henry Cook's Rites Held - Services were at 2 p. m. Friday at First Church of Christ, Oak and Seminary Sts., for Henry W. Cook, 63, of 528 Grant St., who died Wednesday in Lake View Hospital. Rites were conducted by James Strauss, pastor, with burial in Oak Hill Cemetery, Barrick & Sons Funeral Service in charge. Mr. Cook was a veteran bus driver for Danville City Lines and the last of the old street car men still working, having begun such work in Terre Haute more than 40 years ago. Survivors include a sister, Mrs. Betty Briley of Bicknell, Ind., and a stepson, Larry Sayre of Danville. Mr. Cook was preceded in death by his first wife, Beulah Withem Cook, in July, 1953."

HENRY COOK

Funeral services for Henry Cook, formerly of Terre Haute, who died Wednesday at his residence in Danville, Ill., will be at 2 o'clock this afternoon at the Danville Church of Christ. Burial will be in a Danville Cemetery. Surviving are three daughters, a son, three brothers, including George and William Cook, both of Terre Haute and a sister, Mrs Leola Pieper of Terre Haute.

Obituary for Henry Wayne Cook - September 10, 1954
(Terre Haute Star)

Notes for BEULAH MAY WITHEM:

Beulah died on Sunday, July 05, 1953 at a hospital in Danville, Illinois.

Funeral Services: Barrick Funeral Home (now Lakeside-Barrick Funeral Home at 3550 N Vermilion Street) of Danville, Illinois. Services were held Wednesday.

Burial: Wednesday, July 08, 1953 at Oak Hill Cemetery in Danville, Vermilion County, Illinois.

MRS. BEULAH WITHAM COOK.

Word has been received of the death of Mrs. Beulah Witham Cook, who died Sunday at a hospital in Danville, Ill. Mrs. Cook is a former Terre Haute resident. The funeral will be held Wednesday in the Barrick Funreal Home in Danville and the interment will be in a Danville cemetery.

Obituary for Beulah May Withem Cook - July 07, 1953
(Terre Haute Tribune, Obituary for Beulah May Withem Cook)

Children of HENRY WAYNE[3] COOK and BEULAH MAY WITHEM are:

    i.   WILLIAM M.[4] COOK, SR., b. March 31, 1912 in Vigo County, Indiana; d. October 25, 1964 in Danville, Vermilion County, Illinois; m. THELMA LOUISE BATH on November 04, 1935.

    ii. MARY E.[4] COOK, b. May 02, 1915 in Vigo County, Indiana.

    iii. FRANCIS J.[4] COOK, b. April 01, 1917 in Vigo County, Indiana.

    iv. LEOTA MAY[4] COOK, b. September 06, 1919 in Terre Haute, Vigo County, Indiana.

21. WILLIAM "WILLIE" J.[3] COOK *(CAROLINE CARRIE F.[2] MUSS, JOHN[1] MUSS)* was born August 30, 1899 in Lewis, Vigo County, Indiana and died October 02, 1991 in Plainfield, Hendricks County, Indiana. Willie first married NITIS LOUISE FUNK on April 20, 1924 in Patricksburg, Owen County, Indiana, daughter of DANIEL VORHEES FUNK and MANOLA MOYNE FRUMP. Nitis was born on January 08, 1907 in Indiana and died May 19, 2003 in Danville, Hendricks County, Indiana. After his divorce from Nitis Funk, William married IVY MURIAL MCCOY on March 19, 1944 in Lebanon, Boone County, Indiana, daughter of OSCAR EMIL MCCOY and SARAH "SALLIE" JANE ELIZABETH HYPES. Ivy was born July 30, 1907 in Boone County, Indiana and died October 16, 1988 in Lebanon, Boone County, Indiana.

Notes for WILLIAM "WILLIE" J. COOK:

    In the September 12, 1918 World War I draft registration, Willie is listed as a farmer. His father, William M Cook, is listed as his employer and is living in Lewis, Vigo County, Indiana. Willie is also listed as single. Carrie Cook, his mother, is listed as his nearest relative. She is living at Rural Route 2 in Lewis along with Willie. Willie is of medium height and medium build. His eyes are brown and his hair is black.

    In the 1920 Lewis, Clay County, Indiana census (conducted on January 02, 1920) Willie is living with his parents. William M. Cook,

73, is head of the household with Carrie, 66 and Willie J., 20. Willie is listed as a Farm Laborer for a Home Farm.

In the 1930 Terre Haute, Vigo County, Indiana census (conducted on April 16, 1930) Willie J. Cook, 30, is head of the household with Netis L., 21, Paul L., 4 and Betty R., 2. Willie is listed as a Truck Driver for Oakley. Netis is listed as a Store Clerk.

Picture of William "Willie" J. Cook
(Lyle Raymond Cook & Karla Denise Ezell Cook)

More about WILLIAM "WILLIE" J. COOK:

After Willie Cook and Nitis Funk divorced, Paul stayed with Willie and later his new wife, Ivy. Paul was in high school and 18 years old when his father, Willie, remarried to Ivy.

Paul's sister, Betty Cook, was primarily raised by her mother, Nitis, after the divorce.

Willie's obituary was published in the Thursday, October 3, 1991 issue of the Lebanon Reporter, Page 18, Column 1.

Willie worked at Wake Up Oil Company for many years as well as Montgomery Ward; Swiggett Lumber Company of Zionsville, Indiana;

and Marmon-Herrington Company of Lebanon, Indiana until his retirement in 1968.

He was a member of the Otterbein United Methodist Church and enjoyed gardening.

Willie, a long time resident of Lebanon, Indiana, died Wednesday night on October 02, 1954 at Heartland Health Care Center in Plainfield, Indiana after being in failing health for several years. Heartland Health Care Center is a nursing care facility for elderly adults that is located at 445 South County Rd 525 E. in Plainfield, Indiana. Henry was in the nursing home for a couple of years prior to his death.

Funeral Services: Myers Mortuary of Lebanon, Indiana. Services were held at 10:30pm on Monday, October 07, 1991 in the Myers Chapel of Memories at Lebanon, Indiana with the Reverend Charles Hiatt officiating. Myers Funeral Home was established in 1947 at Lebanon, Indiana.

Burial: Monday, October 07, 1991 at Plot 289-33a of Oak Hill Cemetery in Lebanon, Boone County, Indiana.

Notes for NITIS LOUISE FUNK:

After her divorce from William Cook, Nitis married SETH ISAAC HART, son of WILLIAM A. HART and BARBARA "BARBARY" LUCINDA HART. He was born on May 27, 1895 in Saline County, Kansas and died January 24, 1955 in Indiana. There were no known children from this marriage.

More about NITIS LOUISE FUNK:

Nitis was a member of the First Baptist Church in Danville, Indiana and worked in the shipping and packing department at Detroit Diesel Allison Division of General Motors for 25 years. She retired in 1968.

Funeral Services: Conkle Funeral Home of Avon, Indiana. Services were held Saturday, May 22, 2003 in Maple Grove Cemetery at Clay City, Indiana. Conkle Funeral Home has been family owned and operated since 1925.

Burial: Saturday, May 22, 2003 at Maple Grove Cemetery in Clay City, Clay County, Indiana.

NITIS LOUISE (Funk) HART, age 96, Danville died May 19. Graveside services were May 22 in Maple Grove Cemetery, Clay City. Conkle Funeral Home, Avon, handled the arrangements.

Mrs. Hart worked in shipping and packing at Detroit Diesel Allison Division General Motors for 25 years, retiring in 1968.

She was a member of the First Baptist Church of Danville to which memorial contributions may be made.

Se was the widow of Seth I. Hart.

Survivors include daughter, Betty Johnson; son, Paul Cook; bother, Max Funk; nine grandchildren; 25 great-grandchildren and several great-great-grandchildren.

Obituary for Nitis Louise Funk Cook Hart – May 29, 2003
(The Republican)

Notes for DANIEL VORHEES FUNK (Father of NITIS LOUISE FUNK):

Daniel was born on January 04, 1884 in Indiana and died September 15, 1936 in Indiana. He was the son of CASSIUS M. FUNK (b. July 14, 1847 in Ohio) and MARY M. CAIN (b. January 20, 1847 in Ohio; d. September 12, 1909 in Clay County, Indiana).

Daniel married MANOLA MOYNE FRUMP on February 18, 1906 in Clay County, Indiana. Daniel and Manola had 5 known children as follows: NITIS LOUISE FUNK (b. January 08, 1907 in Indiana; d. May 19, 2003 in Danville, Hendricks County, Indiana; m1. WILLIAM "WILLIE" J. COOK on April 20, 1924 in Patricksburg, Owen County, Indiana; m2. REVEREND SETH ISAAC HART on March 28, 1941 in Marion County, Indiana), VIRGIL C. FUNK (b. December 05, 1909 in Lewis, Clay County, Indiana; d. November 17, 1985 in Indiana; m. MARGUERITE PAULINE STICKLES), RUTH R. FUNK (b. about 1912 in Lewis, Clay County, Indiana), RALPH COY FUNK (b. November 09, 1913 in Lewis, Clay County, Indiana'

d. November 18, 1914 in Lewis, Clay County, Indiana), and MAX L. FUNK (b. May 23, 1921 in Lewis, Clay County, Indiana).

Daniel had 6 siblings as follows: JOHN H. FUNK (b. May 1871 in Indiana; m1. ANNA "ANNIE" GRIFFITH on December 08, 1892 in Clay County, Indiana; m2. SARA ELLEN ORMAN on May 26, 1903 in Clay County, Indiana), CORA FUNK (b. November 22, 1875 in Indiana; d. March 29, 1941 in Vigo County, Indiana; m. WILLIAM DENNIS "DENNIS" LUTHER on May 23, 1894 in Clay County, Indiana; buried at Highland Lawn Cemetery in Terre Haute, Vigo County, Indiana), ALLEN FUNK (b. March 09, 1879 in Washington, Clay County, Indiana; m. ADA L. WILLIAMS on September 03, 1899 in Owen County, Indiana), EUNICE FUNK (b. August 1881 in Indiana), IDA JANE FUNK (b. May 04, 1886 in Indiana; m. ELMER NELSON FRANCIS on August 16, 1903 in Clay County, Indiana), and LEWIS ROYER FUNK (b. May 05, 1888 in Clay County, Indiana; d. March 12, 1971 in Bowling Green, Clay County, Indiana; m. OLIVE RUTH SWALLEY on July 15, 1910 in Clay County, Indiana; buried in Swalley Cemetery in Bowling Green, Clay County, Indiana).

Notes for MANOLA MOYNE FRUMP (Mother of NITIS LOUISE FUNK):

Manola was born on October 14, 1884 in Clay County, Indiana and died on November 01, 1964 in Indiana. She was the daughter of JOHN CHARLES FRUMP (b. January 27, 1861 in Parke County, Indiana; d. February 19, 1937 in Clay County, Indiana; m. about 1884) and ELIZABETH "LIZZIE" BERETTA ORMAN (b. December 03, 1864 in Indiana; d. Decmeber 2, 1933 in Indiana).

Manola had 6 siblings as follows: EDNA ROSELLA FRUMP (b. August 1886 in Clay County, Indiana; d. March 31, 1911 in Harrison, Clay County, Indiana; m. DAVID ALBERT STALEY on November 10, 1909 in Clay County, Indiana), CHARLES WILLARD FRUMP (b. November 20, 1887 in Clay County, Indiana; m. GOLDIA M. BEATTY on November 29, 1916 in Owen County, Indiana; buried at Oaklawn Memorial Gardens in Fishers, Hamilton County, Indiana), JOHN RAY FRUMP (b. August 1890 in Clay County, Indiana; d. October 21, 1904 in Bowling Green, Clay County, Indiana), OLIVE MAY FRUMP (b. May 1892 in Clay County, Indiana), GEORGE WASHINGTON FRUMP (b. February 08, 1894 in Bowling Green, Clay County, Indiana; d. April 07, 1974 in Clay County, Indiana; m. NELLIE E. ADAMS on June 25, 1916 in Hot Spring County, Arkansas), and HAZEL B. FRUMP (b. February 1896 in Clay County, Indiana; m. JOSEPH "JOE" C. MOORE on December 23, 1916 in Hot Spring County, Arcansas).

Notes for SETH ISAAC HART:

Seth was first married to EDITH T. SMILEY, daughter of PAYSON A. SMILEY and ANGELINE ZEIGLER. She was born in March 1895 in Daviess County, Indiana. They had 7 children as follows: LORENE E. HART (b. about 1917 in Daviess County, Indiana), MONA M. HART (b. about 1920 in Perry, Marion County, Indiana), LILLIAN G. HART (b. about 1921 in Marion County, Indiana), ELIZABETH HART (b. about 1924 in Indiana), LUELLA K. HART (b. about 1925 in Indiana), DAN SMILEY HART (b. October 22, 1927 in Vigo County, Indiana; d. March 03, 1979 in Saint Petersburg, Pinellas County, Florida), and BERYL RAY HART (b. August 14, 1929 in Terre Haute, Vigo County, Indiana; d. April 20, 2005 in Greenwood, Johnson County, Indiana).

DEATHS

REV. SETH ISAAC HART.

Rev. Seth Isaac Hart, 59 years old, 2553 Napoleon street, Indianapolis, former pastor of the Second Avenue E.U.B. Church of Terre Haute, died Monday morning in Indianapolis. Surviving are the widow, Nitis; six daughters, Mrs. Robert McBride of Indianapolis, Mrs. Ralph Smith of Danville, Ill.; Mrs. Roy Stuffle of Rockport, Mrs. Russell Youngblood of Newcastle, Mrs. Freedman Allen of Plainville and Mrs. Robert Grosse of California; two sons, Ray Hart of Indianapolis and Dan Hart of California; two stepchildren, 17 grandchildren and four step-grandchildren. Funeral services will be at 7:30 o'clock Wednesday evening at the Jordan Funeral Home in Indianapolis with continued services at 1:30 o'clock Thursday afternoon at the Plainville E. U. B. Church. Burial will be in New Bethel cemetery in Daviess county.

Obituary for Seth Isaac Hart – January 25, 1955
(Terre Haute Tribune, Obituary for Seth Isaac Hart)

Notes for EDITH T. SMILEY:
The obituary for Edith G. Hart published on page 6 of the December 09, 1975 issue for the Terre Haute Tribune was not Edith T. Smiley who married Seth Isaac Hart.

Notes for IVY MURIAL MCCOY:
Ivy graduated from Lebanon High School in 1928 and worked at Indiana Bell Telephone for 36 1/2 years until her retirement in 1964. She was a member of the Otterbein United Methodist Church.

More about IVY MURIAL MCCOY:
Ivy's obituary was published in the Monday, October 17, 1988 issue of the Lebanon Reporter.

Ivy died at Sunday, October 16, 1988 in Witham Memorial Hospital in Lebanon, Indiana following a brief illness. Witham Memorial Hospital was established in 1917 through a $15,000 gift from Flavious J. Witham, a Boone County farmer.

Funeral Services: Myers Mortuary of Lebanon, Indiana. Services were held at 10:30pm on Thursday, October 20, 1988 in the Myers Chapel of Memories at Lebanon, Indiana with the Reverend Charles M. Hiatt officiating.

Burial: Thursday, October 20, 1988 at Plot 289-33a of Oak Hill Cemetery in Lebanon, Boone County, Indiana.

Children of WILLIAM "WILLIE" J.[3] COOK and NITIS LOUISE FUNK are:

     i.   PAUL LEROY[4] COOK, b. March 13, 1926 in Lewis, Vigo County, Indiana; m. MYRTLE DORIS DABLEMONT on June 20, 1947 in Bourbonnais, Kankakee County, Illinois.

    ii.   BETTY RUTH[4] COOK, b. April 07, 1928 in Vigo County, Indiana; m. HARRY ALAN JOHNSON.

22. MARTINA CLYDE[3] MUSS *(GEORGE W.[2] MUSS, JOHN[1] MUSS)* was born January 24, 1891 in Louisville, Jefferson County, Kentucky and died March 14, 1952 in Lakeland, Jefferson County, Kentucky.

Notes for MARTINA CLYDE MUSS:
In the 1930 Lakeland, Jefferson County, Kentucky census (conducted on April 07, 1930) Martina C. is a resident of the Central State Hospital for the Insane. Martina is listed with no occupation.

Picture of Martina Clyde Muss
(Lyle Raymond Cook & Karla Denise Ezell Cook)

More about MARTINA CLYDE MUSS:
    Her Kentucky death certificate is #52-05611. Martina is listed as single at the time of her death. She died at 2:10pm.
    Informant: Record – Central State Hospital of Lakeland, Kentucky.
    Parents: George W. Muss and Ella Hannephin.

Cause of death: Cerebral hemorrhage due to hypertension. Other significant conditions were dementia praecox, paranoid type. Cerebral hemorrhage is a medical term that describes a stroke. A stroke happens when blood flow to a part of the brain stops. Hypertension describes high blood pressure. Dementia praecox is a chronic, deteriorating psychotic disorder characterized by rapid cognitive disintegration, usually beginning in the late teens or early adulthood.

Funeral Services: Blanford-Ratterman of 2815 South 4th Street in Louisville, Kentucky.

Burial: March 17, 1952 in Section Y, Lot 14 East Half at Saint Louis Cemetery of Louisville, Jefferson County, Kentucky.

Martina died at Central State Hospital in Lakeland, Kentucky. She is listed as living at 3840 Southern Parkway in Louisville at the time of her death. This is most likely where her mother, Ella W. Hannephin Muss, lived at that time. 3840 Southern Parkway is a 2 story, 2,144 square foot brick duplex home with 2 bedrooms and 2 bathrooms that was built in 1900.

Central State Hospital, a 192-bed adult psychiatric hospital, is located at 10510 LaGrange Road in Louisville, Kentucky and was built in 1869. The hospital is located next to Louisville's E. P. "Tom" Sawyer State Park. The beautiful old, original hospital building was razed in 1996 after a new facility was completed in 1986.

It is believed that Martina developed her mental illness during her late teenage years and as a result of this illness had to live the rest of her life in the Central State Hospital for the Insane.

23. NORA E.[3] MUSS *(CHARLES[2] MUSS, JOHN[1] MUSS)* was born December 1886 in Kentucky and died August 18, 1950 in Chicago, Cook County, Illinois. She married EDWIN MALLIBIEN STOLL on August 17, 1915 in Louisville, Jefferson County, Kentucky, son of DANIEL ALBERT STOLL and LOUISA "LOUISE" C. HABERMAN. He was born April 29, 1887 in White Creek, Montgomery County, Indiana.

Marriage License for Nora E. Muss and Edwin Mallibien Stoll
(Family History Center, Marriage License for Nora E. Muss and Edwin
Mallibien Stoll)

Notes for EDWIN MALLIBIEN STOLL:

On August 16, 1915, Edwin was living in Chicago, Cook County, Illinois when he married NORA E. MUSS. Reverend Wyloff married them.

In the June 05, 1917 World War I draft registration, Edwin is listed as a Railroad Clerk for Illinois Central in Chicago, Cook County, Illinois on South Water Street, and is married with a wife and child under 12 years old. Edwin also indicates that he previously served as a Private in the Infantry for 6 months in Ohio. Edwin is tall and medium build. His eyes are light blue and his hair is dark. He is also listed as being born in White Creek, Montgomery County, Indiana. His registration occurred in the Chicago, Cook County, Illinois.

In the 1920 Chicago, Cook County, Illinois census (conducted on January 02 and 03, 1920) E. M. Stoll, 32, is head of the household with Nora, 32, Rebecca L., 3 1/12 and C. L. Muss, 27. The C. L. Muss in this census that is living with them is Clarence Lee Muss, Nora's younger brother. Edwin is listed as a Railroad Clerk.

In the 1930 Chicago, Cook County, Illinois census (conducted on April 10, 1930) Edwin M. Stoll, 42 is head of the household with Nora M., 41, Becky Low, 13 and Donald E., 5. Edwin is listed as an Adjusting Clerk for the Steam Railroad.

In the 1942 World War II draft registration, Edwin is listed as working for the Illinois Central Railroad. He is living at 63 Dorchester in Chicago, Cook County, Illinois. His wife, Mrs. Nora Stoll, is listed as the person who will always know his address. They are both living at 1117 E 81st Street, Apt. 2E. He is also listed as being born in White Creek, Indiana.

Notes for DANIEL ALBERT STOLL (Father of EDWIN MALLIBIEN STOLL):

Daniel was born on June 21, 1858 in Louisville, Jefferson County, Kentucky and died May 05, 1934 in Louisville, Jefferson County, Kentucky. He was born to CHRISTIAN C. STOLL, SR. (b. April 1823 in Wurtemburg, Germany; d. July 14, 1916 in Jeffersonville, Clark County, Indiana; immigrated. about 1840, m. about 1849) and ELIZABETH CATHERINE ACKER (b. about 1829 in Bavaria, Germany; m. about 1849).

Daniel married LOUISA "LOUISE" C. HABERMAN on November 07, 1883 in Marion County, Indiana. Daniel and Louise had 4 known children as follows: FREDERICK "FRED" WILLIAM STOLL (b. September 18, 1884 in Seymour, Champaign County, Illinois; m. MARY ELIZABETH FLETCHER on October 22, 1912 in Marion County, Ohio), EDWIN MALLIBIEN STOLL (b. April 29, 1887 in White Crek, Montgomery County, Indiana; m. NORA E. MUSS on August 17, 1915 in Louisville, Jefferson County, Kentucky), KARL CHRISTIAN STOLL (b. August 22, 1889 in McKeesport, Allegheny County, Pennsylvania; d. March 1981 in

Rochester, Monroe County, New York; m. ALTA C. DAVIS on August 22, 1916 in Indiana), and HENRY ACKER STOLL (b. December 11, 1895 in McKeesport, Allegheny County, Pennsylvania; d. June 06, 1992 in Richmond County, Georgia; m. LILLY MNU).

Daniel had 6 siblings as follows: LOUISA STOLL (b. about 1852 in Louisville, Jefferson County, Kentucky), WILLIAM STOLL (b. about 1854 in Louisville, Jefferson County, Kentucky), SARAH STOLL (b. September 1856 in Louisville, Jefferson County, Kentucky), CHARLES CHRISTIAN STOLL, JR. (b. April 23, 1861 in Louisville, Jefferson County, Kentucky, d. September 05, 1943 in Louisville, Jefferson County, Kentucky; m. ANNA "ANNIE" CHRISTINE JUNGERMAN on October 20, 1886 in Davidson County, Tennessee; President of the Stoll Oil Refining Company), ELIZABETH "LIZZIE" STOLL (b. about 1863 in Louisville, Jefferson County, Kentucky), and HENRIETTA STOLL (b. about 1868 in Louisville, Jefferson County, Kentucky).

Notes for LOUISA "LOUISE" C. HABERMAN (Mother of EDWIN MALLIBIEN STOLL):

Louise was born on April 11, 1858 in Marion County, Ohio and died April 05, 1947 in Louisville, Jefferson County, Kentucky. Her parents were CHRISTIAN HABERMAN (b. October 06, 1839 in Hesse-Darmstadt, Germany) and GERTRUDE SEAS (b. June 05, 1828 in Baden, Germany. Gertrude immigrated to the United States in 1830 accouding to her 1900 census record, and she immigrated to the United States in 1850 according to her 1910 census record. There may be a family relationship between GERTRUDE SEAS and ELIZABETH "ELIZA" M. CEISE (the matriarch of the Muss family discussed in this book), but this relationship has not been proven.

Marriage License for Christian Haberman and Gertrude Seas
(Family History Center, Marriage License for Christian Haberman and
Gertrude Seas)

Louise was a sister to 8 siblings as follows: CHRISTIAN F. HABERMAN (b. about 1855 in Marion County, Ohio), HENRY HABERMAN (b. about 1856 in Marion County, Ohio), ANNA G. HABERMAN (b. about 1860 in Marion, Marion County, Ohio), AMANDA "MANDY" C. HABERMAN (b.), WILLIAM DAVID HABERMAN (b. about 1864 in in Marion County, Ohio), PHILIP JOSEPH HABERMAN (b. January 15, 1867 in Marion County, Ohio), JOHN A. HABERMAN (b. about 1868 in Marion County, Ohio), and CHARLES W. HABERMAN (b. about 1870 in Marion County, Ohio).

STOLL—Nora Muss Stoll, Aug. 18, 1950, of 1117 E. 81st street, wife of Edwin M., mother of Mrs. Rebecca Sherlock and Donald E. Resting at chapel, Jeffery boulevard at 77th street, until 11:30 a. m. Monday. Services Monday, 2 p. m., at Avalon Community church, 81st and Dante avenue. Interment private. SOuth Shore 8-8822.

Obituary for Nora E. Muss Stoll - August 20, 1950
(Chicago Daily Tribune)

Notes for NORA E. MUSS:
On August 16, 1915, Nora was living in Jacob Park, Jefferson County, Kentucky when she married EDWIN MALLIBIEN STOLL. Reverend Wyloff married them.

According to her obituary, Nora was living at 1117 E 81st Street at the time of her death.

Funeral Services: Avalon Community Church of Chicago, Illinois. Viewing was until 11:30am at a chapel on Jeffrey Boulevard at 77th Street. Services were held at 2:00pm on Monday, August 21, 1950 in the Avalon Community Church at 81st Street and Dante Avenue in Chicago, Illinois.

Her death is corroborated with Illinois Death Certificate # 6057546.

Children of NORA E.[3] MUSS and EDWIN MALLIBIEN STOLL are:

    i.   REBECCA "BECKY" LOUISE[4] STOLL, b. November 14, 1916 in Chicago, Cook County, Illinois; d. December 18, 1994 in Oak Lawn, Cook County, Illinois; m. CHARLES RAYMOND SHERLOCK in Illinois.

        Notes for REBECCA "BECKY" LOUISE STOLL:
        Her birth certificate is listed under Cook County, Illinois Birth Record File Number 6039008.

ii. DONALD EDWIN[4] STOLL, b. July 15, 1924 in Cook County, Illinois; d. August 06, 2000 in Nashville, Davidson County, Tennessee; m. MARGARET JEAN MCCRONE on January 07, 1950 in Cook County, Illinois.

Notes for DONALD EDWIN STOLL:
His birth certificate is listed under Cook County, Illinois Birth Record File Number 6030419.
His marriage license is listed under Cook County, Illinois Marriage File Number 2116307.

24. STELLA E.[3] MUSS *(CHARLES[2] MUSS, JOHN[1] MUSS)* was born July 21, 1890 in Louisville, Jefferson County, Kentucky and died January 05, 1955 in New Albany, Floyd County, Indiana. She first married DAVID FREDERICK DUESING on June 27, 1910 in Louisville, Jefferson County, Kentucky, son of JOHN HENRY DUESING (aka JOHANN HENRICH DUESING) and MARY BELLE STOUT. He was born February 05, 1890 in Louisville, Jefferson County, Kentucky and died July 1972 in Richmond, Henrico County, Virginia. After her divorce from David, Stella married JOSEPH ALEXANDER HICKS on July 10, 1918 in Floyd County, Indiana, son of SAMUEL H. HICKS and ALICE MOORE. He was born on March 05, 1873 in Nashville, Davidson County, Tennessee and died October 13, 1940 in New Albany, Floyd County, Indiana. After the death of Joseph, Stella married JAMES O. MCALLISTER, son of unknown parents.

Notes for STELLA E. MUSS:
On June 27, 1910, Stella was living in Louisville, Jefferson County, Kentucky at the time of her marriage to DAVID FREDERICK DUESING. This was her first marriage. They were married by James S. Keigwin.
On July 10, 1918, Stella was living in Louisville, Jefferson County, Kentucky when she married JOSEPH ALEXANDER HICKS. Her mother was deceased at the time she was married. This was the second marriage for Stella, and she divorced from her previous husband in December 1915 in Louisville, Jefferson County, Kentucky. Reverend W. H. Howerton married Stella and Joseph.
Funeral Services: Seabrook Funeral Home of New Albany, Indiana. Services were held at 2pm on Saturday, January 08, 1955 at the funeral home. Seabrook Funeral Home is now known as Seabrook Dieckmann & Naville Funeral Homes. The Seabrook Funeral Home was founded in 1920 and merged with the Dieckmann Funeral Home (founded in 1848) in 1995 to create the currently named business.
Burial: Saturday, January 08, 1955 at Fairview Cemetery in New Albany, Floyd County, Indiana.
Stella died suddenly at her home at 625 West Market Street in New Albany, Indiana. She was a member of the First Presbyterian

Church in New Albany, Indiana. The home at 625 West Market Street no longer exists. Both 625 and 623 West Market Street are empty lots today that sit between a corner lot, two story home at 629 W Market Street and another, single story home at 619 West Market Street. Today, the owner of 629 West Market Street owns both of the empty lots adjacent to their property.

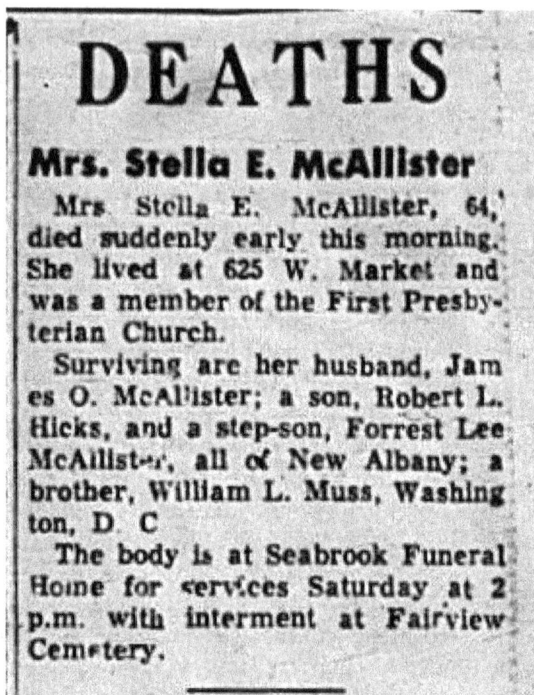

DEATHS

Mrs. Stella E. McAllister

Mrs. Stella E. McAllister, 64, died suddenly early this morning. She lived at 625 W. Market and was a member of the First Presbyterian Church.

Surviving are her husband, James O. McAllister; a son, Robert L. Hicks, and a step-son, Forrest Lee McAllister, all of New Albany; a brother, William L. Muss, Washington, D. C.

The body is at Seabrook Funeral Home for services Saturday at 2 p.m. with interment at Fairview Cemetery.

Obituary for Stella E. Muss Duesing Hicks McAllister – January 06, 1955
(New Albany Tribune, Obituary for Stella E. Muss Duesing Hicks McAllister)

Notes for DAVID FREDERICK DUESING:

In the 1910 Louisville, Jefferson County, Kentucky census (conducted on April 27, 1910) David F. Duesing and his wife are living with David's parents. John H. Duesing, 58, is head of the household with Mary B., 52, David F., 20, Frank, 17 and Ruth, 9. David is listed as a Wallpaper Collector.

On June 27, 1910, David was a clerk and living in Louisville, Jefferson County, Kentucky at the time of his marriage to STELLA E. MUSS. This was his first marriage.

In the June 05, 1917 World War I draft registration, David Frederick Duesing is listed as a wire chief for the Cumberland

Telephone and Telegraph Company in Frankfort, Franklin County, Kentucky, and is single. His mother is listed as a dependent. David is tall and medium build. His eyes are blue and his hair is brown. He is also listed as being born in Louisville, Jefferson County, Kentucky. His registration occurred in the Franklin County, Kentucky.

In the 1920 Ashland, Boyd County, Kentucky census (conducted on February 07, 1920) David Dewsing, 30, is head of the household with Francis, 19 and David Lee, 1. David is listed as a Telephone Operator.

Marriage License for Stella E. Muss and David Frederick Duesing
(Family History Center, Marriage License for Stella E. Muss and David
Frederick Duesing)

More about DAVID FREDERICK DUESING:

He later married FRANCIS "FANNIE" OSBORNE. Together they had at least eleven children as follows: DAVID LEE DUESING (b. February 01, 1919 in Kentucky; d. March 1984 in Richmond, Richmond City, Virginia), FRANK M. DUESING (b. October 09, 1920 in Ashland, Boyd County, Kentucky; d. October 11, 2006 in Bluefield, Mercer County, West Virginia), BESS H. DUESING (b. January 31, 1926?), WILLIAM "BILL" DUESING (b. May 7, 1926?), DONALD "DON" H. DUESING, SR. (b. April 19, 1927 in Virginia; d. February 16, 1991 in Missouri), EMMA G. DUESING (b. July 20, 1933 in Mercer County, West Virginia; d. April 03, 1934 in Mercer County, West Virginia), INFANT DUESING (b. March 08, 1936 in Bluefield, Mercer County, West Virginia; d. March 08, 1936 in Bluefield, Mercer County, West Virginia), JUNE DUESING (b. Unknown), VIRGINIA MAE DUESING (b. Unknown), MARY LOU DUESING (b. Unknown), and MICHAEL DUESING (b. Unknown). Please note that the author is uncertain of some of this information at this time.

Children of STELLA E.[3] MUSS and DAVID FREDERICK DUESING are:

    i.   ROBERT LEE[4] DUESING HICKS, b. December 30, 1910 in Jefferson County, Kentucky; d. December 12, 1955 in Indiana.

    Notes for ROBERT LEE[4] DUESING HICKS:

    He appears to have been later adoped by JOSEPH ALEXANDER HICKS and used the Hicks surname.

Notes for JOSEPH ALEXANDER HICKS:

On July 10, 1918, Joseph was a Conductor for the Southern Railway Company and living at 310 W Fourth Street in New Albany, Floyd County, Indiana when he married STELLA E. MUSS. His mother and father were both deceased at the time he was married. This was the second marriage for Joseph, and his previous wife died in 1913. Reverend W. H. Howerton married Joseph and Stella.

In the 1920 New Albany, Floyd County, Indiana census (conducted January 09, 1920) Joseph A. Hicks, 46, is head of the household with Stella, 29 and Robert L. Duesing, 9. Joseph is listed as a Yardman for the Railroad.

In the 1930 New Albany, Floyd County, Indiana census (conducted April 07, 1930) Joseph A. Hicks, 57, is head of the household with Stella, 39, Samuel H., 35 (son of Joseph) and Robert Lee, 19 (son of Stella). Joseph is listed as a Conductor for Southern Railway.

Marriage License for Stella E. Muss Duesing and Joseph Alexander
Hicks
(Family History Center, Marriage License for Stella E. Muss Duesing
and Joseph Alexander Hicks)

More about JOSEPH ALEXANDER HICKS:

He first married HETTIE GRIGGS RUMSEY on December 14, 1893 in Floyd County, Indiana, daughter of FRANK GRIGGS and INDIANA E MNU. She was born about 1875 in Illinois and died March 14, 1913 in New Albany, Floyd County, Indiana. Hettie died at 9am in the family residence at 239 West Spring Street of New Albany, Indiana after an illness of one year. It is important to note that the home at 239 West Spring Street no longer exists, and is near where the on ramp for Interstate 64 is today at the intersection of West Spring Street and Washington Place. Hettie was a member of the First Presbyterian Church in New Albany, Indiana. Hettie is buried at Fairview Cemetery in New Albany, Floyd County, Indiana. Together Joseph and Hettie had two children as follows: SAMUEL HOLSWORTH HICKS (b. February 06, 1895 in New Albany, Floyd County, Indiana; d. August 1944 in New Albany, Floyd County, Indiana) and NELLIE LOUISE HICKS (b. 1897 in Floyd County, Indiana; d. July 21, 1915 New Albany, Floyd County, Indiana).

Mrs. Hettie Hicks, wife of Joseph Hicks, died this morning at 9 o'clock at the family residence, 239 West Spring street, after an illness of one year. She was thirty-nine years old and besides her husband leaves two children, Samuel and Miss Nellie Hicks. She was a daughter of Mr. and Mrs. Frank Griggs, of this city, and is survived by two brothers and two sisters. They are Edward Griggs, Charles Griggs, Mrs. Amy McKamy and Mrs. Carrie Lottich. She was a member of the First Presbyterian church. The funeral services will be held next Sunday afternoon at 3 o'clock from the residence.

Obituary for Hettie Rumsey Griggs Hicks - March 14, 1913
(New Albany Evening Tribune, Obituary for Hettie Rumsey Griggs Hicks)

Joseph's daughter, NELLIE LOUISE HICKS, died Wednesday afternoon on July 21, 1915 at the age of 18 from tuberculosis. She was staying at the home of her grandparents, Frank M. and Indiana E. Griggs, at the time of her death. Nellie was ill for a year prior to her death. Her father, Joseph Alexander Hicks, was working for Southern Railway Company at the time of her death. Her brother, Samuel Holsworth Hicks, was an employee of the Adams Express Company at the time of her death. Nellie was a member of the First Presbyterian Church in New Albany, Indiana. Reverend E. C. Lucas, from her church, officiated at her funeral.

Burial: Friday, July 23, 1915 at Fairview Cemetery in New Albany, Floyd County, Indiana.

YEAR'S ILLNESS ENDS IN DEATH

Miss Nellie Hicks, Popular Young Woman of West-End, Succumbs to White Plague.

Following a year's illness of tuberculosis, Miss Nellie Hicks, aged 18 years, a well known and greatly beloved young woman of the west end of the city, died last Wednesday afternoon at the home of her grandparents, Mr. and Mrs. Frank Griggs, 710 West Market street. Miss Hicks is the daughter of Joseph A. Hicks, an employe of the Southern Railway Co. Besides her father and grandparents, she leaves one brother, Sam Hicks, an employe of the Adams Express Co. Her mother, Mrs. Hettie Hicks, died about two years ago. Miss Hicks was a member of the First Presbyterian church, where the funeral will be held at 2 o'clock Friday afternoon, with burial in Fairview cemetery. The Rev. E. C. Lucas, pastor of the First Presbyterian church, will officiate.

Obituary 1 for Nellie Louise Hicks – July 23, 1915
(New Albany Weekly Tribune)

Miss Nellie Hicks, daughter of Joseph A. Hicks, an employe of the Southern Railway Company, died Wednesday at the home of her grandparents, Mr. and Mrs. Frank Griggs, 710 West Market street, of tuberculosis, from which she had suffered for the last year. She was 18 years old, and in addition to the relatives mentioned she is survived by a brother, Samuel Hicks, of the Adams Express Company. Her mother died two years ago. She was a member of the First Presbyterian church and the funeral services took place there.

Obituary 2 for Nellie Louise Hicks – July 27, 1915
(Public Press, Obituary 2 for Nellie Louise Hicks)

Joseph's son, SAMUEL HOLSWORTH HICKS, married NORA V. TURNER on May 12, 1934 and they separated on May 18, 1938. A divorce complaint was filed in the Floyd County Circuit Court by Nora on Thursday, May 19, 1938 with cruelty being the charge. Nora was living at 502 West Market Street in New Albany, Indiana at the time the divorce action was filed. According to Samuel's obituary in the New Albany Ledger, he died at 9am on Sunday, July 30, 1944 at Saint Edward's Hospital from internal injuries after being struck by an automobile at about midnight that day. Samuel also sustained fractured arms and legs. Samuel was walking along highway 150 when he was struck by Arnold L. Moser, 23, of Floyd Knobs. Arnold was blinded by the headlights of two approaching automobiles. Arnold did not leave the scene of the accident and was not arrested. Seabrook Funeral Home (now Seabrook Dieckmann & Naville Funeral Home) of New Albany, Indiana was in charge of Samuel's funeral. Samuel was buried at Fairview Cemetery in New Albany, Floyd County, Indiana.

Cruelty Is Charged In Divorce Action

Cruelty was charged by Mrs. Nora V. Hicks, 502 West Market street, in a divorce complaint against Samuel H. Hicks, which was filed Thursday in the Floyd Circuit Court. They were married May 12, 1934, and separated May 18, 1938.

Divorce for Samuel Holsworth Hicks and Nora V. Turner - May 19, 1938
(New Albany Tribune, Divorce for Samuel Holsworth Hicks and Nora V. Turner)

Joseph appears to have adopted the only child from Stella's previous marriage, ROBERT LEE DUESING, and his name was changed to ROBERT LEE HICKS.

Joseph died in his residence on 819 West Market Street at 1:30pm following a long illness. He was 67 years old. Joseph was a member of the First Presbyterian Church in New Albany, Indiana. The home at 819 West Market Street in New Albany, Indiana is a 1,110 square foot, single-family home that was built in 1929 that has 3 bedrooms and 1 bathroom.

Funeral Services: Held at 2:30pm inside Seabrook's Chapel on 1119 East Market Street in New Albany, Indiana.

Burial: Tuesday, October 15, 1940 at Fairview Cemetery in New Albany, Floyd County, Indiana.

Joseph A. Hicks Expires In Home

Joseph A. Hicks, retired switch-man of the Southern Railway, died at 1:30 o'clock Sunday aft-ernoon at the residence, 810 West Market street, following a long illness. He was 67.

He was a member of the Broth-erhood of Railway Trainmen and of the First Presbyterian Church.

Survivors include the widow, Mrs. Stella Hicks; two sons, Sam-uel Hicks and Robert Hicks; a brother, Byron Hicks, Detroit, and one gradchild.

The body is at Seabrook's Chap-el, 1110 East Market street, where funeral services will be held at 2:30 o'clock Tuesday afternoon. Burial will be in Fairview Ceme-tery.

Obituary for Joseph Alexander Hicks - October 14, 1940
(New Albany Tribune, Obituary for Joseph Alexander Hicks)

Headstone for Joseph Alexander Hicks and Hettie Griggs Rumsey
(Douser, Headstone for Joseph Alexander Hicks & Hettie Griggs
Rumsey)

25. CLARENCE LEE[3] MUSS *(CHARLES[2] MUSS, JOHN[1] MUSS)* was born
October 28, 1892 in Kentucky. It is unknown whether he married and
when he died.

Notes for CLARENCE LEE MUSS:
    In the June 05, 1917 World War I draft registration, Clarence Lee
is listed as a salesman for Bush – Krebs Company (Engravers) at 408
W Main Street in Louisville, Jefferson County, Kentucky, and is single.
He is also listed as having served in the Infantry and Artillery for 5
years in the U.S. Army and Kentucky National Guard. Clarence is tall
and medium build. His eyes are brown and his hair is brown. He is
also listed as being born in Louisville, Jefferson County, Kentucky. His
registration occurred in Louisville, Jefferson County, Kentucky. "This
man was in service on registration day, June 05, 1917. Has since been
discharged, honorably."
    In the 1920 Chicago, Cook County, Illinois census (conducted on
January 02 and 03, 1920) E. M. Stoll, 32, is head of the household with
Nora, 32, Rebecca L., 3 1/12 and C. L. Muss, 27. The C. L. Muss in this

census that is living with them is Clarence Lee Muss, Nora's younger brother. Clarence is listed as a Clerk for the Packing House.

In the 1930 Chicago, Cook County, Illinois census (conducted on April 02, 1930) Clarence Lee Muss is a boarder. Walter C. Royce, 44, is head of the household with Beulah, 30 Martin, 7/12, and Clarence L. Muss, 37. Clarence is listed as a Freight Clerk for the Railroad.

More about CLARENCE LEE MUSS:
Clarence died prior to January 1955 since he is not listed in the obituary for his sister, Stella E. Muss Duesing Hicks McAllister.

26. WILLIAM NATHAN[3] MUSS *(CHARLES[2] MUSS, JOHN[1] MUSS)* was born February 14, 1896 in Harrison County, Indiana and died February 20, 1957 in Virginia. He married MARY KATHERINE LAUGHLIN about 1925 in Kentucky, daughter of unknown parents. She was born about 1897 in Kentucky.

Notes for WILLIAM NATHAN MUSS:
In the June 05, 1917 World War I draft registration, William Nathan is listed as a clerk for Louisville Nashville Railroad in Louisville, Jefferson County, Kentucky at a Field Office at 9th and Madison, and is single. William is medium height and medium build. His eyes are brown and his hair is brown. He is also listed as being born in Harrison County, Indiana. His registration occurred in Allison, Jefferson County, Kentucky.

In the 1920 Allison, Jefferson County, Kentucky census (conducted on January 12 and 13, 1920) William Muss is a boarder. Henry J. Forst, 66, is head of the household with Mary, 66, George I., 26, Louise Caragan (daughter), 30, Mary E. Forst, 28, William Caragan (son-in-law), Morris Caragan (grandson), 3 10/12, Emmett W. Caragan (grandson), 5/12 and William Muss, 24. William is listed as a Clerk for the Steam Railroad.

In the 1930 Winchester, Clark County, Kentucky census (conducted on April 17, 1930) William N. Muss, 34 is head of the household with Mary K., 33 and Betty A., 3 10/12. William is listed as a Traffic Manager for the Roller Mills.

Headstone for William Nathan Muss (McInturff)

More about WILLIAM NATHAN MUSS:
He enlisted in the military on June 28, 1918 in Louisville, Jefferson County, Kentucky and served as a Sergeant in World War I.
Burial: February 1957 at Arlington National Cemetery in Arlington, Arlington County, Virginia.

Children of WILLIAM NATHAN[3] MUSS and MARY KATHERINE LAUGHLIN are:
     i.   BETTY A. MUSS, b. June 08, 1926 in Fayette County, Kentucky.

27. JAMES CLYDE[3] DORIOT *(MARY EMMA[2] MUSS, JOHN[1] MUSS)* was born in April 1893 in Bullitt County, Kentucky. No additional information can be found on him at this time.

28. NANNIE M.[3] DORIOT *(MARY EMMA[2] MUSS, JOHN[1] MUSS)* was born August 25, 1895 in Bullitt County, Kentucky and died May 18, 1970 in Louisville, Jefferson County, Kentucky. It is believed that she never married. No additional information can be found on her at this time.

29. Morna[3] Doriot *(Mary Emma[2] Muss, John[1] Muss)* was born in March 1900 in Bullitt County, Kentucky. No additional information can be found on her at this time.

30. David P.[3] Doriot *(Mary Emma[2] Muss, John[1] Muss)* was born in 1903 in Bullitt County, Kentucky and died September 17, 1957 in Jefferson County, Kentucky. No additional information can be found on him at this time.

Notes for David P. Doriot :
David died at 4:45am on September 17, 1957 in Kentucky Baptist Hospital. At the time of his death, he lived at 1730 Blanton Lane. David was a bus driver for Mill Creek School on Dixie Highway and an insurance agent. He was also a member of the Masonic Lodge and Valley Hi -Twelve Club.

Funeral Services: Hardy Funeral Home of Valley Station, Kentucky. Services were held at 3pm on Friday, September 20, 1957. Hardy Funeral home was originally established by the same W. G. Hardy that handled services for most of the members of this family.

Burial: Friday, September 20, 1957 at Louisville Memorial Gardens in Louisville, Jefferson County, Kentucky.

Obituary for David P. Doriot – September 19, 1957
(Louisville Courier-Journal, Obituary for David P. Doriot)

31. LONNIE[3] DORIOT *(MARY EMMA[2] MUSS, JOHN[1] MUSS)* was born in 1906 in Jefferson County, Kentucky and died February 13, 1919 in Frankfort, Franklin County, Kentucky.

Notes for LONNIE DORIOT:
His Kentucky death certificate is #19-05655. Lonnie is listed as 10 years old at the time of his death. He died at 9am and had stayed in the hospital for 7 months and 6 days. He died in what is now the Franklin Regional Medical Center.
Informant: F. M. I. (Hospital) Records of Frankfort, Kentucky.
Parents: "No history" of "No history" and Mary -- of "No history".
Cause of Death: Measles complicated with lobar pneumonia for 4 days. Measles is a very contagious infection of the respiratory system due to a virus that causes a rash, cough, sore throat, fever, runny nose, sore muscles and bloodshot eyes. Lobar pneumonia is a form of pneumonia that affects a large and continuous area of the lobe of a lung.
Funeral Services: W. G. Hardy of West Point, Kentucky.
Burial: Friday, February 14, 1919 on the hospital grounds in Frankfort, Franklin County, Kentucky.

More about LONNIE DORIOT:
He was buried on the hospital grounds, and "None" is listed for the undertaker.

32. LOUIS EDWARD "ED"[3] APPLEGATE *(ELIZABETH "BETTIE"[2] MUSS, JOHN[1] MUSS)* was born March 15, 1890 in Riverview, Jefferson County, Kentucky and died October 05, 1969 in Shelby County, Kentucky. He married LILLIAN "LILLIE" MAY MERKER about 1913 in Kentucky, daughter of CHARLES "CHARLEY" MERKER, JR. and JULIA IDA "IDA" DILLON. She was born October 03, 1892 in Kentucky and died June 23, 1972 in Jefferson County, Kentucky.

Marriage License for Louis Edward "Ed" Applegate and Lillian "Lillie" May Merker
(Family History Center, Marriage License for Louis Edward "Ed" Applegate and Lillian "Lillie" May Merker)

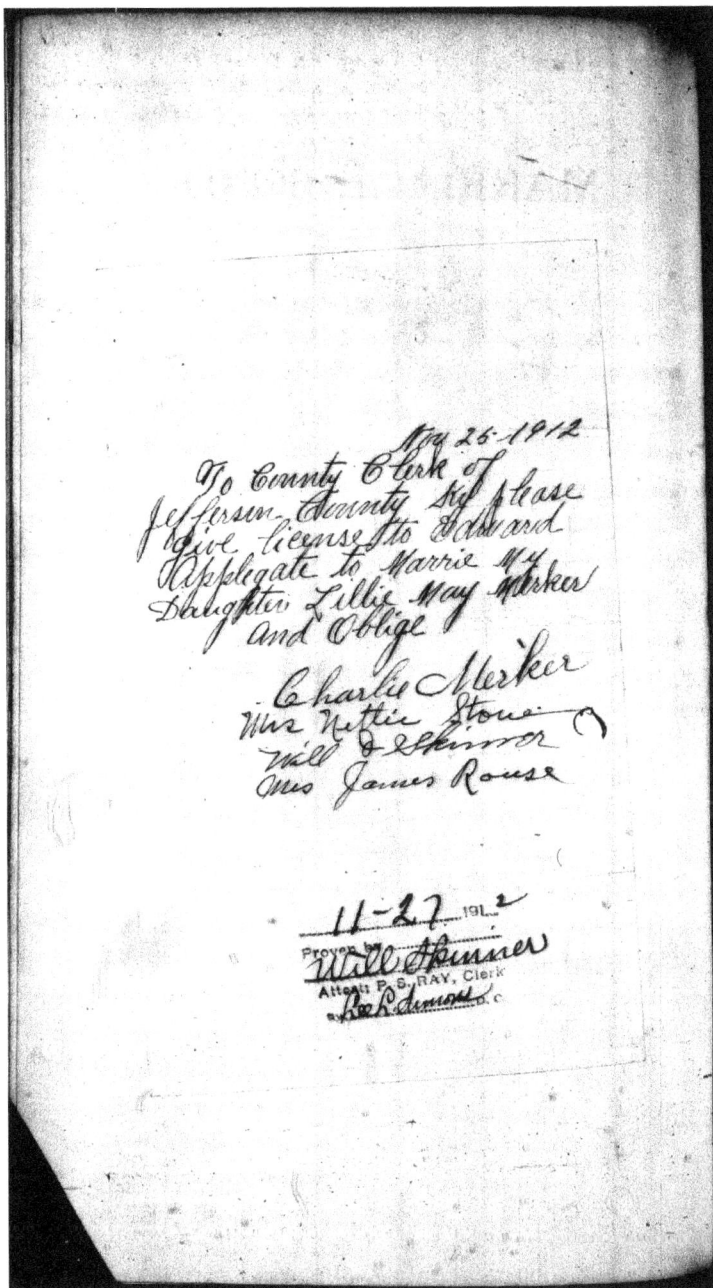

Marriage Consent for Louis Edward "Ed" Applegate and Lillian "Lillie"
May Merker
(Family History Center, Marriage Consent for Louis Edward "Ed"
Applegate and Lillian "Lillie" May Merker)

Notes for LOUIS EDWARD "ED" APPLEGATE:
On November 27, 1912, Ed was living in West Point, Hardin County, Kentucky when he married LILLIAN "LILLIE" MAY MERKER. Reverend Alderman married Ed and Lillie. WILLIAM "WILL" O. SKINNER co-signed the marriage bond with Ed. Will may be related to ELIZABETH "ELIZA" J. SKINNER, who was the mother of REBECCA JANE MOORE. Will Skinner was living in Highland Park, Jefferson County, Kentucky when he co-signed on the marriage bond.
In the June 05, 1917 World War I draft registration, Louis Edward Applegate is listed as a self-employed farmer in West Point, Bullitt County, Kentucky, and is married. He has a wife and one child. Lewis is medium height and stout build. His eyes are brown and his hair is black. He is also listed as being born in Riverview, Jefferson County, Kentucky. His registration occurred in Bullitt County, Kentucky.
In the 1920 Shepherdsville, Bullitt County, Kentucky census (conducted on January 10, 1920) L. E. Applegate, 29, is head of the household with Lillie, 27, Thelma, 6, Aline, 2 and Ednamay, 1/12. Lewis is listed as a Farmer.
In the 1930 Blandville, Hardin County, Kentucky census (conducted on April 04, 1930) Louis E. Applegate, 40, is head of the household with Lillie M., 68, Thelma P., 16, Aline, 12, Adna M., 10, Mary C., 6 and Linda M., 4 2/12. Lewis is listed as an Overseer of the Saw Mill.

More about LOUIS EDWARD "ED" APPLEGATE :
Burial: Mount Eden Cemetery in Shepherdsville, Bullitt County, Kentucky.

Notes for LILLIAN "LILLIE" MAY MERKER:
She died on Friday, June 23, 1972 at 2:45pm in the Kentucky Baptist Hospital of Louisville, Kentucky.
Funeral Services: W. G. Hardy at 10907 Dixie Highway in Valley Station, Kentucky. Funeral services were held at 2pm on Monday, June 26, 1972 in the Knob Creek Union Church at Cupio, Kentucky.
Burial: Monday, June 26, 1972 at Mount Eden Cemetery in Shepherdsville, Bullitt County, Kentucky.

APPLEGATE, Mrs. Lillie Mc? (nee Merker)

Of the Masonic Widow's and Orphan's Home, passed away in her 80th year, Friday, June 23, 1972, at 2:45 p.m. at the Kentucky Baptist Hospital. Devoted mother of Mrs. Robert (Thelma) Henderson, Mrs. James (Aire) Funk, St. Clair Shores, Mich., Mrs. Joe (Katherine) Hedges, Brooks, Ky.; Mrs. Robert (Linda) Durrett Mr. Charles Edward, West Point, Ky. and Mrs. Frank Applegate, Westland, Mich.; sister of Mrs. Minnie Heath, Mrs. Ethel Snellen, Mrs. Hazel Cund..t and Mrs. Nellie Miller; also survived by 12 grandchildren and 16 great-grandchildren. Remains are at the W. G. Hardy Valley Chapel, 10907 Dixie Hgwy. after 5 p.m. Saturday. Funeral services Monday at 2 p.m. at the Knob Creek Church. Bullitt County, Ky. Interment in Mount Eden Cemetery.

Obituary for Lillian "Lillie" May Merker Applegate - June 24, 1972
(Louisville Courier-Journal, Obituary for Lillian "Lillie" May Merker Applegate)

Notes for CHARLES "CHARLEY" M. MERKER, JR. (Father of LILLIAN "LILLIE" MAY MERKER):

Charles, Jr. was born on September 09, 1867 in Bullitt County, Kentucky and died May 10, 1937 in Cupio, Bullitt County, Kentucky. He was the son of CHARLES MERKER, SR. (b. January 1816 in France; d. about 1900; m. September 01, 1848 in Bullitt County, Kentucky) and MARY ELIZABETH "ELIZABETH" STIBBINS (b. January 1829 in Kentucky; d. January 07, 1904 in Jefferson County, Kentucky).

Charles, Jr. first married LAURA HARSHFIELD on February 18, 1890 in Bullitt County, Kentucky. There were no known children from this marriage, and Laura died on Feburary 19, 1891 in Bullitt County, Kentucky. After the death of his first wife, Charles, Jr. married JULIA IDA "IDA" DILLON on January 13, 1892 in Louisville, Jefferson County,

Kentucky. Charles, Jr. and Ida had 6 known children as follows:
LILLIAN "LILLIE" MAY MERKER (b. October 03, 1892 in Kentucky; d. June
23, 1972 in Jefferson County, Kentucky; m. LOUIS EDWARD "ED"
APPLEGATE on November 27, 1912 in Louisville, Jefferson County,
Kentucky), MINNIE MYRTLE MERKER (b. June 12, 1894 in Kentucky; d.
December 05, 1976 in Shepherdsville, Bullitt County, Kentucky; m.
WILLIAM "WILL" F. HEATH about 1921; buried at Knob Creek Union
Church Cemetery in Cupio, Bullitt County, Kentucky), GARNET "GARNIE"
MERKER (b. August 15, 1896 in Bullitt County, Kentucky; d. March 13,
1959 in Jefferson County, Kentucky; m. NANNIE PEARL "PEARL"
RAYMOND on April 16, 1918 in Clark County, Indiana; buried at Knob
Creek Union Church Cemetery in Cupio, Bullitt County, Kentucky),
ETHEL MERKER (b. June 18, 1900 in Bullitt County, Kentucky; d. March
21, 1973 in Jefferson County, Kentucky; m. PLEASANT SNELLEN on
December 17, 1917 in Clark County, Indiana), HAZEL MERKER (b. July
24, 1904 in Bullitt County, Kentucky; d. 1976 in Kentucky; m. WILLIAM
CLARENCE "CLARENCE" ARMSTRONG on December 13, 1924 in Clark
County, Indiana; buried at Hebron Cemetery in Brooks, Bullitt County,
Kentucky), and NELLIE MERKER (b. May 09, 1907 in Bullitt County,
Kentucky; m. ERNEST MILLER on October 23, 1926 in Clark County,
Indiana).

Charles, Jr. had 6 siblings as follows: WILLIAM HENRY "HENRY"
MERKER (b. July 1950 in Bullitt County, Kentucky; d. August 25, 1926
in Cupio, Bullitt County, Kentucky; believed to have never married;
buried in Merker Cemetery), CLARISA "CLARA" MERKER (b. March 15,
1852 in Bullitt County, Kentucky; d. March 13, 1932 in Louisville,
Jefferson County, Kentucky; m. JAMES T. FERGUSON on March 10, 1872
in Bullitt County, Kentucky), M. ELIZA MERKER (b. June 28, 1854 in
Bullitt County, Kentucky; d. June 07, 1931 in Cupio, Bullitt County,
Kentucky; m. SANFORD SCOTT on December 23, 1875 in Bullitt County,
Kentucky; divorced by the 1880 census; buried in Merker Cemetery),
MARGARET "MAGGIE" A. MERKER (b. July 60, 1856 in Bullitt County,
Kentucky; d. October 19, 1927 in Louisvile, Jefferson County,
Kentucky; m1. B. H. MILLER on February 07, 1906 in Bullitt County,
Kentucky; m2. SAMUEL "SQUIRE" T. PINKSTON about 1922; buried at
Knob Creek Cemetery in Cupio, Bullitt County, Kentucky), MARTHA
ANN MERKER (b. June 15, 1859 in Bullitt County, Kentucky; d.
November 20, 1878 in Bullitt County, Kentucky; m. MATTHEW MORRIS
HIBBS on December 27, 1877 in Bullitt County, Kentucky), and JACOB
MERKER (b. February 18, 1862 in Bullitt County, Kentucky; d.
December 15, 1942 in Bullitt County, Kentucky; m. MARY B. SKINNER on
March 21, 1886 in Bullitt County, Kentucky).

Burial: Knob Creek Union Cemetery in Cupio, Bullitt County,
Kentucky.

Notes for JULIA IDA "IDA" DILLON (Mother of LILLIAN "LILLIE" MAY MERKER:
Ida was born on September 09, 1868 in Jefferson County, Kentucky and died on June 08, 1933 in Cupio, Bullitt County, Kentucky. She was the daughter of WILLIAM DILLON (b. August 07, 1829 in Spencer County, Kentucky; d. January 13, 1908 in Kentucky; buried at Wilson-Snawder Cemetery in Valley Station, Jefferson County, Kentucky; m. CLEMENTINE SNAWDER on December 04, 1851 in Jefferson County, Kentucky) and CLEMENTINE SNAWDER (b. November 17, 1829 in Jefferson County, Kentucky; d. April 29, 1910 in Jefferson County, Kentucky; buried at Wilson-Snawder Cemetery in Valley Station, Jefferson County, Kentucky).

Ida had 6 siblings as follows: MANDEVILLE "AMANDA" V. DILLON (b. March 15, 1852 in Jefferson County, Kentucky; d. July 03, 1885 in Jefferson County, Kentucky; m. FRED SEYBOLT on February 15, 1882 in Jefferson County, Kentucky; buried at Wilson-Snawder Cemetery in Valley Station, Jefferson County, Kentucky), MARY ANN DILLON (b. December 29, 1854 in Jefferson County, Kentucky; d. January 06, 1936 in Louisville, Jefferson County, Kentucky; m. MATTHEW MORRIS HIBBS on December 22, 1883 in Jefferson County, Kentucky; buried at Resthaven Memorial Park Cemetery in Louisville, Jefferson County, Kentucky), MARTHA "MATTIE" DILLON (b. May 1858 in Jefferson County, Kentucky; m. JOHN W. GATEWOOD on December 23, 1882 in Jefferson County, Kentucky), REBECCA DILLON (b. May 1860 in Salina, Jefferson County, Kentucky; m. WILLIAM "WILLIE" SNAWDER on May 05, 1886 in Jefferson County, Kentucky), BELLE DILLON (b. about 1863 in Jefferson County, Kentucky; m. W. M. STONE on October 17, 1889 in Jefferson County, Kentucky), and ALICE DILLON (b. May 22, 1867 in Jefferson County, Kentucky; d. February 07, 1918 in Jefferson County, Kentucky; buried in Orell, Jefferson County, Kentucky; m. DENNIS MITCHELL, JR. on January 12, 1888 in Bullitt County, Kentucky).

MATTHEW MORRIS HIBBS first married MARTHA ANN MERKER, and later married MARY ANN DILLON after Martha died.

Burial: Knob Creek Union Cemetery in Cupio, Bullitt County, Kentucky.

Children of LOUIS EDWARD[3] APPLEGATE and LILLIAN "LILLIE" MAY MERKER are:

    i.   THELMA PEARL[4] APPLEGATE, b. September 06, 1913 in Jefferson County, Kentucky; d. October 18, 2008 in New Albany, Floyd County, Indiana; m. ROBERT B. HENDERSON on September 8, 1931 in Jeffersonville, Clark County, Indiana.

    ii. ALINE[4] S. APPLEGATE, b. August 18, 1917 in Bullitt County, Kentucky; d. December 14, 2007 in Louisville, Jefferson County, Kentucky; m. JAMES OSCAR FUNK.

    iii.   EDNA MAE[4] APPLEGATE, b. November 19, 1919 in Shepherdsville, Bullitt County, Kentucky; m. HENRY LEE ARNOLD on July 18, 1938 in Bartholomew County, Indiana.

    iv.   MARY KATHERINE "KATHERINE"[4] APPLEGATE, b. March 12, 1924 in Bullitt County, Kentucky; m1. JOSEPH "JOE" HEDGES; m2. EDWARD M. ROY.

    v.   LINDA M.[4] APPLEGATE, b. February 25, 1926 in Bullitt County, Kentucky; m. ROBERT "BOB" O. DURRETT.

33. ROY WALKER[3] APPLEGATE *(ELIZABETH "BETTIE"[2] MUSS, JOHN[1] MUSS)* was born August 31, 1892 in West Point, Bullitt County, Kentucky and died April 30, 1976 in West Point, Bullitt County, Kentucky. He married ZULA COOK on December 25, 1920 in Kentucky, daughter of ROBERT T. COOK and ROXANA FUNK. She was born August 26, 1902 in Indiana and died January 15, 1983 in West Point, Hardin County, Kentucky.

Notes for ROY WALKER APPLEGATE:

In the May 26, 1917 World War I draft registration, Roy Walker is listed as a farmer for R. D. McNutt in Arvada, Jefferson County, Colorado, and is single. R. D. McNutt must be living in Arvada, Colorado but owned farm land in the area at this time. Lewis is medium height and medium build. His eyes are brown and his hair is black. He is also listed as being born in West Point, Bullitt County, Kentucky. His registration occurred in the Bullitt County, Kentucky.

In the 1930 Bullitt County, Kentucky census (conducted on April 29, 1930) Roy W. Applegate, 37, is head of the household with Lula, 27. Roy is listed as a Farmer.

Marriage License for Roy Walker Applegate and Zula Cook
(Family History Center, Jefferson County, Kentucky Marriages)

More about ROY WALKER APPLEGATE:
It is believed that Roy and Zula did not have any children.
Roy was a veteran of World War I and a retired farmer. He was a member of the Miles Masonic Lodge 341 and Order of Amaranth.

He died on Saturday, May 01, 1976 at 1pm in Saints Mary and Elizabeth Hospital in Louisville, Kentucky.

Funeral Services: W. G. Hardy at 10907 Dixie Highway in Valley Station, Kentucky. Funeral services were held at 1pm on Monday, May 03, 1976 in the Knob Creek Union Church at Cupio, Kentucky.

Burial: Monday, May 03, 1976 at Bethany Memorial Cemetery in Louisville, Jefferson County, Kentucky.

> **Roy W. Applegate,** 83, of West Point Rt. 1, died at 1 p.m. Friday at SS. Mary & Elizabeth Hospital.
>
> He was a retired farmer and a member of Miles Masonic Lodge 341 and Order of Amaranth. He was a veteran of World War I.
>
> Survivors include his wife, the former Zula Cook.
>
> The funeral will be at 1 p.m. Monday at Knob Creek Union Church on KY 44, with burial in Bethany Cemetery.
>
> The body will be at the W.G. Hardy Valley Funeral Home, 10907 Dixie Highway, until noon Monday when it will be taken to the church.

Obituary for Roy Walker Applegate – May 1, 1976
(Louisville Courier-Journal, Obituary for Roy Walker Applegate)

Notes for ZULA COOK:

Zula was a member of the Knob Creek Baptist Church at Cupio, Kentucky.

She died on Saturday, January 15, 1983 in the Georgetown Manor Nursing Home of Louisville, Kentucky.

Funeral Services: W. G. Hardy at 10907 Dixie Highway in Valley Station, Kentucky. Funeral services were held at 1:30pm on Wednesday, January 19, 1983 at the funeral home.

Burial: Wednesday, January 19, 1983 at Bethany Memorial Cemetery in Louisville, Jefferson County, Kentucky.

Zula Cook Applegate, 80, of Georgetown Manor Nursing Home, died there Saturday.

She was a member of Knob Creek Baptist Church. -

The funeral will be at 1:30 p.m. Wednesday at W. G. Hardy Valley Funeral Home, 10907 Dixie Highway, with burial in Bethany Cemetery.

Visitation at the funeral home will be after 2 p.m. Monday.

Obituary for Zula Cook Applegate – January 17, 1983
(Louisville Courier-Journal, Obituary for Zula Cook Applegate)

Notes for ROBERT T. COOK (Father of ZULA COOK):

Robert was born on October 15, 1851 in Bullitt County, Kentucky and died on March 03, 1924 in Cupio, Bullitt County, Kentucky. His parents were JAMES COOK (b. about 1817 in Spencer County, Kentucky) and MARY JANE CONGROVE (b. about 1832 in Kentucky).

Robert was the brother of MARTHA A. COOK, MARY C. COOK, LILLIE M. COOK, ADA E. COOK, CHARLES "CHARLEY" C. COOK, and ABEL L. COOK as well as the half-brother of WILLIAM MALCOLM COOK, SARAH C. COOK, and MARY E. COOK. WILLIAM MALCOLM COOK married CAROLINE "CARRIE" F. MUSS, and this family is discussed in detail in the earlier section of the book that covers WILLIAM MALCOLM COOK and CAROLINE "CARRIE" F. MUSS .

Robert married ROXANA FUNK on October 22, 1873 in Bullitt County, Kentucky. Robert and Roxana had 6 known children as follows: MAYME COOK (b. August 13, 1874 in Bullitt County, Kentucky; d. April 19, 1945 in Hardin County, Kentucky; buried at Knob Creek Union Church Cemetery in Cupio, Bullitt County, Kentucky; m. SYDNEY A. ANDERSON on December 31, 1896 in Jeffersonville, Clark County, Indiana), ALVIN "ALVA" E. COOK (b. April 01, 1876 in Bullitt County, Kentucky; m. HATTIE OGLE on Auaugst 26, 1897 in Jeffersonville, Clark County, Indiana), THOMAS COOK (b. about 1878 in Bullitt County, Kentucky; m. KATE LANNIGAN on February 20, 1899 in Jeffersonville, Clark County, Indiana), MATTIE L. COOK (b. December 1886 in Shepherdsville, Bullitt County, Kentucky; d. March 11, 1966 in Bullitt County, Kentucky; buried at Knob Creek Union Church Cemetery in Cupio, Bullitt County, Kentucky; m. KEARN FUNK on June 10, 1906 in Bullitt County, Kentucky), ETHEL A. COOK (b. August 21, 1889 in Shepherdsville, Bullitt County, Kentucky; m. WILLIAM HENRY BISHOP on October 10, 1928 in Clark County, Indiana), and ZULA COOK (b. August 26, 1902 in Kentucky; d. January 15, 1983 in Louisville, Jefferson

County, Kentucky; m. ROY WALKER APPLEGATE on December 25, 1920 in Kentucky).

Burial: Knob Creek Union Cemetery in Cupio, Bullitt County, Kentucky.

Notes for ROXANA FUNK (Mother of ZULA COOK):

Roxana was born on October 21, 1852 in Bullitt County, Kentucky and died on May 13, 1930 in Cupio, Bullitt County, Kentucky. She was the daughter of WILLIAM ROBERT FUNK (b. January 18, 1822 in Nelson County, Kentucky; d. October 27, 1896 in Bullitt County, Kentucky; buried at Mount Eden Cemetery in Shepherdsville, Bullitt County, Kentucky; m. SARAH ANN MCDANIEL on January 12, 1852 in Jefferson County, Kentucky) and SARAH ANN MCDANIEL (b. Jul 08, 1832 in Jefferson County, Kentucky; d. March 14, 1893 in Bullitt County, Kentucky; buried at Mount Eden Cemetery in Shepherdsville, Bullitt County, Kentucky).

Roxana had 6 siblings as follows: JAMES THOMAS FUNK (b. July 16, 1854 in Bullitt County, Kentucky; d. December 12, 1913 in Bullitt County, Kentucky; buried at Mount Eden Cemetery in Shepherdsville, Bullitt County, Kentucky; it is believed that he never married), WEEDEN F. FUNK (b. October 03, 1856 in Bullitt County, Kentucky; d. July 28, 1909 in Kentucky; m. SALLIE COOK on May 11, 1877 in Jeffersonville, Clark County, Indiana; buried at South Jefferson Cemetery in Louisville, Jefferson County, Kentucky), ALVARADO ERWIN FUNK (b. June 17, 1859 in Bullitt County, Kentucky; d. September 22, 1920 in Bullitt County, Kentucky; m1. ALICE VICTORIA HOLSCLAW on February 22, 1883 in Bullitt County, Kentucky; m2. EUGENIA H. HOLSCLAW on August 08, 1886 in Bullitt County, Kentucky; buried at Hebron Cemetery in Books, Bullitt County, Kentucky), ROBERT A. FUNK (b. August 05, 1861 in Bullitt County, Kentucky; d. June 09, 1864 in Bullitt County, Kentucky; buried in Mount Eden Cemetery in Shepherdsville, Bullitt County, Kentucky), CHARLES "CHARLEY" EDGAR FUNK (b. November 20, 1864 in Bullitt County, Kentucky; d. September 20, 1940 in Cupio, Bullitt County, Kentucky; buried at South Jefferson Cemetery in Louisville, Jefferson County, Kentucky; m. MARTHA "MATTIE" E. RAMSEY on November 21, 1889 in Bullitt County, Kentucky), and SAMUEL EDWARD FUNK (b. November 15, 1866 in Bullitt County, Kentucky; d. March 02, 1932 in Louisville, Jefferson County, Kentucky; buried at South Jefferson Cemetery in Louisville, Jefferson County, Kentucky; m. LAURA B. CARPENTER on October 18, 1894 in Cupio, Buliitt County, Kentucky).

ALICE VICTORIA HOLSCLAW and EUGENIA H. HOLSCLAW were the daughters of WILLIAM HARDIN HOLSCLAW (b. February 08, 1820 in Mount Washington, Bullitt County, Kentucky; d. February 26, 1902 in Louisville, Jefferson County, Kentucky; buried at Hebron Cemetery in Brooks, Bullitt County, Kentucky; m. November 24, 1842 in Bullitt

County, Kentucky) and CATHERINE JANE "JANE" GRAHAM (b. March 06, 1824 in Indiana; d. December 04, 1911 in Zoneton, Bullitt County, Kentucky; buried at Hebron Cemetery in Brooks, Bullitt County, Kentucky; m. November 24, 1842 in Bullitt County, Kentucky).

Burial: Knob Creek Union Cemetery in Cupio, Bullitt County, Kentucky.

34. JAMES WESLEY[3] APPLEGATE, SR. *(ELIZABETH "BETTIE"[2] MUSS, JOHN[1] MUSS)* was born June 07, 1898 in Bullitt County, Kentucky and died June 22, 1979 in Louisville, Jefferson County, Kentucky. He married ANNABEL "ANNA" B. STOVALL about 1923 in Kentucky, daughter of ROBERT MATTHEW STOVALL and SALLY B. HORNE. She was born May 13, 1900 in Indiana and died November 19, 1990 in Jefferson County, Kentucky.

Notes for JAMES WESLEY APPLEGATE, SR.:

In the September 12, 1918 World War I draft registration, James is listed as a farmer for Charles Applegate (his father) in Valley Station, Jefferson County, Kentucky, and is married. He has a wife and one child. Lewis is medium height and medium build. His eyes are brown and his hair is dark. His registration occurred in Bullitt County, Kentucky and he is living in Valley Station, Jefferson County, Kentucky.

In the 1930 Louisville, Jefferson County, Kentucky census (conducted on April 11, 1930) James is living with his mother-in-law and listed as a servant. Sally B. Stovall, 69, is head of the household with James W. Applegate (servant), 31, Annabel Applegate (James' wife), 29 and James W. (James' son), 2 11/12. James is listed as a Cashier for the Broker Office.

More about JAMES WESLEY APPLEGATE, SR.:

James lived at 1914 Strathmoor Boulevard at the time of his death. He was a retired personnel director at Farm Credit Bank and member of the Bethany Baptist Church. James was also a member of the Saint Matthews Hi 12 Club and past master of Masonic Lodge 348.

The home at 1914 Strathmoor Boulevard is a 1,552 square foot, 1 bedroom and 1.5 bathroom single family home with a detached garage that was built in 1939.

He died on Friday, June 22, 1979 at 3pm in Suburban Hospital in Louisville, Kentucky.

Funeral Services: Highlands Funeral Home at 3331 Taylorsville Road in Louisville, Kentucky. Funeral services were held at 11am on Monday, June 25, 1979 in the funeral home.

Burial: Monday, June 25, 1979 at Resthaven Memorial Park Cemetery in Louisville, Jefferson County, Kentucky.

SATURDAY, JUNE 23, 1979

LOUISVILLE AR

J. Wesley Applegate Sr., 81, of 1914 Strathmoor Blvd., died at 3 p.m. Friday at Suburban Hospital.

He was retired personnel director at Farm Credit Bank, a member of the Bethany Baptist Church and St. Matthews Hi 12 Club and past master of Masonic Lodge 348.

Survivors include his wife, the former Annabel Stoval; a son, James W. Applegate Jr.; a daughter, Mrs. William H. Dohrman Jr.; and five grandchildren.

The funeral will be at 11 a.m. Monday at Highlands Funeral Home, 3331 Taylorsville Road, with burial in Resthaven Memorial Park.

Visitation at the funeral home will be from 7 to 9 p.m. Saturday and from 2 to 5 and 7 to 9 p.m. Sunday.

Obituary for James Wesley Applegate, Sr. – June 23, 1979 (Louisville Courier-Journal, Obituary for James Wesley Applegate, Sr.)

Notes for Annabel "Anna" B. Stovall:

Annabel was a member of the Bethany Baptist Church at 2319 Taylorsville Road in Louisville, Kentucky.

She died on Monday, November 19, 1990 in the Episcopal Church Home at 7504 Westport Road in Louisville, Kentucky.

Funeral Services: Pearson's Funeral Home at 149 Breckenridge Lane in Saint Matthews, Kentucky. Funeral services were held at 10am on Friday, November 23, 1990 at the funeral home.

Burial: Friday, November 23, 1990 in the Mausoleum at Resthaven Memorial Park Cemetery of Louisville, Jefferson County, Kentucky.

Mrs. J. Wesley Applegate Sr.,
90, of Episcopal Church Home, formerly of Strathmoor Boulevard, died Monday at Baptist Hospital East.
She was the former Annabel Stovall and a member of Bethany Baptist Church and Highland Woman's Club.
Survivors: a son, James W. Applegate; a daughter, Norma A. Dohrman; five grandchildren; and four great-grandchildren.
Funeral: 10 a.m. Friday, Pearson's, 149 Breckinridge Lane. Entombment: Resthaven Mausoleum. Visitation: 2-5 and 7-9 p.m. Wednesday.

Obituary for Annabel "Anna" B. Stovall Applegate
(Louisville Courier-Journal, Obituary for Annabel "Anna" B. Stovall Applegate)

Children of JAMES WESLEY[3] APPLEGATE, SR. and ANNABEL "ANNA" B. STOVALL are:

    i.   JAMES WESLEY[4] APPLEGATE, JR., b. April 17, 1927 in Jefferson County, Kentucky.

    ii.   NORMA A.[4] APPLEGATE, b. February 27, 1934 in Jefferson County, Kentucky; m. WILLIAM H. DOHRMAN, JR.

35. CHARLES EMORY "JACK"[3] APPLEGATE *(ELIZABETH "BETTIE"[2] MUSS, JOHN[1] MUSS)* was born July 22, 1906 in Bullitt County, Kentucky and died May 18, 1967 in Louisville, Jefferson County, Kentucky. He married KATHERINE "KITTY" MNU. She was born in 1906 and died December 30, 1979 in Jefferson County, Kentucky.

Notes for CHARLES EMORY "JACK" APPLEGATE:
Based upon his obituary, it is believed that Jack and Kitty did not have any children.
Jack died at 5am on Thursday, May 18, 1967 in Saints Mary and Elizabeth Hospital in Louisville, Kentucky.

Funeral Services: Maraman Funeral Home of Shepherdsville, Kentucky. Services were held at 2pm on Friday, May 19, 1967 in the funeral home. Maraman Funeral Home was established in 1880 and today operates under the name Maraman-Billings Funeral Home. The funeral home is located at 605 South Preston Highway in Shepherdsville, Kentucky.

Burial: Friday May 19, 1967 at Hebron Cemetery in Brooks, Bullitt County, Kentucky. His wife, Kitty, is buried next to him in Hebron Cemetery. A picture of their headstone is available on the Find a Grave web site.

APPLEGATE, Mr. Charles Emory "Jack"

Age 60, Thurs., May 18th, 1967, 5 a.m. SS. Mary and Elizabeth Hospital. Survived by wife Catherine "Kitty" Applegate, Shepherdsville, Ky.; 3 brothers Mr. Edward Applegate, Brooks, Ky., Mr. Roy Applegate, West Point Route ; Mr. Wesley Applegate, Louisville; also several nieces and nephews. Mr. Applegate is at the Maraman Funeral Home Shepherdsville, Ky. Services in chapel Sun. May 21, 2 p.m. Interment Hebron Cemetery. Friends may call after noon Fri. May 19th.

Obituary for Charles Emory "Jack" Applegate – May 19, 1967 (Louisville Courier-Journal, Obituary for Charles Emory "Jack" Applegate)

Generation No. 4: Descendants of Kate Muss

It is unclear what happened to Kate Muss, but it is believed that she died while still a child and did not marry. Therefore, there were no 4th generation descendants of John Muss through the Kate Muss branch of the family.

Generation No. 4: Descendants of John Carroll Muss

36. ANNA VAUGHN⁴ MUSS *(WILLIAM JOSEPH³ MUSS, JOHN CARROLL² MUSS, JOHN¹ MUSS)* was born on March 03, 1908 in Bullitt County, Kentucky and died on September 12, 1985 in Mount Clemens, Macomb County, Michigan. She first married LLOYD NELSON MARTIN on July 29, 1923 in Clark County, Indiana, son of HARMON ELI MARTIN and REBECCA FLORENCE CRENSHAW. He was born on September 14, 1892 in Florida. It is unknown at this time what happened to this marriage. Anna later married THEODORE EMMETT OBERHAUSEN about 1927, son of JOSEPH OBERHAUSEN and MARY A. MNU. He was born on February 21, 1903 in Jefferson County, Kentucky and died on March 24, 1980 in Mount Clemens, Macomb County, Michigan.

Notes for ANNA VAUGHN MUSS:
Anna was living in Ira, Saint Clair County, Michigan at the time of her death, and died in a hospital located in Mount Clemens, Macomb County, Michigan. This was most likely the Mount Clemens Regional Medical Center.

Notes for THEODORE EMMETT OBERHAUSEN:
He was living in Ira, Saint Clair County, Michigan at the time of his death, and died in a hospital located in Mount Clemens, Macomb County, Michigan. This was most likely the Mount Clemens Regional Medical Center.

37. CHESTER LOUIS⁴ MUSS *(WILLIAM JOSEPH³ MUSS, JOHN CARROLL² MUSS, JOHN¹ MUSS)* was born December 04, 1913 in Bullitt County, Kentucky and died August 04, 1985 in Louisville, Jefferson County, Kentucky. He married HILDA PAULENE MERKER about 1938, daughter of WILLIAM L. MERKER and GERTRUDE "GERTIE" MARTIN. She was born August 15, 1922 in Bullitt County, Kentucky and died September 16, 2010 in Louisville, Jefferson County, Kentucky.

Notes for CHESTER LOUIS MUSS:
Chester served in the Navy.
Chester is listed on one of the T.C. Carroll land plats that are stored at the Bullitt County Clerk's office in large plastic envelopes. The listing can be found on Slide # 186, Map # 259 (along with Mr. Ferguson, James Foster, Mr. McNutt, Mr. Merker, and Annie E. Muss). The address for the Bullitt County Clerk's Office is: 149 N. Walnut, Shepherdsville, KY, 40165.

More about CHESTER LOUIS MUSS:
Burial: Knob Creek Union Church Cemetery in Cupio, Bullitt County, Kentucky.

Notes for HILDA PAULENE MERKER:
Hilda's grandfather was JACOB MERKER. Jacob was the brother of CHARLES "CHARLEY" MERKER, JR.. Charles was the father of LILLIAN "LILLIE" MAY MERKER who married LOUIS EDWARD "ED" APPLEGATE.

Obituary Notes for HILDA PAULENE MERKER:
Published in The Courier-Journal on September 19, 2010
"MUSS, HILDA, 88, was called home to be with her Lord on Wednesday, September 16, 2010. She was retired from Brown & Williamson Tobacco Co. Hilda was preceded in death by her husband, Chester Louis; daughter, Glenda Stephenson; grandson, Chris Muss. Her survivors include her sons, Donnie (Marilyn), Jerry (Kathy) and Tim (Bekki) Muss; son-in-law, Jack Stephenson; 11 grandchildren; 29 great-grandchildren; nine great-great grandchildren; and her best bud, Jenny. Hilda's remains were donated to the U of L School of Medicine. A memorial service will be held at Knob Creek Baptist Church, 10439 Hwy 44W, West Point, KY 40177 in her honor on Monday at 7 p.m. Family will receive friends from 5-7 p.m. Monday. In lieu of flowers donations can be made to Knob Creek Baptist Church. W.G. Hardy Funeral Home is in charge of arrangements. W.G. Hardy Funeral Home and Cremation Service; 10907 Dixie Hwy; Louisville, Kentucky; 502-937-6400; www.hardyfuneral.com"

Children of CHESTER LOUIS[4] MUSS and HILDA PAULENE MERKER are:
  i.   DONALD "DONNIE" L.[5] MUSS, b. January 04, 1939 in Bullitt County, Kentucky; m. MARILYN J. MILLS About 1956.
  ii. GLENDA DARLENE[5] MUSS, b. August 22, 1940 in Jefferson County, Kentucky; m. JACK STEPHENSON About 1958; d. February 16, 2009.

    Obituary Notes for GLENDA DARLENE MUSS:
    Published in The Courier-Journal on February 18, 2009
    "STEPHENSON, GLENDA DARLENE MUSS, passed away February 16, 2009 after an extended illness. She was a slave to Jesus Christ, a loving wife and a thoughtful mother and grandmother. She leaves behind her husband of more than 51 years, Jack; sons, Joey and Jammie (Mary); mother, Hilda Muss; brothers, Donald, Jerry and Tim Muss; mother-in-law, Louise Stephenson; grandchildren, Austin, Jacob, Madeline, Abigail and Quentin; plus numerous sisters-in-law, brothers-in-law, cousins, nieces, nephews, relatives and caring friends. She had a zest for life, was an avid bowler, sportsperson, animal lover and professional seamstress. She was known and loved by

countless friends. A memorial service is scheduled at the World Cafe at Highview Baptist Church, 7711 Fegenbush Lane in Louisville on Saturday, February 21, 2009 from 1-4 p.m."

    iii. JERRY B.[5] MUSS, b. March 23, 1945 in Jefferson County, Kentucky; m1. CAROL S. FLOYD about 1964; m2. KATHY JEAN BOSTON on July 06, 1979 in Clay County, Tennessee; m3. KATHY JEAN BOSTON (for a second time) on August 04, 1986 in Jefferson County, Kentucky.

    iv. TIM BARRON[5] MUSS, SR., b. December 18, 1953 in Jefferson County, Kentucky; m. BEKKI A. WOLFE on April 04, 1981 in Jefferson County, Kentucky.

38. MARY PEARL[4] MUSS *(WILLIAM JOSEPH[3] MUSS, JOHN CARROLL[2] MUSS, JOHN[1] MUSS)* was born May 09, 1918 in Cupio, Bullitt County, Kentucky and died May 09, 1918 in Cupio, Bullitt County, Kentucky.

Notes for MARY PEARL MUSS:
    Her Kentucky death certificate is #18-12423. Mary is listed as 1 day old at the time of her death.
    Informant: Joseph Muss of Valley Station, Kentucky.
    Parents: Joseph Muss of Bullitt County, Kentucky and Mattie Muss of Bullitt County, Kentucky.
    Cause of death: 6 months old when born. Her mother was in her forties.
    Funeral Services: not listed.
    Burial: May 1922 at Vaughn Burying Ground in Bullitt County, Kentucky.
    Mary's mother, MARTHA "MATTIE" ROBERTS VAUGHN, was actually 38 years old when Mary was born. It appears as though the death certificate is indicating that Mattie was in her 40s and that the baby was premature at only 6 months when born. Those are the two reasons given that Mary did not live beyond birth.

39. WILLAM "WILLIE" RAY[4] MUSS *(WILLIAM JOSEPH[3] MUSS, JOHN CARROLL[2] MUSS, JOHN[1] MUSS)* was born May 28, 1919 in Bullitt County, Kentucky and died February 26, 1980 in Bullitt County, Kentucky. He married VIOLA J. GLASS on June 05, 1937 in Clark County, Indiana, daughter of THEODORE A. GLASS and DELIA C. WHEATLEY. She was born on November 03, 1917 in Louisville, Jefferson County, Kentucky and died October 19, 1997 in Louisville, Jefferson County, Kentucky.

More about VIOLA J. GLASS:
    After the death of William "Willie" Ray Muss, Viola married CORNLUS KEITH on September 01, 1990 in Bullitt County, Kentucky.

Children of WILLAM "WILLIE" RAY[4] MUSS and VIOLA J. GLASS are:
> i. SHIRLEY A.[5] MUSS (female), b. August 16, 1938 in Jefferson County, Kentucky.
> ii. RAYMOND E.[5] MUSS, b. May 25, 1941 in Jefferson County, Kentucky.
> iii. RICHARD L.[5] MUSS, b. March 08, 1944 in Jefferson County, Kentucky.

40. EULA ANNA[4] "POLLY" MUSS (*JOHN E.[3] MUSS, JOHN CARROLL[2] MUSS, JOHN[1] MUSS*) was born November 30, 1922 in Kentucky and died October 01, 1993 in Somerset, Perry County, Ohio. She married WILLIAM "BILL" RAYMOND DALEY, SR. about 1938, son of JAMES ALEXANDER DALEY and FANNY BISHOP. He was born February 25, 1916 in Hardin County, Kentucky and died December 04, 1976 in Meade County, Kentucky.

Children of EULA ANNA[4] "POLLY" MUSS and WILLIAM "BILL" RAYMOND DALEY, SR. are:
> i. FANNIE A. "TINY"[5] DALEY, b. September 03, 1939 in Hardin County, Kentucky; m. Mr. POWELL.
> ii. WILLIAM RAYMOND[5] DALEY, JR., b. February 09, 1943 in Hardin County, Kentucky.

> Notes for WILLIAM RAYMOND DALEY, JR.:
> Living in Glenford, Perry County, Ohio about 1992.

41. MILDRED J.[4] MUSS (*JOHN E.[3] MUSS, JOHN CARROLL[2] MUSS, JOHN[1] MUSS*) was born September 09, 1935 in Bullitt County, Kentucky. No additional information can be found on her at this time.

42. EARL B.[4] MUSS (*JOHN E.[3] MUSS, JOHN CARROLL[2] MUSS, JOHN[1] MUSS*) was born October 09, 1928 in West Point, Hardin County, Kentucky and died January 06, 1933 in Hardin County, Kentucky.

Notes for EARL B. MUSS:
> His Kentucky death certificate is #33-03905. Earl is listed as an infant at the time of his death. He died at 5:30am.
> Informant: J. E. Muss of Bullitt County, Kentucky.
> Parents: J. E. Muss of Bullitt County, Kentucky and Anna Crabtree of Brackenridge County, Kentucky.
> Cause of death: Acute Nephritis contributed to by Scarlet Fever. Acute nephritis is an inflammation of the tissues and blood vessels in the kidneys that often occurs after an infectious disease. Scarlet fever is a disease caused by the strep throat bacteria. Symptoms include a rash, abdominal pain, chills, fever, headache, sore muscles, sore throat, swollen tongue and vomiting.

Funeral Services: W. G. Hardy of West Point, Kentucky.

Burial: Saturday, January 07, 1933 at Knob Creek Union Church Cemetery in Cupio, Bullitt County, Kentucky.

Headstone for Earl B. Muss
(Browning, Headstone for Earl B. Muss)

43. CHARLES E.[4] MUSS, SR. *(JOHN E.[3] MUSS, JOHN CARROLL[2] MUSS, JOHN[1] MUSS)* was born June 19, 1931 in Bullitt County, Kentucky. No additional information can be found on him at this time.

44. ROY F.[4] MUSS *(JAMES ROY "ROY" TYLINGS[3] MUSS, JOHN CARROLL[2] MUSS, JOHN[1] MUSS)* was born May 14, 1933 in Cupio, Bullitt County, Kentucky and died May 25, 1933 in Cupio, Bullitt County, Kentucky.

Notes for ROY F. MUSS:

His Kentucky death certificate is #33-13046. Roy is listed as an 11 day old infant at the time of his death. He died at 1am.

Informant: R. T. Muss of Bullitt County, Kentucky.

Parents: R. T. Muss of Bullitt County, Kentucky and Daisy Foster of Bullitt County, Kentucky.

Cause of death: Malnutrition, Mitral Insufficiency. Malnutrition is a condition that occurs when the body does not get enough nutrients. Mitral insufficiency is a disorder in which the heart's mitral valve suddenly does not close properly causing blood to flow backward into the upper heart chamber.

Funeral Services: W. G. Hardy of West Point, Kentucky.
Burial: Thursday, May 25, 1933 at Knob Creek Union Church
Cemetery in Cupio, Bullitt County, Kentucky.

45. EDWARD GUTHRIE "GUTHRIE"[4] MUSS (JAMES ROY "ROY" TYLINGS[3] MUSS, JOHN CARROLL[2] MUSS, JOHN[1] MUSS) was born October 30, 1934 in Bullitt County, Kentucky. No additional information can be found on him at this time.

46. COLA MARGARET[4] MUSS (JAMES ROY "ROY" TYLINGS[3] MUSS, JOHN CARROLL[2] MUSS, JOHN[1] MUSS) was born November 13, 1939 in Bullitt County, Kentucky and died May 27, 2002 in West Point, Hardin, Kentucky. No additional information can be found on her at this time.

Notes for COLA MARGARET MUSS:
Burial: Knob Creek Union Church Cemetery in Cupio, Bullitt County, Kentucky.

Headstone for Cola Margaret Muss
(Browning, Headstone for Cola Margaret Muss)

47. EULA MAY[4] CARBY (ANNA "ANNIE" ADRESS[3] MUSS, JOHN CARROLL[2] MUSS, JOHN[1] MUSS) was born March 19, 1916 in Jefferson County, Kentucky and died September 01, 1988 in Buena Park, Orange County, California. She married WILLIAM "BILL" HOWE HARPOOL on an unknown date, son of EUGENE IDOLPHOS HARPOOL and FANNIE E. SETTLES. He was born March 23, 1898 in Hardin County, Kentucky and died June 13, 1985 in Montclair, San Bernardino County, California.

Children of EULA MAY[4] CARBY and WILLIAM "BILL" HOWE HARPOOL are:
    i.   ADRESS ETHEL MAE "SISSY"[5] HARPOOL, b. November 09, 1946
        in Jefferson County, Kentucky; m. JESSE ALLEN "BUD" JOHNSON;
        d. December 09, 1968 in Los Angeles County, California.

        Notes for ADRESS ETHEL MAE "SISSY" HARPOOL:
            She was an adopted child and sister by blood of WANDA FAY
        CIRESI.

48. CLARA LEE[4] CARBY *(ANNA "ANNIE" ADRESS[3] MUSS, JOHN CARROLL[2] MUSS, JOHN[1] MUSS)* was born December 27, 1917 in Jefferson County, Kentucky and died September 24, 1994 in Sun Valley, Los Angeles County, California. She first married WILLIAM "BILL" SMITH about 1936. Clara later married MICHAEL EDWARD CIRESI about 1941 in Louisville, Jefferson County, Kentucky, son of TONY CIRESI and LULA MCHUGH. He was born May 01, 1916 in Jefferson County, Kentucky and died October 14, 1986 in Sun Valley, Los Angeles County, California.

Notes for CLARA LEE CARBY:
    She served as a Corporal (CPL) in the US Army during World War II and started service on October 28, 1943.
    Burial: Riverside National Cemetery in Riverside, Riverside County, California alongside her husband who was also a veteran. Section F, 0, Site 158.

Notes for MICHAEL EDWARD CIRESI and CLARA LEE CARBY:
    Burial: Section F, Site 158 of Riverside National Cemetery in Riverside, Riverside County, California.

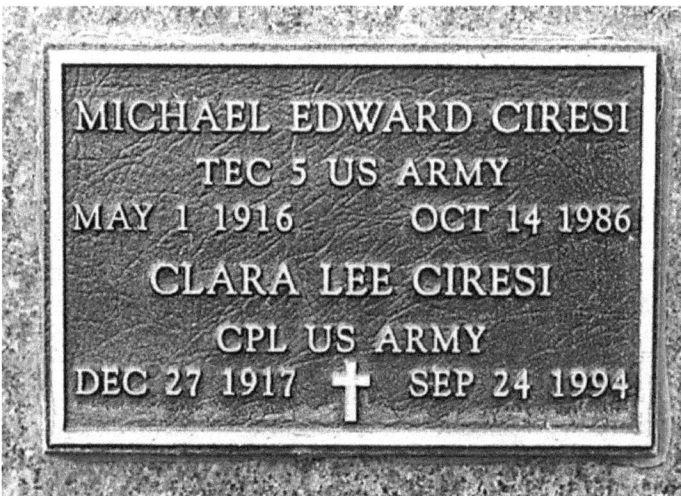

Headstone for Michael Edward Ciresi and Clara Lee Ciresi (Robinson)

Children of CLARA LEE[4] CARBY and MICHAEL EDWARD CIRESI are:

    i.   WANDA FAY[5] CIRESI, b. October 31, 1945 in Jefferson County, Kentucky; m1. TOMMY B. SUMNER on February 28, 1965 in Los Angeles County, California; divorce1. November 1968 in Los Angeles, Los Angeles, California; m2. FRANK R. VANHECKE, SR. on February 23, 1968 in Reno, Washoe County, Nevada; d. January 29, 1993 in Los Angeles County, California.

        Notes for WANDA FAY CIRESI:

        Wanda was an adopted child and sister by blood to ADRESS ETHEL MAE "SISSY" HARPOOL.

        Wanda had 2 children with her first husband, TOMMY B. SUMNER, as follows: LISA MARLENE SUMNER (b. October 14, 1964 in Los Angeles County, California; m. WILLIAM E. GERBER, JR. on November 20, 1980 Clark County, Nevada) and MICHAEL A. SUMNER (b. October 20, 1964 in Los Angeles County, California).

        Wanda had 4 children with her second husband, FRANK R. VANHECKE, SR. as follows: FRANK R. VANHECKE, JR. (b. May 17, 1969 in Los Angeles County, California; m. LINDA M. WICKE on January 15, 1999 in Minnesota), VERONICA VANHECKE (b. about 1972 in Los Angeles County, California), and JASON E. VANHECKE (b. January 25, 1975 in Los Angeles County, California), and AMANDA L. VANHECKE (b. November 10, 1976 in Los Angeles County, California).

49. ORVILLE EMMITT "J. R."[4] CARBY, JR. *(ANNA "ANNIE" ADRESS[3] MUSS, JOHN CARROLL[2] MUSS, JOHN[1] MUSS)* was born February 28, 1919 in Jefferson County, Kentucky and died March 17, 1960 in Los Angeles, Los Angeles County, California. He first married BETTY HALE on December 20, 1941 in Phenix City, Russell County, Alabama, daughter of ERNEST HALE and ANNIE MAE GRANT. She was born August 20, 1916 in Alabama. Orville later married FRANCES COFFEY. In mid to late 1943, Orville started dating GEORGIA LEE GRIFFITH, daughter of GEORGE EATON GRIFFITH and CHLOE BELL GROSS. She was born November 25, 1913 in Corbin, Whitley County, Kentucky and died April 05, 1991 in Greensboro, Guilford County, North Carolina. Orville later married RITA BLANCHE MULKINS on October 08, 1949 in Floyd County, Indiana, daughter of JESSE OMAR MULKINS, SR. and ANNA BELLE HINES.

Notes for BETTY HALE:

    Betty was first married to a MR. MILNER, and divorced him in 1940 in Alabama.

    Betty and Frances may be the same woman, and Frances could be a middle name.

Marriage License for Orville Emmitt "J. R."Carby, Jr. and Betty Hale
Milner
(Alabama Vital Records)

Notes for ORVILLE EMMITT "J. R." CARBY, JR.:
He died at Los Angeles County General Hospital, 1200 North State Street. The Los Angeles County Hospital and the University of Southern California Medical School (USC) were first affiliated in 1885. This was five years after USC was founded. Today the hospital is a 600 bed public teaching hospital that is jointly operated by Los Angeles County and the USC.

His cause of death was ventricular fibrillation (a severely abnormal heart rhythm) due to calcific aortic stenosis (aging and "wear and tear" of the aortic valve) of the bicuspid valve.

Burial: Section W, Site 5 of Fort Rosecrans National Cemetery in San Diego, San Diego County, California.

Headstone for Orville Emitt "J. R."Carby, Jr.
(Browning, Headstone for Orville Emmitt "J. R." Carby, Jr.)

Obituary Notes for ORVILLE EMMITT "J. R." CARBY, JR.:

Interment.

CARBY, JR., ORVILLE E., of Sepulveda, passed away Mar. 17, 1960. Survived by his wife, Rita Carby; 3 sons, Robert, Richard & Ronald Carby; 2 daughters, Misses Patricia & Pamela Carby his mother, Mrs. Adress Carby of Manhattan Beach; father, Orville E. Carby Sr, of San Diego 2 brothers, Roy of San Fernando & Harel Carby of Sylmar; 6 sisters, Mrs. Eula Harpool of Manhattan Beach, Mrs. Clara Cireal of Sylmar, Mrs. Violet Flake of North Long Beach, Mrs. Dorothy Wilbur of Victorville, Mrs. Glenna Barrett of Sylmar & Mrs. Juanita Roberts of Long Beach. Services were Mon., Mar. 21 at 2 p.m. J. T. OSWALD SAN FERNANDO CHAPEL Rev. I. Stanley Polk, officiating. Interment Ft. Rosecrans National Cemetery, San Diego, J. T. OSWALD MORTUARY, San Fernando, directors.

Obituary for Orville Emmitt "J. R." Carby, Jr. – March 24, 1960
(San Fernando Valley Sun)

Death Certificate for Orville Emmitt "J. R." Carby, Jr.
(California Department of Public Health)

Notes for RITA BLANCHE MULKINS:
Rita was born on September 09, 1927 in Louisville, Jefferson County, Kentucky and died on September 17, 2004 in Escondido, San Diego County, California. She was the daughter of JESSE OMAR MULKINS, SR. and ANNA BELLE HINES.

Rita was the sister of ROSEMARY MULKINS. Rosemary married HAREL LYN CARBY, SR., and Harel was the brother of ORVILLE EMMITT "J. R." CARBY, JR.

Rita first married JAMES ALBERT CURL (b. March 19, 1924; d. December 06, 199 in Louisville, Jefferson County, Kentucky) on January 17, 1946 in Louisville, Jefferson County, Kentucky. Together they had 2 children as follows: LARRY L. CURL (b. Septebmer 10, 1946 in Jefferson County, Kentucky; m. NORMA C. MNU) and STEPHEN WILLIAM CURL (b. February 24, 1948 in Jefferson County, Kentucky; d. December 30, 1980 in New York, New York County, New York).

Rita next married ORVILLE EMMITT "J. R." CARBY, JR. on October 08, 1949 in Floyd County, Indiana.

Obituary Notes for RITA BLANCHE MULKINS:
Published in the North County Times on September 28, 2004
"ESCONDIDO - Rita Blanche Carby, 77, died Friday, Sept. 17, 2004, at Palomar Medical Center of a heart attack. Born Sept. 9, 1927, in Louisville, Kentucky, she lived in Escondido for 31 years. She enjoyed taking long car rides. Mrs. Carby was preceded in death by her husband; parents Annabell Hines and Jesse Omar Mulkins; sons Stephen William Curl and Richard Emmitt Carby; brothers Jesse Omar Mulkins, Jr., and William Mulkins; and grandson Keven Anthony Spencer. She is survived by her sons, Larry Curl of Paduka, Kentucky, and Robert Carby and Ronald Carby, both of Yelm, Wash.; daughters Patricia Carby of Medford, Ore., and Pamela Carby-Blackemore of Escondido; sister Rosemary Carby of New Braunsels; 18 grandchildren; and 24 great-grandchildren. Private graveside service at Fort Rosecrans National Cemetery was held."

Headstone for Rita Blanche Mulkins
(Browning, Headstone for Rita Blanche Mulkins)

Notes for JESSE OMAR MULKINS, SR. (Father of RITA BLANCHE MULKINS and ROSEMARY MULKINS):

Jesse was born on July 04, 1895 in Hardin County, Kentucky and died on June 16, 1952 in Jefferson County, Kentucky. He was the son of ABRAHAM "ABE" MCCAULEY MULKINS (b. July 01, 1874 in Harrison County, Indiana; d. January 20, 1948 in Louisville, Jefferson County, Kentucky; buried at Bethany Memorial Cemetery in Louisville, Jefferson County, Kentucky) and ADA VIOLA BLEVINS (b. August 02, 1877 in West Point, Hardin County, Kentucky; d. December 25, 1965 in Louisville, Jefferson County, Kentucky).

Jesse. had five siblings as follows: WILBUR DEWEY MULKINS (b. July 02, 1898 in Hardin County, Kentucky; d. March 23, 1988 in Louisville, Jefferson County, Kentucky; m1. LETTIE DAUGHERTY on February 25, 1922 in Clark County, Indiana; m2. EDITH FAY DANGERFIELD on September 28, 1942 in Kirkwood, Saint Louis County, Missouri), WILLIAM T. MULKINS (b. January 06, 1904 in West Point, Hardin County, Kentucky; d. July 07, 1950 in Louisville, Jefferson County, Kentucky; m. NELLIE AIKIN on December 03, 1925 in Clark County, Indiana), LENA VIOLA MULKINS (b. January 13, 1905 in Jefferson County, Kentucky, d. June 24, 1997 in Metairie, Jefferson Parish, Louisiana; m1. ROBERT LEE GOODE; m2. MR. BIRDWELL), MABEL EDITH MULKINS (b. November 25, 1908 in West Point, Hardin County, Kentucky; d. August 27, 1950 in Louisville, Jefferson County, Kentucky; m. EDWIN VIVIAN SMITH on October 14, 1925 in Clark County, Indiana), and NELLIE JANE BELL MULKINS (b. October 28, 1911 in West Point, Hardin County, Kentucky; d. December 22, 1989 in Louisville, Jefferson County, Kentucky; m. GARNER YANCY VALLANDINGHAM).

Jesse first married ANNA BELLE HINES on May 29, 1923 in Clark County, Indiana. Together they had 5 children as follows: CHESTER MULKINS (b. August 10, 1924 in Louisville, Jefferson County, Kentucky; August 10, 1924 in Louisville, Jefferson County, Kentucky), JESSE OMAR MULKINS, JR. (b. December 24, 1925 in Jefferson County, Kentucky; d. January 20, 1990 in Illinois; m. BETTY WEBB on September 28, 1949 in Cape Girardeau, Cape Girardeau County, Missouri), RITA BLANCHE MULKINS (b. September 09, 1927 in Louisville, Jefferson County, Kentucky; d. September 17, 2004 in Escondido, San Diego County, California; m1. JAMES ALBERT CURL on January 17, 1946 in Louisville, Jefferson County, Kentucky; divorce 1. in March 1949; m2. ORVILLE EMMITT "J. R." CARBY, JR. on October 08, 1949 in Floyd County, Indiana), EDWARD B. MULKINS (b. March 07, 1930 in Jefferson County, Kentucky; d. August 24, 1930 in Jefferson County, Kentucky), and ROSEMARY MULKINS (b. March 08, 1930 in Louisville, Jefferson County, Kentucky; m. HAREL LYN CARBY, SR.).

ROSEMARY MULKINS and EDWARD B. MULKINS were twins that were born during the midnight hour. Edward was born before midnight and Rosemary, right after midnight

Jesse next married THELMA KEMP about 1932. Together they had one child as follows: WILLIAM LLOYD MULKINS (b. March 03, 1933 in Louisville, Jefferson County, Kentucky; d. July 05, 1999 in Spingfield, Sangamon County, Illinois).

Notes for ANNA "Annie" BELLE HINES (Mother of RITA BLANCHE MULKINS and ROSEMARY MULKINS):

Anna was born on July 10, 1904 in Louisville, Jefferson County, Kentucky. She was the daughter of ANDREW WYNFIELD HINES (b. June 28, 1879 in Ohio; d. October 06, 1914 in Louisville, Jefferson County, Kentucky) and ANNA MAY TOTTEN (b. August 23, 1883 in Newport, Campbell County, Kentucky; d. June 27, 1966 in Louisville, Jefferson County, Kentucky; m1. ANDREW WYNFIELD HINES about 1902; m2. HUMPHREY GILBERT "GILBERT" GLASCOE on March 12, 1921 in Clark County, Indiana).

Anna had 5 siblings as follows: MARY E. HINES (b. January 27, 1903 in Louisville, Jefferson County, Kentucky; m1. THOMAS G. SKELTON on December 16, 1918 in Kentucky; m2. JOSEPH T. DEVINE on June 18, 1927 in Clark County, Indiana; m3. WILLIAM F. WEBER on October 19, 1934 in Clark County, Indiana), THEODORE ROOSEVELT HINES (b. May 12, 1907 in Louisville, Jefferson County, Kentucky; d. April 23, 1980 in Louisville, Jefferson County, Kentucky; m. HELEN WEINSTOCK on July 17, 1931 in Clark County, Indiana), NELLIE N. HINES (b. June 14, 1909 in Louisville, Jefferson County, Kentucky; m. HENRY LATHAM on November 21, 1925 in Jeffersonville, Clark County, Indiana), BOYCE WYNFIELD HINES (b. February 24, 1912 in Louisville, Jefferson County, Kentucky; d. October 18, 1990 in Louisville, Jefferson County, Kentucky), and JENNIE LEE HINES (b. January 01, 1915 in Louisville, Jefferson County, Kentucky).

Children of ORVILLE EMMITT "J. R."[4] CARBY, JR. and GEORGIA LEE GRIFFITH are:

    i.   SANDRA RAE[5] CARBY COYLE, b. June 28, 1945 in Louisville, Jefferson County, Kentucky; m. HABURN/HAYBURN RUBE "H. R." BROWNING, JR. on August 21, 1965 in Louisville, Jefferson County, Kentucky.

        Notes for SANDRA RAE CARBY COYLE:
        She was married in the parsonage of Saints Simon and Jude Church in Louisville, Jefferson County, Kentucky.
        HABURN/HAYBURN RUBE "H. R." BROWNING, JR. was Baptist and SANDRA RAE CARBY COYLE was Catholic.

Interdenominational marriages were not allowed inside a
Catholic Church.

Notes for HABURN/HAYBURN RUBE "H. R." BROWNING, JR.
      Hayburn was the son of HABURN/HAYBURN RUBE "RUBE"
BROWNING, SR. and ANNA LAURA "LAURA" CRAIG.

Children of ORVILLE EMMITT "J. R."[4] CARBY, JR. and RITA BLANCHE MULKINS
are:
      i.   ROBERT "ROBBY" "BOB" CALVIN[5] CARBY, b. November 04, 1949
              in Louisville, Jefferson County, Kentucky; m1. PATRICIA "PAT"
              ANN EAST on January 26, 1968 in Las Vegas, Clark County,
              Nevada; m2. DEBORAH YVONNE MCKAY CASE on April 01, 1978;
              m3. LORI QUINN in 1991.

              Notes for PATRICIA "PAT" ANN EAST:
                  She was born on May 28, 1951 in Highland Park, Lake
              County, Illinois. Pat was the daughter of LEE EDWARD EAST and
              CONSTANCE BERNICE PHIPPS.

      ii.   RICHARD "RICKY" EMMITT[5] CARBY, SR., b. September 28, 1950 in
              Jeffersonville, Clark County, Indiana; m. CANDACE "CANDY"
              MARIE ANDERSON on January 16, 1970 in Rancho Cucamonga,
              San Bernardino County, California; d. September 14, 1991 in
              Magalia, Butte County, California.

Headstone for Richard "Ricky" Emmitt Carby, Sr.
(Browning, Headstone for Richard "Ricky" Emmitt Carby, Sr.)

Notes for RICHARD "RICKY" EMMITT CARBY, SR.:
      Richard died under unusual circumstances. He was shot
and killed by a Butte County, California Deputy in his home
after the police had been called to his residence. Apparently,
Richard had been firing off a gun in the back yard of his home
earlier that night, and neighbors called the police to report the

gun fire. This part of the story appears to be agreed upon by all parties. However, the story appears to be different depending upon who you talk to after deputies arrived at the home and were let in.

News reports (Chico Enterprise-Record), with information provided by the Butte County Sheriff's Office, indicate that Richard became hostile after he was awakened from sleep, grabbed a pistol from one of the deputy's holsters, aimed it at the deputies, and tried to fire the gun. The gun was reported to have the safety on, and thus did not fire. The deputies then shot and killed Richard.

Reports from family members indicate that Richard was awakened from sleep in his waterbed, the deputies were on edge and could not see well in the dark, when Richard made a movement in the dark, the deputies opened fire on Richard and killed him. Richard was shot 6 times at close range in the chest. That appears to have been an excessive reaction in the author's opinion. It is important to note that one of the deputies involved in the incident was only a reserve deputy. It is said that law suits were filed by the family, and offers to settle out of court were extended to the family by the Sherriff's department. This was a very tragic and sad incident.

Notes for CANDACE "CANDY" MARIE ANDERSON:
She was born on September 28, 1950 in Los Angeles, Los Angeles County, California. Candy was the daughter of DONALD FRANCIS ANDERSON and LOIS ELAINE SIMMONS.

iii. PATRICIA "PATTIE" ANN[5] CARBY, b. January 17, 1953 in Louisville, Jefferson County, Kentucky; m1. WILLIAM "BILL" GRAHAM about 1972 in Saint Louis, Missouri; m2. JOHN R. BJORLING about 1983 in California (they were never actually married, but had a child together); m3. WILLIAM "BILL" LEA about 1986 in California (they were never actually married, but had a child together); d. August 26, 2005 in Seattle, King County, Washington.

Notes for PATRICIA "PATTIE" ANN CARBY:
Her ashes were scattered on Mount Rainier.

iv. PAMELA KAY[5] CARBY, b. May 18, 1954 in Los Angeles, Los Angeles County, California; m1. DANIEL J. SPENCER on October 21, 1972 in Springfield, Sangamon County, Illinois; d1. DANIEL J. SPENCER on June 05, 1978 in San Diego County, California; m2. UNKNOWN (they were never actually married, but had a child together); m3. ROBERT "BOB" ALAN BLAKEMORE on January 01, 2000; d. February 21, 2006 in Escondido, San Diego County, California.

Obituary Notes for PAMELA KAY CARBY:
Please note that there are several inaccuracies in this obituary.

Pamela Blakemore, 51

ESCONDIDO — Pamela Kay Blakemore, 51, died Tuesday, Feb. 21, 2006.

Born May 18, 1954, in Long Beach, she lived in San Diego County for 30 years. She was a private duty nurse.

Mrs. Blakemore was preceded in death by her son, Kevin Carby. She is survived by her husband of 20 years, Bob Blakemore of Escondido; sons Jason Carby and Steven Paul Carby, both of North Carolina, and Joshua Carby of Escondido; brothers Larry Curly of Kentucky, and Bob Carby and Ron Carby, both of Washington; and one grandchild.

No services will be held at the request of the deceased. A private cremation is planned.

McLeod Mortuary is handling arrangements.

Obituary for Pamela Kay Carby Blakemore – February 24, 2006 (North County Times)

v. RONALD LYNN[5] CARBY, b. November 02, 1955 in Louisville, Jefferson County, Kentucky; m1. DALE ROUPE about 1974 in California; m2. DENISE DANIELS STEDMAN on April 01 in San Diego County, California, 1981; m3. DIANE LORRAINE RUSHALL on October 25, 1987 in Las Vegas, Clark County, Nevada.

Notes for DIANE LORRAINE RUSHALL:
She was born on January 31, 1952 in Los Angeles, Los Angeles County, California.

50. VIOLET "VI" OPAL[4] CARBY *(ANNA "ANNIE" ADRESS[3] MUSS, JOHN CARROLL[2] MUSS, JOHN[1] MUSS)* was born September 15, 1922 in Jefferson County, Kentucky. She married JAMES EDWARD FLAKE, SR. on April 14,

1948, son of JAMES FRANKLIN "FRANK" FLAKE and JESSIE JULY WILSON. He was born July 21, 1922 in Wildersville, Henderson County, Tennessee and died March 10, 2007 in Russellville, Pope County, Arkansas.

Children of VIOLET "VI" OPAL[4] CARBY and JAMES EDWARD FLAKE, SR. are:
    i.   SHARON RHEA[5] FLAKE, b. November 29, 1948 in Louisville, Jefferson County, Kentucky; d. November 30, 1948 in Louisville, Jefferson County, Kentucky.

        Notes for SHARON RHEA FLAKE:
           She died at 10:35pm in Kentucky Baptist Hospital due to a premature birth.

    ii. SONDRA "SANDY" D.[5] FLAKE, b. September 07, 1950 in Indiana; m1. NEIL TRACY CRABTREE on November 04, 1968 in Los Angeles, Los Angeles County, California; m2. MICHAEL "MIKE" R. KERR on September 17, 1977 in Orange County, California.
    iii. JAMES "JIM" EDWARD[5] FLAKE, JR., b. November 02, 1951 in Indiana; m. MS. CAREY.
    iv. CHERYL DENISE[5] FLAKE, b. January 21, 1956 in Chambers County, Texas; m. WILLIAM R. RIERA on September 02, 1978 in Los Angeles County, California.
    v. RANDEL "RANDY" WAYNE[5] FLAKE, b. December 21, 1960 in Los Angeles County, California; d. July 12, 2008 in Bakersfield, Kern County, California.

51. DOROTHY VIRGINIA[4] CARBY *(ANNA "ANNIE" ADRESS[3] MUSS, JOHN CARROLL[2] MUSS, JOHN[1] MUSS)* was born August 26, 1924 in Jefferson County, Kentucky and died November 03, 1998 in Lexington, Fayette County, Kentucky. She first married a Mr. ARWOOD about 1943. Dorothy later married STANLEY DONALD WILBUR on August 03, 1946, son of ARTHUR LEE WILBUR and MINTA "MINNIE" J. CANTERBURY. He was born December 07, 1912 in Illinois and died November 20, 1980 in Victorville, San Bernardino County, California.

Notes for DORTOHY VIRGINIA CARBY:
    Dorothy enlisted in the army during World War II as a Private in the Women's Army Corps on September 04, 1944 in Louisville, Jefferson County, Kentucky. Her education at the time of enlistment was 1 year of high school. Her civil occupation was a waitress, except private family. She was married to a Mr. Arwood when she enlisted.
    Dorothy showed up for duty on September 25, 1944 and was released from duty on March 24, 1946.
    She died at the veteran's home in Lexington, Fayette County, Kentucky.

Funeral Services: Kerr Brothers Funeral Home.

Dorothy's ashes were taken to Victorville, San Bernardino County, California and spread out by her brother, Roy Edwin "Pete" Carby.

52. ROBERT EARL[4] CARBY (ANNA "ANNIE" ADRESS[3] MUSS, JOHN CARROLL[2] MUSS, JOHN[1] MUSS) was born May 14, 1926 in Louisville, Jefferson County, Kentucky and died May 14, 1926 in Louisville, Jefferson County, Kentucky.

Notes for ROBERT EARL CARBY:

His Kentucky death certificate is #26-13266. Robert is listed still born at the time of his death. He died at 7:20pm.

Informant: O. E. Carby of 3618 Kahlert Avenue in Louisville, Kentucky.

Parents: O. E. Carby of Kentucky and Adress Muss of Kentucky.

Cause of death: Still born.

Funeral services: McDaniel Bros. of Louisville, Kentucky.

Burial: May 25, 1933 at South Jefferson Cemetery in Louisville, Jefferson County, Kentucky in an unmarked grave.

3618 Kahlert Avenue in Louisville, Kentucky is an 812 square foot, 1 bedroom and 1 bathroom home that was built in 1920.

53. DAVID CALVIN[4] CARBY (ANNA "ANNIE" ADRESS[3] MUSS, JOHN CARROLL[2] MUSS, JOHN[1] MUSS) was born April 26, 1927 in Louisville, Jefferson County, Kentucky and died June 18, 1949 in Louisville, Jefferson County, Kentucky.

Notes for DAVID CALVIN CARBY:

He served in the U.S. Navy Reserves during World War II as a Seaman First Class.

His Kentucky death certificate is #49-12059. David is listed as single and an instructor at the time of his death. He died at 3:34am.

Informant: Mr. Orville Carby, Sr.

Parents: Orville Carby and Anna C. Muss.

Cause of death: Fractured skull and internal injury due to an "auto accident vs auto truck" at 18th (Dixie Highway) and Hale Avenue.

Funeral Services: Blanford-Ratterman Funeral Home, 2815 South 4th Street in Louisville, Kentucky. Services were conducted at 2pm on Tuesday, June 21, 1949 in the Blanford-Ratterman Funeral Home.

Burial: Tuesday, June 21, 1949 at Zachary Taylor National Cemetery, Plot: C, 111 in Louisville, Jefferson County, Kentucky.

David lived at 1901 Llytle at the time of his death. This is an 896 square foot home with 1 bedroom and 1 bathroom that was built in 1900.

David died in General Hospital, and was dead on arrival. His cause of death was a fractured skull and internal injuries due to an auto accident with truck at 18th Street (Dixie Highway) and Hale Avenue. He was a passenger in an auto that hit the back of a truck traveling in the same direction. The time of the accident was 3:34am.

David is buried in Zachary Taylor National Cemetery, Section C, Site 111. He was buried on June 21, 1949.

Obituary for David Calvin Carby – June 19, 1949
(Louisville Courier-Journal, Obituary for David Calvin Carby)

More about DAVID CALVIN CARBY:

David, along with the rest of the occupants in the car involved in the accident, was working at the Arthur Murray School of Dancing as a dance instructor when he died. The Arthur Murray Dance Studios were located at 450 South Third Street when the accident occurred. Arthur Murray Dance Studios still operates in the Louisville, Kentucky area today, and is located now located at 201 Breckenridge Lane.

David was the only person in the car that was not trapped in the car after the accident. He fell out of the car when the police arrived and pried open the passenger side front door.

The convertible at the scene of the accident – June 18, 1949
(Louisville Times, The convertible at the scene of the accident)

The following passengers inside the 1940 Ford convertible died in the accident: BETTIE JEAN THOMPSON of 963 Charles St, MARY LAVONNE "BONNIE LEE" CRAIG of 1219 Eastern Parkway, CHARLES C. EVERHART of 4543 Stoltz Street, WORDIE ADAMS, JR. of 2718 Elliott Street, and DAVID CALVIN CARBY of 4400 Stoltz Street. Skull fractures, broken necks, and internal injuries were the causes of death listed for all those who died in the accident. The following passengers of the convertible were injured in the accident: JOHN J. PLEASANT of 944 Dixie

Highway and EARL K. FRASHER of 916 S 29th Street. The convertible was owned by WORDIE ADAMS, JR.

EARL K. FRASHER, who had driven the car earlier that night, indicated that the brakes were bad on the convertible. EARL K. FRASHER was born on October 02, 1926 in Jefferson County, Kentucky and died on May 16, 1992 in Jefferson County, Kentucky. Earl was the son of MARY GREENWELL, and later became a doctor.

JOHN J. PLEASANT was born on June 23, 1925 and died on September 30, 1975 in Louisville, Jefferson County, Kentucky.

Photos of those who died in the automobile accident – June 19, 1949 (Louisville Courier-Journal, Photos of those who died in the automobile accident)

The driver of the car that was involved in the fatal accident was HARVEY G. WIGGINS of 2590 E Burnett Street, son of HARVEY RANDOL WIGGINS and MARY KINNANT. Harvey was not killed in the accident, but he died less than 6 months later on December 13, 1949 at 1:05pm in the Veterans Administration Hospital of Louisville, Kentucky from acute, purulent meningitis. Meningitis is a bacterial infection and inflammation of the protective membranes covering the brain and spinal cord, and the term "purulent" means containing, consisting of, or being pus. It is interesting to note the other conditions that were noted on Harvey's death certificate included an old, frontal skull fracture as well as bilateral, terminal, bronchial pneumonia. The skull fracture would have been from the accident that occurred 6 months earlier. Harvey most likely died 6 months after the accident as a result of the injuries that he sustained during the accident.

Harvey was charged with five manslaughter charges along with drunken driving, drunkenness in a public place and reckless driving. It is unclear at this time what the results of these charges were since Harvey died 6 months later.

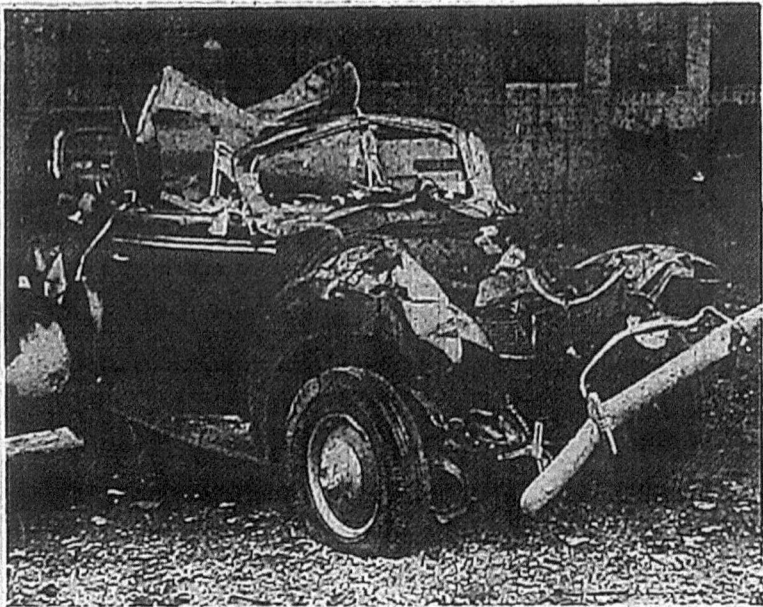

DEATH CAR WHICH RAMMED TRUCK, KILLING FIVE AND INJURING FOUR.
The convertible that was involved in the accident – June 19, 1949
(Louisville Courier-Journal, The convertible that was involved in the
accident)

David Carby, Charles Everhart, and Miss Craig were in the front
seat of the car with Harvey Wiggins. Miss Thompson, Wordie Adams,
John Pleasant, and Earl Frasher were in the back seat. Adams, Carby
and Miss Craig were killed immediately. Everhart died at 4am, and
Miss Thompson died at 5am, both at General Hospital. Wiggins and
Frasher were treated at General Hospital and later released. Pleasant
was taken to Nicholas Hospital and later released. The driver of the
cattle truck; CLIFFORD HOBBS of Huntsville, Alabama; that was struck
from behind was not injured. The passenger in the cattle truck; JOE
HELT of Columbus, Indiana; was only slightly injured when his head
struck the windshield. The 59 cattle that were being transported in
the tractor trailer were not injured in the accident.

Five city squad cars, two county cruisers, and city firemen were
all called to the crash scene. It was estimated that the convertible
driven by Wiggins was traveling at between 75 and 80 miles per hour,
and the truck that Wiggins struck was traveling at 20 to 25 miles per
hour.

On the night of the accident and after leaving work, the eight
Arthur Murray employees had first gone to the American Legion Club
at Seelbach, then later to the New Mill night club on Cane Run Road.

The eight had left the New Mill night club on Cane Run Road just before the accident.

Headstone for David Calvin Carby (Bailey)

54. HAREL LYN[4] CARBY, SR. *(ANNA "ANNIE" ADRESS[3] MUSS, JOHN CARROLL[2] MUSS, JOHN[1] MUSS)* was born May 07, 1929 in Louisville, Jefferson County, Kentucky and died March 09, 2011 in McQueeney, Guadalupe County, Texas. Harel was born as HAROLD LLOYD CARBY and later changed his name to HAREL LYN CARBY. He first married ROSEMARY MULKINS on November 23, 1949 in Jeffersonville, Clark County, Indiana, daughter of JESSE OMAR MULKINS, SR. and ANNA BELLE HINES. She was born March 08, 1930 in Louisville, Jefferson County, Kentucky. Harel later married THELMA LOUISE ROCHELLE on October 07, 1983 in Clark County, Nevada. Harel later married SHIRLEY BURCH on July 17, 1992 in Harris County, Texas. Shirley was born about 1946. Harel later married FLORETTA "FLO" COMLEY on March 17, 1994 in Harris County, Texas, daughter of EDWARD FLOYD COMLEY and THERESA GRACE MCGHEE. Flo was born December 07, 1936 in Tarrant County, Texas.

Notes for FLORETTA "FLO" COMLEY:
Flo was first married to ROBERT EUGENE WARE on April 17, 1967 in Tarrant County, Texas.

Notes for ROSEMARY MULKINS:

Rosemary was not raised by her biological Mulkins parents during a portion of her childhood. She was not adopted by the Wittekin family that helped raise her, but chose to use the maiden name of Wittekin until some time after she was married. The birth certificate for HAREL LYN CARBY, JR. indicates that his mother was MS. WITTEKIN. The explanation for Harel, Jr.'s birth record is that Rosemary used the surname for her family that raised her when she filled out Harel, Jr.'s birth certificate.

Notes for HAREL LYN CARBY, SR.:

Harel was born as HAROLD LLOYD CARBY.

He died after suffering from a long illness.

Burial: Section 71, Site 539 of Fort Sam Houston National Cemetery in San Antonio, Bexar County, Texas.

Harel had additional marriages, but their names are unknown at this time.

Headstone for Harel Lyn Carby, Sr. (Kenny & Julie)

Children of HAREL LYN[4] CARBY, SR. and ROSEMARY MULKINS are:

    i.   HAREL LYN "LYN"[5] CARBY, JR., b. April 09, 1959 in Los Angeles County, California; m1. ROSE DODD; m2. SHELLIE MNU.

ii. LYNDA DARLENE[5] CARBY, b. December 01, 1964 in Los Angeles, Los Angeles County, California; m1. JAMES WESLEY SLAY on April 14, 1984 in Travis County, Texas and divorced on May 28, 1984 in Travis County, Texas; m2. RICHARD "RICK" HOMER HEGGY on July 15, 1997 in Guadalupe County, Texas. JAMES WESLEY SLAY was born on June 24, 1960 in Hunt County, Texas and died on July 08, 1987 in Hopkins County, Texas. RICHARD "RICK" HOMER HEGGY was born on July 20, 1959 in Houston, Harris County, Texas.

Notes for LYNDA DARLENE CARBY:
   She was an adopted child.

55. ROY EDWIN "PETE"[4] CARBY *(ANNA "ANNIE" ADRESS[3] MUSS, JOHN CARROLL[2] MUSS, JOHN[1] MUSS)* was born January 21, 1931 in Jefferson County, Kentucky and died April 13, 2004 in Lexington, Fayette County, Kentucky. He married MARGARET "MARGIE" L. GREGORY about 1953, daughter of CHESTER WILLIAM GREGORY and LILLIE MAY DRESCHEL. She was born July 10, 1934 in Jefferson County, Kentucky.

Notes for ROY EDWIN "PETE" CARBY:
   Pete served as a Private First Class (PFC) in the 101st Airborne Division of the Army during the Korean War from June 01, 1954 to May 31, 1956.
   He was retired from General Telephone Company at the time of his death.
   Roy died at Hospice of the Bluegrass, 2312 Alexandria Drive, Lexington, KY 40504.
   Funeral Services: Kerr Brothers Funeral Home.
   Burial: April 2004 in Section T, Lot 132 of Camp Nelson National Cemetery at Nicholasville, Jessamine County, Kentucky.

Notes for ROY EDWIN "PETE" CARBY:
   Published in the Lexington Herald-Leader (KY) on April 15, 2004
   "PFC in the United States Army from June 01, 1954 to May 31, 1956. Roy E. 'Pete' Carby, age 73, husband of Margie Carby, was called to rest on Tuesday, April 13, 2004 while residing at the Hospice Care Center in Lexington, Kentucky. Mr. Carby was the son of Anna Adress Muss Carby and Orville Emmett Carby, Sr. Mr. Carby was survived by a son, Gregg Carby, Lexington, Kentucky, and two daughters; Mrs. Laura R. Carby Smith (Greg), Louisville, Kentucky, and Karen L. Carby of Lexington, Kentucky. In addition, Pete was survived by two sisters; Violet Flake, Russellville, Arkansas, and Juanita Dixon of Sulphur Springs, Texas; a brother, Harel L. Carby, McQueeny, Texas; four grandchildren, Matthew Tungate, Louisville, Kentucky, Lindsay and Christina Smith also of Louisville, Kentucky,

and Trisha Tungate of Lexington, Kentucky; a great granddaughter, Zoe Tungate, of Louisville, Kentucky. He was also survived by brothers-in-law that were like brothers to him and sisters-in-law that meant the world to him, as well as numerous nieces and nephews along with so many special friends. Pete was a member of the 101st Airborne Division of the Army. He retired from General Telephone Company in 1990. He served his country as a PFC in the United States Army from June 01, 1954 to May 31, 1956. Funeral services were held Friday, April 15, 2004 at Kerr Brothers Funeral Home, Main Street, Lexington, Kentucky. Services were conducted by Reverend Terrence Freeman. Burial was in Camp Nelson National Cemetery."

Children of ROY EDWIN "PETE"[4] CARBY and MARGARET "MARGIE" L. GREGORY are:

    vi.   GREGORY "GREG" ALLEN[5] CARBY, b. May 16, 1955 in Jefferson County, Kentucky.

    iii.   LAURA R.[5] CARBY, b. December 20, 1955; m1. GREG SMITH.

    iv.   KAREN L.[5] CARBY, b. August 17, 1957; m1. CLARENCE E. NORMAN on January 14, 1977 in Fayette County, Kentucky; m2. CLIFFORD E. DIXON on July 18, 1980 in Fayette County, Kentucky.

56. GLENNA IRENE[4] CARBY *(ANNA "ANNIE" ADRESS[3] MUSS, JOHN CARROLL[2] MUSS, JOHN[1] MUSS)* was born November 22, 1932 in Louisville, Jefferson County, Kentucky and died April 15, 1999 in Buena Park, Orange County, California. She married NORMAN LEE BARRETT, JR., son of NORMAN LOREN BARRETT and IDA NELL PHILLIPS. He was born August 02, 1928 in Englewood, Arapahoe County, Colorado.

Notes for GLENNA IRENE CARBY:
    Glenna died from cancer.

Children of GLENNA IRENE[4] CARBY and NORMAN LEE BARRETT, JR. are:

    i.   DEBORAH D.[5] BARRETT, b. August 22, 1956 in Buena Park, Orange County, California; m. WILLIAM F. WIESEN on July 12, 1975 in Orange County, California.

    ii.   DANA DIANE[5] BARRETT, b. June 01, 1957 in Los Angeles County, California; d. April 02, 2004 in Buena Park, Orange County, California.

        Notes for DANA DIANE BARRETT:
           She died from bone cancer.

57. JUANITA ROSE "TINY"[4] CARBY *(ANNA "ANNIE" ADRESS[3] MUSS, JOHN CARROLL[2] MUSS, JOHN[1] MUSS)* was born March 15, 1938 in Jefferson County, Kentucky. She first married a BOYD ALAN ROBERTS on July 10,

1954 in Wichita, Sedgwick, Kansas, son of MR. ROBERTS and MS. GAREY. Boyd was born on April 26, 1935 in Santa Monica, Los Angeles County, California and died March 29, 2005 in Atwater, Merced County, California. Juanita later married DOYLE LEE "LEE" LYNCH on March 03, 1962 in Los Angeles County, California, son of CHARLES "CHARLIE" LAWTON LYNCH and SARAH JANE WILLIAMS. Juanita and Doyle divorced during June 1966 in Los Angeles County, California. Doyle was born on April 23, 1935 in Lynch, Harlan County, Kentucky and died in Frankfort, Frankfurt am Main, Hessen, Germany on May 15, 2003. Juanita later married L. C. DIXON on October 09, 1970 in Sulphur Springs, Hopkins County, Texas, son of CLAUDE DIXON and LAVIRLE GLOSSUP. Lee was born on March 17, 1929 in Posey, Hopkins County, Texas and died on December 22, 2010 in Sulphur Springs, Hopkins County, Texas.

Notes for BOYD ALAN ROBERTS:
Boyd served in the Air Force from April 15, 1954 to April 30, 1974.
He later married MARCELLA E. CASH on April 17, 1970 in Merced County, California.
Boyd later married CAROL M. PALMER on July 2, 1983 in Merced County, California.

Notes for DOYLE LEE "LEE" LYNCH:
Doyle served as a Sergeant First Class (SFC) in the Army during the Vietnam War.
He died in Frankfort, Frankfurt am Main, Hessen, Germany while he was working at the U.S. Consulate.
Doyle is buried in Wilhelm Wacker Kg Cemetery located in Neuberg, Muhldorf am Inn, Bayern, Germany.

Notes for L. C. DIXON:
L. C. was first married to MARY MARGARET TOLES. They had 4 children together: GLENN RAY DIXON (b. November 24, 1950 in Dallas County, Texas), MARY KATHRYN DIXON (b. April 15, 1957 in Dallas County, Texas), TERRY WAYNE DIXON (b. April 05, 1958 in Dallas County, Texas), and BOBBY LEE DIXON (b. Jul 10, 1959 in Dallas County, Texas).
L. C. was next married to WANDA JOHNSON. They had 1 child together: DAVID WAYNE DIXON (b. August 15, 1963 in Los Angeles County, California).

Obituary Notes for L. C. DIXON:
West Oaks Funeral Home site, www.westoaksfuneralhome.com
Dateline: December 23, 2010
Born: March 17, 1929. Died: December 22, 2010
Died: Wednesday, December 22, 2010, in Sulphur Springs, Texas
"L. C. Dixon, age 81, of Sulphur Springs passed away Wednesday, December 22, 2010 at Hopkins County Memorial Hospital. There will be no formal services. A private burial will take place at a later date. Visitation will be from 5:00 to 8:00 p.m., Thursday, December 30, 2010 at West Oaks Funeral Home. Honorary pallbearers will be LeRoy Dixon, Richard Waldrup, Dickey Scroggins, Joe Thomas, David Dougan, Danny Underwood, Sr., and Terry Burns. Mr. Dixon was born on March 17, 1929 in Posey, TX, the son of Claude and Lavirle (Glossup) Dixon. He married Juanita Lynch on October 09, 1970 in Sulphur Springs. She survives. Mr. Dixon and his wife owned and operated Dixon's HI-LO Grocery for 36 years. He was a member of First Baptist Church. He is survived by his wife, sons, Glen Dixon and wife Daniela of Garland, Terry Dixon of Mesquite, Bobby Dixon and wife Judy of Rockwall, Alan Roberts and wife Leisha of Sulphur Springs, David Wayne Dixon of Los Angeles, CA, daughters, Mary Chapman and husband Ronnie of Mesquite, April Lynch of Alba, Kelli Matheson and husband Stacy of Quitman, 18 grandchildren and 10 great-grandchildren. He was preceded in death by brothers, Kenneth Dixon and Douglas Dixon, sister, Hazel Shugart. Arrangements are under the direction of West Oaks Funeral Home. Date: Thursday, December 30, 2010. Time: 5:00 to 8:00 p.m. Location: West Oaks Funeral Home."

Children of JUANITA ROSE "TINY"[4] CARBY and BOYD ALAN ROBERTS are:
    i.   ALAN D.[5] ROBERTS, b. July 28, 1956 in Travis Air Force Base, Solano County, California.

Children of JUANITA ROSE "TINY"[4] CARBY and DOYLE LEE "LEE" LYNCH are:
    i.   APRIL LEANN[5] LYNCH, b. May 28, 1962 in Santa Monica, Los Angeles County, California; d. September 12, 2011 in Tyler, Smith County, Texas; m1. FOUAD MOHAMMAD BDEIR on July 03, 1981 in Lamar County Texas; d1. November 24, 1987 in Hopkins County, Texas. m2. DANNY TRAVIS UNDERWOOD on December 30, 1987 in Hopkins County, Texas.
    ii.   KELLI RAE[5] LYNCH, b. April 17, 1963 in Santa Monica, Los Angeles County, California; m1. THOMAS E. HARBIN on August 18, 1989 in Hopkins County, Texas; m2. STACY MATHESON.

58. MARY L.[4] MUSS (*CLAUDE LEE[3] MUSS, JOHN CARROLL[2] MUSS, JOHN[1] MUSS*) was born May 18, 1921 in Jefferson County, Kentucky. No additional information can be found on her at this time.

59. CATHERINE V.[4] MUSS *(CLAUDE LEE[3] MUSS, JOHN CARROLL[2] MUSS, JOHN[1] MUSS)* was born March 08, 1923 in Jefferson County, Kentucky. No additional information can be found on her at this time.

60. AGNES INEZ "INEZ"[4] MUSS *(CLAUDE LEE[3] MUSS, JOHN CARROLL[2] MUSS, JOHN[1] MUSS)* was born June 10, 1925 in Jefferson County, Kentucky. No additional information can be found on her at this time.

61. NANCY M.[4] MUSS *(CLAUDE LEE[3] MUSS, JOHN CARROLL[2] MUSS, JOHN[1] MUSS)* was born July 13, 1927 in Jefferson County, Kentucky and died May 20, 1998 in Jefferson County, Kentucky. She had at least 3 children, all believed at this time to be with a MR. SNOWDEN. It is unclear whether she married MR. SNOWDEN.

Children of NANCY M.[4] MUSS and MR. SNOWDEN are:
  i.   JOSEPH[5] MUSS MARX, b. August 07, 1954 in Louisville, Jefferson County, Kentucky; d. May 20, 1998. Joseph was put up for adoption.
  ii. ROBERT "BOBBY"[5] SNU, b. Louisville, Jefferson County, Kentucky.
  iii. ROBIN MARIE[5] SNOWDEN, b. February 05, 1962; m. DEWEY L. CRISWELL on July 21, 1984 in Jefferson County, Kentucky.

62. JOHN W.[4] SNELLEN *(SARAH "SALLIE" ELIZABETH[3] MUSS, JOHN CARROLL[2] MUSS, JOHN[1] MUSS)* was born May 31, 1920 in Kentucky and died June 11, 1995 in Louisville, Jefferson County, Kentucky. No additional information can be found on him at this time.

63. ARLEY R.[4] MUSS *(GOLDA "GOLDIE" NAOMI "NAOMI"[3] MUSS, JOHN CARROLL[2] MUSS, JOHN[1] MUSS)* was born April 24, 1922 in Bullitt County, Kentucky and died March 01, 1987 in Louisville, Jefferson County, Kentucky. He married MARY LEOLA DOWNS on June 15, 1941 in Campbell County, Tennessee. No additional information can be found on him at this time.

Children of ARLEY R.[4] MUSS and MARY LEOLA DOWNS are:
  i.   GLENN DAVID[5] MUSS, b. October 11, 1946 in Jefferson County, Kentucky; d. January 10, 1967 in Quang Nam, Vietnam.

       Notes for GLENN DAVID MUSS:
            Glenn enlisted in the U S Marine Corps on January 20, 1965 in Louisville, Jefferson County, Kentucky.
            Lance Corporal Glenn David Muss served under the 2nd Platoon, India Company, 3rd Battalian, 7th Marines, 1st Marine Division.

Glenn died from hostile, small arms fire in the Vietnam War while serving for the U S Marines. His body was recovered.

Glenn is honored on Panel 14 E, Row 6 of the Vietnam Veterans Memorial.

Burial: Section 22, Row 80, Grave 8 in Calvary Cemetery of Louisville, Jefferson County, Kentucky.

Headstone for Glenn David Muss
(McClure)

64. LINDSEY W.[4] MUSS *(GOLDA "GOLDIE" NAOMI "NAOMI"[3] MUSS, JOHN CARROLL[2] MUSS, JOHN[1] MUSS)* was born October 29, 1927 in Jefferson County, Kentucky and died February 27, 1993 in Louisville, Jefferson County, Kentucky. No additional information can be found on him at this time.

65. WILLIAM HENRY[4] ARMES, JR. *(GOLDA "GOLDIE" NAOMI "NAOMI"[3] MUSS, JOHN CARROLL[2] MUSS, JOHN[1] MUSS)* was born May 26, 1929 in Jefferson County, Kentucky. No additional information can be found on him at this time.

66. JOHN C.[4] ARMES *(GOLDA "GOLDIE" NAOMI "NAOMI"[3] MUSS, JOHN CARROLL[2] MUSS, JOHN[1] MUSS)* was born October 24, 1943 in Jefferson County, Kentucky. No additional information can be found on him at this time.

67. JAMES T.[4] ARMES *(GOLDA "GOLDIE" NAOMI "NAOMI"[3] MUSS, JOHN CARROLL[2] MUSS, JOHN[1] MUSS)* was born October 24, 1943 in Jefferson County, Kentucky. No additional information can be found on him at this time.

Generation No. 4: Descendants of Caroline "Carrie" F. Muss

68. JAMES W.[4] COOK *(GEORGE W.[3] COOK, CAROLINE "CARRIE" F.[2] MUSS, JOHN[1] MUSS)* was born on July 03, 1917 in Indiana and died February 17, 1998 in Indiana. Based upon the obituaries for his mother and father, James had 2 children. No additional information can be found on him at this time.

69. ELLEN ARLENA[4] COOK *(GEORGE W.[3] COOK, CAROLINE "CARRIE" F.[2] MUSS, JOHN[1] MUSS)* was born about December 08, 1921 in Vigo County, Indiana and died December 28, 1960 in Saint Louis, Saint Louis County, Missouri, but she was living in Terre Haute, Vigo County, Indiana at the time of her death. Ellen married JAMES LEON CORZINE on September 18, 1942 in Vigo County, Indiana, son of JAMES EARL CORZINE and SARAH ELNORA HOWELL. He was born on March 19, 1921 in Balcom, Union County, Illinois and died on August 16, 1997 in Lecanto, Citrus County, Florida.

Notes for ELLEN ARLENA COOK:
     Ellen died at 5:00pm Wednesday in Saint Luke's Hospital in Saint Louis, Missouri. Saint Luke's Hospital was found on February 28, 1866 by a group of concerned Episcopalians, and joined by the Presbyterians in 1948. Today, Saint Luke's is part of the healing ministry for the Episcopal and Presbyterian churches. Saint Luke's Hospital is located at 232 South Woods Mill Road in Chesterfield, Missouri.
     She lived at 2530 North Fourteenth and One-Half Street at the time of her death, and was a member of the Eighth Avenue Baptist Church. The home at 2530 North 14th 1/2 Street in Terre Haute, Indiana is a 1,862 square foot single family home built in 1910 that has 2 bedrooms and 1 bathroom.
     Services were held at 2:30pm on Saturday December 31, 1960 at the Thomas Funeral Home. The Reverend Donald Edward and Reverend Esmond Elliott officiated.
     Funeral Services: Thomas Funeral Home of Terre Haute, Indiana.
     Burial: June 21, 1949 in Section H, Lot 256, Spaces 9 & 10 (along with her huband JAMES LEON CORZINE) at Roselawn Memorial Park of Terre Haute, Vigo County, Indiana.

MRS. ELLEN ARLENA CORZINE

Mrs. Ellen Arlena Corzine, 39 years old, of 2530 North Fourteenth and One-half street, died at 5 o'clock Wednesday evening at St. Luke's Hospital in St. Louis. She was a member of the Eighth Avenue Baptist Church. Surviving are the husband, James L.; a daughter, Miss Jane Ellen Corzine and a son, James George Corzine, both at home; the parents, Mr. and Mrs. George W. Cook of Terre Haute, and a brother, James W. Cook of Terre Haute. Service arrangements are pending at the Thomas Funeral Home.

Obituary 1 for Ellen Arlena Cook Corzine – December 29, 1960
(Terre Haute Tribune, Obituary 1 for Ellen Arlena Cook Corzine)

MRS. ELLEN ARLENA CORZINE

Services for Mrs. Ellen Arlena Corzine, 39 years old, of 2530 North Fourteenth and One-half street, who died Wednesday, will be at 2:30 o'clock Saturday afternoon at the Thomas Funeral Home. The Rev. Donald Edwards and the Rev. Esmond Elliott will offiate and burial will be in Roselawn Memorial Park. Friends may call.

Obituary 2 for Ellen Arlena Cook Corzine – December 30, 1960
(Terre Haute Tribune, Obituary 2 for Ellen Arlena Cook Corzine)

Headstone for Ellen Arlena Cook Corzine
(Atkinson, Headstone for Ellen Arlena Cook Corzine)

Notes for JAMES LEON CORZINE:
 After the death of his wife, Ellen Arlena Cook, James married MARY JO HAASE about 1962 in Vigo County, Indiana. Together they had 2 children as follows: KEVIN CORZINE (b. November 01, 1963 in Vigo County, Indiana) and PATRICIA COLLEEN "COLLEEN" CORZINE (b. September 15, 1968 in Vigo County, Indiana; m. MICHAEL JOHN MCGILLICUDDY on March 30, 1991 in Citrus County, Florida).
 Funeral Services: Mattox-Wood Funeral Home of Terre Haute, Indiana.
 Burial: August 20, 1997 in Section H, Lot 256, Spaces 9 & 10 (along with his wife ELLEN ARLENA COOK) at Roselawn Memorial Park of Terre Haute, Vigo County, Indiana.

Obituary Notes for JAMES LEON CORZINE:
 Published on Page 2 of the Terre Haute Tribune Star on Monday, August 18, 1997
"James L. Corzine, 76, of Lecanto, Fla., and formerly of Terre Haute died at 6:30 a.m. Saturday, Aug. 16, 1997, in Mariner Health Care Center in Florida. He retired as a maintenance supervisor for Anaconda. He was born March 19, 1921 in Union County, Ill., to James E. Corzine and Elnora Howell Corzine. His first wife, Arlena Corzine, died in 1961. Survivors include his wife, Mary Haase Corzine; two daughters, Jane Julien of River Ranch, Fla., and Patricia McGillicuddy of Carthage, Tenn.; two sons, James G. Corzine of Lyons and Kevin Corzine of Terre Haute; three sisters, Vivian Boyd and Colleen Garrott both of Anna, Ill., and Betty Snyder of Springhill, Fla.; eight grandchildren; four great-grandchildren; and several nieces and nephews. He was a Navy veteran of World War II. Services are 10 a.m. Wednesday in Mattox-Wood North Terre Haute Chapel. Burial is in Roselawn Memorial Park. Visitation is 4 to 8 p.m. Tuesday."

Headstone for James Leon Corzine
(Atkinson, Headstone for James Leon Corzine)

Children of ELLEN ARLENA[4] COOK and JAMES LEON CORZINE are:

    i.   JANE ELLEN[5] CORZINE, b. October 15, 1943 in Vigo County, Indiana; m1. MR. SHELL in Indiana; m2. BRUCE BARR GRALOW, JR. on April 25, 1975 in Pinellas County, Florida; m3. DONALD ARTHUR JULIEN on September 07, 1986 in Pinellas County, Florida.

          Notes for JANE ELLEN CORZINE:
              Jane lived in Clermont, Lake County, Florida and Saint Petersburg, Pinellas, Florida. She was last known to be living in River Ranch, Polk County, Florida.

   ii.   JAMES GEORGE[5] CORZINE, b. March 22, 1947 in Vigo County, Indiana.

          Notes for JAMES GEORGE CORZINE:
              James lived in Bloomington, Monroe County, Indiana. He was last known to be living in Lyons, Greene County, Indiana.

70. JANE ELLEN[4] BRILEY *(BETTY MAE[3] COOK, CAROLINE "CARRIE" F.[2] MUSS, JOHN[1] MUSS)* was born March 12, 1920 in Linton, Greene County, Indiana and died March 12, 1920 in Linton, Greene County, Indiana.

Notes for JANE ELLEN BRILEY:
    According to the birth index available at the Bloomfield-Eastern Green County Public Library, the birth record for Jane Ellen was recorded by the Green County Health Department in Book CHO-2, Page 69.
    According to the death index available at the Bloomfield-Eastern Green County Public Library, the death record for Jane Ellen was

recorded by the Green County Health Department in Book CHO-1, Page 66.

Burial: March 1920 at Fairview Cemetery in Linton, Greene County, Indiana.

71. WILLIAM M.⁴ COOK, SR. *(HENRY WAYNE³ COOK, CAROLINE "CARRIE" F.²* *MUSS, JOHN¹ MUSS)* was born on March 31, 1912 in Vigo County, Indiana and died on October 25, 1964 in Danville, Vermilion County, Illinois. He married THELMA MARIE BATH on November 04, 1935, most likely in Illinois, daughter of FREDERICK "FRED" DAVID BATH and MAMIE ALBERS. Thelma was born on June 11, 1917 in Danville, Vermillion County, Illinois and died on September 21, 2009 in Danville, Vermilion County, Illinois.

Notes for WILLIAM M. COOK, SR.:
Burial: Oak Hill Cemetery in Danville, Vermilion County, Illinois.

Notes for THELMA MARIE BATH:
After the death of her first husband, WILLIAM M. COOK, SR., Thelma married WILLIAM JOSEPH HARTMAN, SR. on May 15, 1971 in Illinois, son of unknown parents. William Hartman was born March 30, 1917 and died on September 29, 1999 in Danville, Vermillion County, Illinois. He is buried in Danville National Cemetery.

More about THELMA MARIE BATH:
Burial: Oak Hill Cemetery in Danville, Vermilion County, Illinois.

Obituary Notes for THELMA MARIE BATH:
Published in the Commercial-News (Danville, Illinois) on September 21, 2009

"Thelma Marie Hartman, 92, of Danville, passed away at 12:50 p.m. Monday, Sept. 21, 2009, at North Logan Healthcare, where she had resided since May 2004. Mrs. Hartman was born June 11, 1917, in Danville, to Frederick and Mamie (Albers) Bath. She married William M. Cook, Sr. on Nov. 4, 1935. To this union there were two children born, Melva Louise (Cook) Bryant (deceased) and William M. Cook, Jr. On May 15, 1971, she married William J. Hartman, Sr., who passed away Sept. 29, 1999. She is survived by her son, William M. (Gay) Cook, Jr. of Smithville, Texas; brother, Theo (Ruth) Bath of Danville; sister, Julia Vehlewald of Danville; eight grandchildren; 11 great-grandchildren; 16 great-great grandchildren; and several nieces, nephews, great-nieces and great-nephews. Mrs. Hartman was preceded in death by her parents; both husbands; daughter, Melva Bryant; sister, Mary; brother, Earl; half brother, Clarence; great-grandson, Joey Williams; two nephews, Larry Bath and Matt Moll; niece, Dianna Moll; sister-in-law, Marie; and brother-in-law, Howard.

She graduated from Rose Hill Grade School and was a sales clerk and waitress. She and her late husband retired from management of Motel 6 in Wisconsin in 1981. She was a member of the Ladies of the Moose for 65 years. Her hobbies were flowers and crafts and dearly loved to spend time with her grandchildren and babysit her great-grandchildren. A special thanks to all employees of N.L.H., especially her granddaughter, Hope Bryant and great-grandson, Chris. A graveside service for Thelma Marie Hartman will be at 2:30 p.m. Wednesday, Sept. 23, 2009 at Oakhill Cemetery, with Pastor June Moll officiating. Visitation will be from noon to 2 p.m. Wednesday at Sunset Funeral Home and Cremation Center. Memorials may be made to hospice. E-mail condolences may be sent to the family at: www.sunsetfuneralhome.com."

Children of WILLIAM M.⁴ COOK, SR. and THELMA MARIE BATH are:
    i.   MELVA LOUISE⁵ COOK, b. July 28, 1937 in Illinois; d. January 18, 2005 in Danville, Vermilion County, Illinois; m. MR. BRYANT.

        Notes for MELVA LOUISE COOK:
            Burial: Oak Hill Cemetery in Danville, Vermilion County, Illinois.

    ii.   WILLIAM M.⁵ COOK, JR., b. July 24, 1939 in Illinois; m. GAY LYNICE HURLEY on August 19, 1979 in Travis County, Texas.

        Notes for WILLIAM M. COOK, JR.:
            His marriage to Gay may not have been his first marriage.

72. MARY E.⁴ COOK *(HENRY WAYNE³ COOK, CAROLINE "CARRIE" F.² MUSS, JOHN¹ MUSS)* was born on May 02, 1915 in Vigo County, Indiana. No additional information can be found on her at this time.

73. FRANCIS J.⁴ COOK *(HENRY WAYNE³ COOK, CAROLINE "CARRIE" F.² MUSS, JOHN¹ MUSS)* was born on April 01, 1917 in Vigo County, Indiana. No additional information can be found on her at this time.

74. LEOTA MAY⁴ COOK *(HENRY WAYNE³ COOK, CAROLINE "CARRIE" F.² MUSS, JOHN¹ MUSS)* was born on September 06, 1919 in Terre Haute, Vigo County, Indiana. She married KEITH ANTHONY ELLIOTT on July 25, 1939 in Vigo County, Indiana, son of ARTHUR ELLIOTT and ETHEL CASSELL. He was born March 07, 1922 in Oakland, Gibson County, Indiana and died July 1986 in Spartanburg, Spartanburg County, South Carolina.

75. PAUL LEROY⁴ COOK *(WILLIAM "WILLIE" J.³ COOK, CAROLINE "CARRIE" F.² MUSS, JOHN¹ MUSS)* was born on March 13, 1926 in Lewis, Vigo

County, Indiana. He married MYRTLE DORIS "DORIS" DABLEMONT on June 20, 1947 in Bourbonnais, Kankakee County, Illinois, daughter of EARL ROLLIN DABLEMONT and INEZ LEOTA REEDER. She was born on April 21, 1927 in Lincoln Park, Wayne County, Michigan.

Notes for PAUL LEROY COOK:
Paul enlisted in the U.S. Army during World War II on June 5, 1944 at Fort Benjamin Harrison, Marion County, Indiana.
He moved his family to California in 1964.
Paul owned Dressel Print Shop in Vallejo, Solano County, California from about 1965 to 1990.
He was living in Vallejo, Solano County, California on October 16, 1988 according to the obituary for his stepmother, Ivy Murial McCoy.
In 1990, Paul and Doris moved to South Africa as lay missionaries. They were there until 2007.
Paul was living in South Africa on October 02, 1991 according to the obituary for his father, William "Willie" J. Cook.
Paul and Doris currently live in Rolla, Phelps County, Missouri and have 5 children, 23 grandchildren, and 22 great-grandchildren.

Children of PAUL LEROY[4] COOK and MYRTLE DORIS DABLEMONT are:

    i.   NANCY JANE COOK, b. April 08, 1952 in Kankakee, Kankakee County, Illinois; m. MARSHALL MARVIN MOSLEY on August 20, 1971 in Nampa, Canyon County, Idaho.

        Notes for MARSHALL MARVIN MOSLEY:
        He was born on May 28, 1951 in Worland, Washakie County, Wyoming.

    ii.   LESLIE ALLEN COOK, b. May 28, 1953 in Kankakee, Kankakee County, Illinois; m. DONNA LOU CLEVENGER on January 25, 1980 in Santa Clara County, California.

        Notes for DONNA LOU CLEVENGER:
        She was born on January 04, 1962.

    iii.   LOREN WAYNE COOK, b. February 17, 1957 in Wood River, Madison County, Illinois; m. SUSAN "SUE" LEE GARDNER on June 12, 1976 in San Jose, Santa Clara County, California.

        Notes for SUSAN "SUE" LEE GARDNER:
        She was born on September 06, 1956 in Santa Clara County, California.

    iv.   LEROY DAVID COOK, b. January 16, 1959 in Wood River, Madison County, Illinois; m. CARLA JEAN NUSZ on August 18, 1979 in Wichita, Sadgwick County, Kansas.

Notes for CARLA JEAN NUSZ:
> She was born on November 09, 1960 in Wichita, Sedgwick County, Kansas.

v.   LYLE RAYMOND⁵ COOK, b. August 03, 1964 in Dinuba, Tulare County, California; m. KARLA DENISE EZELL on November 02, 1985 in West Plains, Howell County, Missouri.

Notes for KARLA DENISE EZELL:
> She was born on November 24, 1965 in Jennings, Jefferson Davis Parish, Louisiana.

76. BETTY RUTH⁴ COOK *(WILLIAM "WILLIE" J.³ COOK, CAROLINE "CARRIE" F.² MUSS, JOHN¹ MUSS)* was born on April 07, 1928 in Lewis, Vigo County, Indiana. She married HARRY ALAN JOHNSON on September 10, 1948 in Marion County, Indiana, son of HARRY E. JOHNSON and LELA GALE NUDING. He was born on May 15, 1928 in Marion County, Indiana.

Children of BETTY RUTH⁴ COOK and HARRY ALAN JOHNSON are:
   i.   HARRY LEROY JOHNSON, b. January 31, 1951 in Marion County, Indiana; m1. SUSAN BOYLE on September 30, 1973 in Marion County, Indiana; m2. JANE KUNKEL on October 22, 1994 in Marion County, Indiana.

Notes for SUSAN BOYLE:
> She was born on June 06, 1960.

   ii. KAREN LOUISE JOHNSON, b. April 07, 1952 in Marion County, Indiana; m. GLENN MALCOLM RAY on June 18, 1972 in Dakota County, Minnesota.

Notes for GLENN MALCOLM RAY:
> He was born on December 20, 1949.

   iii. SHARON GAIL JOHNSON, b. October 01, 1955 in Marion County, Indiana; m. JOHN FINLAY on July 08, 1977 Marion County, Indiana.

Notes for JOHN FINLAY:
> He was born on May 30, 1955.

   iv. JAY ALAN JOHNSON, b. November 27, 1961 in Marion County, Indiana; m. KAREN BALDOCK on August 16, 1986 in Warren County, Kentucky.

Notes for KAREN BALDOCK:
   She was born on April 04, 1965.

Generation No. 4: Descendants of George W. Muss

The only child of GEORGE W. MUSS and ELLEN "ELLA" W. HANNEPHIN, MARTINA CLYDE MUSS, never married and did not have children. For this reason, there were no 4th generation descendants of John Muss through the George W. Muss branch of the Muss family tree.

Generation No. 4: Descendants of Charles Muss

77. REBECCA "BECKY" LOUISE[4] STOLL *(NORA E.[3] MUSS, CHARLES[2] MUSS, JOHN[1] MUSS)* was born on November 14, 1916 in Chicago, Cook County, Illinois and died December 18, 1994 in Oak Lawn, Cook County, Illinois. She married CHARLES RAYMOND SHERLOCK on April 17, 1942 in Cook County, Illinois, son of HARRY ANTHONY SHERLOCK and GERTRUDE V. ROBERTSON. He was born on June 10, 1918 in Chicago, Cook County, Illinois and died on September 26, 1982 in Cook County, Illinois.

Notes for REBECCA "BECKY" LOUISE STOLL:
Her birth is provided according to Illinois birth certificate file # 6039008.

Her marriage to Charles Raymond Sherlock is provided according to Illinois marriage certificate file # 1726939.

Funeral Services: Blake-Lamb Funeral Home of Oak Lawn, Illinois. Her funeral was held at 9am in Saint Catherine of Alexandria Church with visitation from 2 to 10pm on Wednesday, December 21, 1994.

Burial: Thursday, December 22, 1994 at Holy Sepulchre Cemetery in Alsip, Cook County, Illinois.

SHERLOCK
Rebecca L. Sherlock, 78 years, wife of the late Charles Raymond; mother of Louise (Joseph) Moffatt, Richard, William and Barbara; grandmother of Elizabeth Moffatt Rollins, Joseph Moffatt III and Jeddy Rae Sherlock; great-grandmother of one. Funeral Thursday 9 a.m. from Blake-Lamb Funeral Home, 4727 W. 103rd St., Oak Lawn, to St. Catherine of Alexandria Church. Mass 9:45 a.m. Interment Holy Sepulchre Cemetery. Visitation Wednesday 2 to 10 p.m. Memorials to Love Letters, P.O. Box 416875, Chicago, IL 60641. Info, 708-636-1193 or 312-735-4242.

Obituary for Rebecca "Becky" Louise Stoll Sherlock - December 21, 1994
(Chicago Tribune)

Notes for CHARLES RAYMOND SHERLOCK:
Charles enlisted as a Warrant Officer during World War II on June 30, 1942 in Chicago, Cook County, Illinois and reported for duty on

July 13, 1942. He served until he was released on November 18, 1945.

Children of REBECCA "BECKY" LOUISE[4] STOLL and CHARLES RAYMOND SHERLOCK are:

i. LOUISE[5] SHERLOCK, b. Cook County, Illinois; m. JOSEPH MOFFATT, JR.
ii. RICHARD[5] SHERLOCK, b. Cook County, Illinois.
iii. WILLIAM[5] SHERLOCK, b. Cook County, Illinois.
iv. BARBARA[5] SHERLOCK, b. Cook County, Illinois.

78. DONALD EDWIN[4] STOLL *(NORA E.[3] MUSS, CHARLES[2] MUSS, JOHN[1] MUSS)* was born about July 15, 1924 in Cook County, Illinois and died August 06, 2000 in Nashville, Davidson County, Tennessee. He married MARGARET JEAN MCCRONE on January 07, 1950 in Cook County, Illinois, daughter of WALTER COX MCCRONE, SR. and BESSIE MCGOWAN. She was born on January 04, 1926 in Buffalo, Erie County, New York and died on February 09, 1991 in Nashville, Davidson County, Tennessee.

Notes for DONALD EDWIN STOLL:
His birth is provided according to Illinois birth certificate file # 6030419.
His marriage to Margaret Jean McCrone is provided according to Illinois marriage certificate file # 2116307.
Donald received his architectural degree from the University of Illinois.
He served in World War II with the 731st Engineer Company.
Donald was a scout master of Boy Scouts of America troop number 136, a 32nd degree Mason, and a Kentucky Colonel.
Funeral Services: Marshall-Donnelly-Combs Funeral Home of Nashville, Tennessee. His funeral was held at 4:30pm in on Thursday, August 10, 2000 with visitation one hour prior to the service.

Nashville, TN

STOLL, Mr. Donald Edwin
A.I.A.— Age 76. August 6,
2000. Survived by sons,
Steve Stoll, Chuck Stoll,
Rick Stoll all of Nashville,
TN, David Stoll, Atlanta, GA;
grandchildren, Brigg, Tim,
Alisa and Brandon Stoll. Mr.
Stoll received his architectural degree from the University of Illinois. Served in
WWII with the 731st Engi-
neer Company. Formed ar-
chitecture business with
Tom Clark, 'Clark and Stoll
Architects', in 1956. Founded Donald E. Stoll and Asso-
ciates Architects Inc. in
1957. Founded D.S.A. De-
signs, Inc. in 1960. He was a
member of the American In-
stitute of Architects, an ac-
tive member of Greenhills
YMCA and Scout Master of
BSA Troop No. 136. He was
a 32nd Degree Mason, and a
Kentucky Colonel. Memorial
service will be held 4:30
P.M. Thursday at Marshall-
Donnelly-Combs Funeral-
Home, with visitation one
hour prior to service. MAR-
SHALL-DONNELLY-
COMBS, Nashville, TN,
615-327-1111.

Obituary for Donald Edwin Stoll - August 08, 2000
(The Tennessean, Obituary for Donald Edwin Stoll)

Notes for MARGARET JEAN MCCRONE:
Funeral Services: Marshall-Donnelly-Combs Funeral Home of Nashville, Tennessee. Her funeral was held at 2:30pm in on Wednesday, February 13, 1999.

> **STOLL, Margaret Jean**—February 9, 1991 at her residence. Survived by sons, Charles Wayne Stoll, Clearwater Beach, FLA., David Donald Stoll, Atlanta, GA., Richard Steven Stoll and Stephen Edwin Stoll both of Nashville; three grandchildren; brother, Walter McCrone, Chicago, ILL.; sisters, Sylvia Graft, Frankfort, ILL., Mary Lou Capps, Chattanooga, TN. and Phyllis Painter, Westbend, WISC. A memorial service will be held 2:30 p.m., Wednesday at Marshall Donnelly Combs, 201 25th Avenue, North. In lieu of flowers, please send donations to American Heart Association, 209 23rd Avenue, North, Nashville, TN., 37203. MARSHALL DONNELLY COMBS, 327-1111

Obituary for Margaret Jean McCrone Stoll – February 11, 1991
(The Tennessean, Obituary for Margaret Jean McCrone Stoll)

Children of DONALD EDWIN[4] STOLL and CHARLES MARGARET JEAN MCCRONE are:

    i.   CHARLES "CHUCK" WAYNE[5] STOLL, b. January 21, 1951 in Cook County, Illinois.

    ii. RICHARD "RICK" STEVEN[5] STOLL, b. February 10, 1953 in Cook County, Illinois; m1. Unknown; m2. Unknown; m3. PAMELA M. WOHLLEB on September 16, 1989 in Jefferson County, Kentucky.

    iii. STEPHEN "STEVE" EDWIN[5] STOLL, b. September 02, 1955 in Cook County, Illinois; m. KIBBY FELECIA PATTERSON on September 07, 1979 in Williamson County, Tennessee.

Notes for STEPHEN "STEVE" EDWIN STOLL:
Stephen and Kibby lived in the same apartment complex in Hermitage, Tennessee at the time of their marriage.

iv. DAVID DONALD[5] STOLL, b. October 13, 1959 in Cook County, Illinois; d. October 27, 2002 in Marietta, Cobb County, Georgia.

79. ROBERT LEE[4] DUESING HICKS *(STELLA E.[3] MUSS, CHARLES[2] MUSS, JOHN[1] MUSS)* was born December 30, 1910 in Jefferson County, Kentucky and died December 12, 1955 in Indiana.

Notes for ROBERT LEE DUESING HICKS:
On June 6, 1941 Robert enlisted in the U.S. Army for World War II at Louisville, Jefferson County, Kentucky. He is listed as single with 3 years of high school. His civil occupation at the time of enlistment is a Baker.

Robert was living at 819 West Market Street in New Albany, Indiana at the time he was drafted into the U.S. Army. The residence at 819 West Market Street is a 1,100 square foot, single family home with 3 bedrooms and 1 bathroom that was built in 1929.

26 COUNTY BOYS CALLED JUNE 9 TO JOIN COLORS

Group Will Include Draftees Of City And Rural District For Ninth Quota

NEW RULES WILL BE STUDIED

Twenty-six Floyd County youths will be inducted into the United States Army June 9 for a year's training under the Selective service Act, local draft officials announced Monday.

Comprising the ninth call, the group will meet at the New Albany Armory at 7:45 o'clock in the morning and will be transported to the induction station in the Louisville Post Office for federal physical examination.

The selectees follow:

Richard Elmer Borkeheim, 142 Locust street.

Charles William Kreutzer, 1215 East Elm street.

Marvin Vollney Oakes, 1813 Shelby street.

Parvin Russell Sperzel, 1829 East Oak street.

Charles Ivan Loebig, 1745 West Spring street.

Earl LaVerne Winders, 722 West Spring street.

Norman A. Gonder, 916 East Market street.

Carl Daniel Gresham, 1314 Culbertson avenue.

Robert Lee Hicks, 819 West Market street.

Oalos Everett Dixon, 412 East Market street.

Charles William ZurSchmiede, 707 West Spring street.

Theodore David Hammer, 2415 Shelby street.

Andrew J. Schlageter, 1217 Culbertson avenue.

World War II Draft for Robert Lee Duesing Hicks – June 02, 1941 (New Albany Tribune, World War II Draft for Robert Lee Duesing Hicks)

More about ROBERT LEE DUESING HICKS:

Funeral Services: Kraft Funeral Home of New Albany, Indiana. His funeral was held in the funeral home at 2:00pm on Wednesday, December 14, 1955.

Burial: Wednesday. December 14, 1955 at Fairview Cemetery in New Albany, Floyd County, Indiana.

Robert died suddenly at his residence in the Stag Hotel of New Albany, Indiana. He was working at the New Albany Box and Basket Company at the time of his death.

Deaths

Robert Lee Hicks

Robert Lee Hicks, 46, veteran of World War II, died suddenly Monday morning at the Stag Hotel where he made his residence.

He was an employee of the New Albany Box and Basket Factory.

Hicks is survived by an uncle, William N. Muss of Washington, D. C.

The body is at the Kraft Funeral Home. Funeral arrangements will be announced later.

Obituary 1 for Robert Lee Duesing Hicks – December 12, 1955
(New Albany Tribune, Obituary 1 for Robert Lee Duesing Hicks)

Page Three

Deaths

Robert Lee Hicks

Funeral service for Robert Lee Hicks, 46, veteran of World War II, will be held Wednesday at 2 p.m. at the Kraft Funeral Home. Military burial services will be held at Fairview Cemetery.

Hicks died suddenly Monday morning at the Stag Hotel where he made his residence.

Obituary 2 for Robert Lee Duesing Hicks – December 13, 1955
(New Albany Tribune, Obituary 2 for Robert Lee Duesing Hicks)

Headstone for Robert Lee Duesing Hicks
(Douser, Headstone for Robert Lee Hicks)

80. BETTY A.[4] MUSS *(WILLIAM NATHAN[3] MUSS, CHARLES[2] MUSS, JOHN[1] MUSS)* was born on June 08, 1926 in Fayette County, Kentucky. No additional information can be found on her at this time.

Generation No. 4: Descendants of Mary Emma Muss

It is unknown at this time whether there were any 4th generation descendants of John Muss through this branch of the family. It is very likely that this branch of the family did not continue to the 4th generation. It is believed that NANNIE M. DORIOT did not marry. DAVID P. DORIOT appears to have not had children based upon his obituary. JAMES CLYDE DORIOT and MORNA DORIOT are the most probable possibilities that the family continued down the Doriot branch. Unfortunately, JAMES CLYDE DORIOT cannot be located in any census records after 1910 so he may have died shortly after that census. Additionally, MORNA DORIOT can only be found in the 1900 census so she very likely died shortly after that census.

Generation No. 4: Descendants of Elizabeth "Bettie" Muss

85. THELMA PEARL⁴ APPLEGATE *(LEWIS EDWARD "ED"³ APPLEGATE, ELIZABETH "BETTIE"² MUSS, JOHN¹ MUSS)* was born on September 06, 1913 in Jefferson County, Kentucky and died on October 18, 2008 in New Albany, Floyd County, Indiana. She married ROBERT B. HENDERSON on September 08, 1931 in Jeffersonville, Clark County, Indiana, son of MATT B. HENDERSON and BETSY "BETTIE" FRANCIS J. TRENT.

Children of THELMA PEARL⁴ APPLEGATE and ROBERT B. HENDERSON are:
    i.   NANCY C.⁵ HENDERSON, b. January 05, 1938 in Jefferson County, Kentucky.

86. ALINE⁴ S. APPLEGATE *(LEWIS EDWARD "ED"³ APPLEGATE, ELIZABETH "BETTIE"² MUSS, JOHN¹ MUSS)* was born on August 18, 1917 in Jefferson County, Kentucky and died December 14, 2007 in Louisville, Jefferson County, Kentucky. She married JAMES OSCAR FUNK, believed to be the son of HARRY E. FUNK and MYRTA V. GUNTERMAN. No additional information can be found on her at this time.

87. EDNA MAE⁴ APPLEGATE *(LEWIS EDWARD "ED"³ APPLEGATE, ELIZABETH "BETTIE"² MUSS, JOHN¹ MUSS)* was born on November 19, 1919 in Jefferson County, Kentucky. She married HENRY LEE ARNOLD on July 18, 1938 in Bartholomew County, Indiana, son of SEYMOUR ARNOLD and MARY EMMA WRIGHT. He was born on January 20, 1917 in Bullitt County, Kentucky and died on October 03, 1943 in Jefferson County, Kentucky.

Children of EDNA MAE⁴ APPLEGATE and HENRY LEE ARNOLD are:
    i.   PHILLIP L.⁵ ARNOLD, b. June 22, 1941 in Jefferson County, Kentucky.

88. MARY KATHERINE "KATHERINE"⁴ APPLEGATE *(LEWIS EDWARD "ED"³ APPLEGATE, ELIZABETH "BETTIE"² MUSS, JOHN¹ MUSS)* was born on March 12, 1924 in Bullitt County, Kentucky. She first married JOSEPH "JOE" HEDGES. Katherine later married EDWARD M. ROY on June 05, 1884 in Bullitt County, Kentucky, son of OLIVER MCKINLEY ROY and ROSA ETHEL GODBEY. Edward was born on August 31, 1920 in Casey County, Kentucky and died on October 07, 1991 in Grayson County, Kentucky.

Children of MARY KATHERINE "KATHERINE"[4] APPLEGATE and JOSEPH "JOE" HEDGES are:

    i.   ROBERT L.[5] HEDGES, b. July 12, 1940 in Jefferson County, Kentucky.

    ii.   BETTIE S.[5] HEDGES, b. August 27, 1941 in Bullitt County, Kentucky.

89. LINDA M.[4] APPLEGATE *(LEWIS EDWARD "ED"[3] APPLEGATE, ELIZABETH "BETTIE"[2] MUSS, JOHN[1] MUSS)* was born on February 25, 1926 in Bullitt County, Kentucky. She married ROBERT "BOB" O. DURRETT, son of an unknown father and ALTA MARCUM. No additional information can be found on her at this time.

90. JAMES WESLEY[4] APPLEGATE, JR. *(JAMES WESLEY[3] APPLEGATE, ELIZABETH "BETTIE"[2] MUSS, JOHN[1] MUSS)* was born on April 17, 1927 in Jefferson County, Kentucky. He married FRANCES MENJER, daughter of unkown parents.

Children of JAMES WESLEY[4] APPLEGATE, JR. and FRANCES MENJER are:

    i.   DR. JAMES WESLEY[5] APPLEGATE III, b. December 03, 1953 in Jefferson County, Kentucky; d. November 28, 2000 in Jefferson County, Kentucky; m. JEANNE M. KRENEK on October 14, 1989 in Jefferson County, Kentucky.

91. NORMA A.[4] APPLEGATE *(JAMES WESLEY[3] APPLEGATE, ELIZABETH "BETTIE"[2] MUSS, JOHN[1] MUSS)* was born on February 27, 1934 in Jefferson County, Kentucky. She married WILLIAM H. DOHRMAN, JR., son of WILLIAM H. DOHRMAN, SR. and IRENE MAGEE.

Children of NORMA A.[4] APPLEGATE and WILLIAM H. DOHRMAN, JR. are:

    i.   WILLIAM MARK DOHRMAN, b. August 17, 1959 in Jefferson County, Kentucky; m. MICHELE E. MCCAULEY on November 10, 1989 in Jefferson County, Kentucky.

    ii.   SUSAN ELIZABETH DOHRMAN, b. August 30, 1964 in Jefferson County, Kentucky; m. RICHARD E. WHITE on December 23, 1995 in Jefferson County, Kentucky.

Generation No. 4: Descendants of Joseph P. Muss

It is believed that JOSEPH P. MUSS never had children from his marriage. For this reason, there were no 4th generation descendants of John Muss through the Joseph P. Muss branch of the Muss family tree.

References

Alabama Vital Records. Marriage Certificate for Orville Emmitt "J. R." Carby, Jr. and Betty Hale Milner. Alabama Department of Public Health, Montgomery, AL.

Atkinson, David M. Headstone for Ellen Arlena Cook Corzine. Find a Grave. Roselawn Memorial Park, Section H, Lot 256, Spaces 9 & 10. Terre Haute, IN, 2012. Memorial# 82705498.

Atkinson, David M. Headstone for James Leon Corzine. Find a Grave. Roselawn Memorial Park, Section H, Lot 256, Spaces 9 & 10. Terre Haute, IN, 2012. Memorial# 82639152.

Bailey, Christopher. Headstone for David Calvin Carby. Find a Grave. Zachary Taylor National Cemetery. Louisville, KY, 2011. Memorial# 3296976.

Ballard, Julie. Headstone for James F. Hannephin, Sr. Find a Grave. Saint Louis Cemetery. Louisville, KY, 2012. Memorial# 81276706.

Bellows, Jamie. Headstone for Anna "Annie" Adress Muss Carby. Find a Grave. Inglewood Park Cemetery. Inglewood, CA, 2011. Memorial# 63546118.

Browning, Mark D. Headstone for Alexander Francis Carby and Elnora "Nora" Bell Hunt. White Mills Community Cemetery. White Mills, KY, 2010. Memorial# 59661027 & 59659956.

Browning, Mark D. Headstone for Cola Margaret Muss. Find a Grave. Knob Creek Union Church Cemetery. Cupio, KY, 2010. Memorial# 60541687.

Browning, Mark D. Headstone for Earl B. Muss. Find a Grave. Knob Creek Union Church Cemetery. Cupio, KY, 2010. Memorial# 60122888.

Browning, Mark D. Headstone for James Roy "Roy" Tylings Muss and Daisy E. Foster. Find a Grave. Knob Creek Union Church Cemetery. Cupio, KY, 2010. Memorial# 60066125 & 60066137.

Browning, Mark D. Headstone for John Carroll Muss & Anna "Annie" Eliza Hopewell. Find a Grave. Knob Creek Union Church Cemetery. Cupio, KY, 2010. Memorial# 60065927 & 60065945.

Browning, Mark D. Headstone for John Earl Muss & Sally Annis "Annis" Crabtree. Find a Grave. Knob Creek Union Church

Cemetery. Cupio, KY, 2010. Memorial# 60122418 & 60122577.

Browning, Mark D. Headstone for Orville Emmitt "J R" Carby, Jr. Find a Grave. Fort Rosecrans National Cemetery. San Diego, California, 2010. Memorial# 3391095.

Browning, Mark D. Headstone for Orville Emmitt "J. R." Carby, Jr. Find a Grave. Fort Rosecrans National Cemetery. San Diego, CA, 2010. Memorial# 3391095.

Browning, Mark D. Headstone for Richard "Ricky" Emmitt Carby, Sr. Find a Grave. Fort Rosecrans National Cemetery. San Diego, CA, 2010. Memorial# 3391096.

Browning, Mark D. Headstone for Rita Blanche Mulkins. Find a Grave. Fort Rosecrans National Cemetery. San Diego, CA, 2010. Memorial# 63507681.

Browning, Mark D. Headstone for William Joseph "Joe" Muss and Martha "Mattie" Roberts Vaughn. Find a Grave. Knob Creek Union Church Cemetery. Cupio, KY, 2010. Memorial# 60066028 & 60066003.

Bushman, Kathy. Headstone for Orville Emmitt "Slim" Carby, Sr. Find a Grave. Glen Haven Memorial Park. Sylmar, CA, 2011. Memorial# 63545789.

California Department of Public Health. Death Certificate for Orville Emmitt "J. R." Carby, Jr. Vital Records - MS 5103, Sacramento, CA.

Chicago Daily Tribune. Obituary for Nora E. Muss Stoll. Sunday August 20 Issue. Chicago, IL, 1950. Page B26.

Chicago Tribune. Obituary for Rebecca "Becky" Louise Stoll Sherlock. Wednesday December 21 Issue. Chicago, IL, 1994. Section 2, Page 9, Column 2.

Chico Enterprise-Record. News Story for Richard "Ricky" Emmitt Carby, Sr. Monday September 16 Issue. Chico, CA, 1991. Section A, Pages 1 and 8.

Corydon Democrat. Charles Muss Kills Wife at Louisville. Wednesday, June 24 Issue. Corydon, IN, 1914. Page 7, Column 3.

Daniels, Karen. Headstone for James Foster, Jr. and Martha "Marthy" C. Walls. Find a Grave. Knob Creek Union Church Cemetery. Cupio, KY, 2012. Memorial# 79676064 & 79676453.

Daniels, Karen. Headstone for Samuel Joseph Bryant. Find a Grave. Knob Creek Union Church Cemetery. Cupio, KY, 2012. Memorial# 78522343.

Dayton Daily Journal. Obituary for John Muss. Saturday March 26 - Volume 41, Issue 208. Dayton, OH, 1904. Page 5, Column 1.

Douser. Headstone for Joseph Alexander Hicks & Hettie Griggs Rumsey. Find a Grave. Fairview Cemetery. New Albany, IN, 2011. Memorial# 81322077 & 81520493.

Douser. Headstone for Robert Lee Hicks. Find a Grave. Fairview Cemetery. New Albany, IN, 2011. Memorial# 80077741.

Family History Center. Bullitt County, Kentucky Marriages. The Church of Jesus Christ of Latter-day Saints. Marriage License for Charles Muss and Rebecca Jane Moore. Salt Lake City, UT, 1886. Source Film Number: 482691, Page 34.

Family History Center. Bullitt County, Kentucky Marriages. The Church of Jesus Christ of Latter-day Saints. Marriage License for Samuel Joseph Bryant and Caroline "Carrie" F. Muss. Salt Lake City, UT, 1878. LDS Source Film Number: 482691, Page 233.

Family History Center. Bullitt County, Kentucky Marriages. The Church of Jesus Christ of Latter-day Saints. Marriage License for William Malcolm Cook and Caroline "Carrie" F. Muss. Salt Lake City, UT, 1881. LDS Source Film Number: 482691, Page 192.

Family History Center. Clark County, Indiana Marriages. The Church of Jesus Christ of Latter-day Saints. Marriage License for Charles Muss and Lida C. Flanigan. Salt Lake City, UT, 1913. LDS Source Film Number: 1415920, Page 324, Image 522.

Family History Center. Jefferson County, Kentucky Marriages. The Church of Jesus Christ of Latter-day Saints. Marriage License for Roy Walker Applegate and Zula Cook. Salt Lake City, UT, 1920. Film Number: 2024996, Marriage Book 5, Certificate Number 177.

Family History Center. Jefferson County, Kentucky Marriages. The Church of Jesus Christ of Latter-day Saints. Marriage License for George W. Muss & Ellen "Ella" W. Hannephin. Salt Lake City, UT, 1997. Source Film Number: 813385.

Family History Center. Jefferson County, Kentucky Marriages. The Church of Jesus Christ of Latter-day Saints. Marriage License for James H. Doriot and Mary Emma Muss. Salt Lake City, UT, 1889. Source Film Number: 482716, Page 320.

Family History Center. Jefferson County, Kentucky Marriages. The Church of Jesus Christ of Latter-day Saints. Marriage License for Elizabeth "Bettie" Muss & Charles L. Applegate. Salt Lake City, UT, 1889. Source Film Number: 813388.

Family History Center. Kentucky Marriages, 1785-1979. The Church of Jesus Christ of Latter-day Saints. Marriage License for John Carroll Muss and Anna "Annie" Eliza Hopewell. Salt Lake City, UT, 1785-1979. Film Number: 482691, Page 14.

Family History Center. Kentucky Marriages, 1785-1979. The Church of Jesus Christ of Latter-day Saints. Marriage License for Matthew Hopewell and Sarah A. Foster. Salt Lake City, UT, 1785-1979. Film Number 482690, Book 1A, Page 135.

Family History Center. Kentucky Marriages, 1785-1979. The Church of Jesus Christ of Latter-day Saints. Marriage License for William Joseph "Joe" Muss and Martha "Mattie" Roberts Vaughn. Salt Lake City, UT, 1785-1979. Film Number: 482691, Page 189.

Family History Center. Kentucky Marriages, 1785-1979. The Church of Jesus Christ of Latter-day Saints. Marriage License for Anna "Annie" Address Muss and Orville Emmitt "Slim" Carby, Sr. Salt Lake City, UT, 1785-1979. Film Number: 817765, Page 129.

Family History Center. Marriage Consent for Louis Edward "Ed" Applegate and Lillian "Lillie" May Merker. The Church of Jesus Christ of Latter-day Saints. Jefferson County, Kentucky Marriage Records. Clerk of the County Court. Salt lake City, UT, 1912. Film Number: 827351, Marriage License # 220, Back side of previous license.

Family History Center. Marriage License for Christian Haberman and Gertrude Seas. The Church of Jesus Christ of Latter-day Saints. Ohio, County Marriages, 1790-1950. Salt Lake City, UT, 1853. Film Number: 384239, Reference Number: 136, Image Number: 616.

Family History Center. Marriage License for Louis Edward "Ed" Applegate and Lillian "Lillie" May Merker. The Church of Jesus Christ of Latter-day Saints. Jefferson County, Kentucky Marriage Records. Clerk of the County Court. Salt Lake City, UT, 1912. Film Number: 827351, Marriage License # 220.

Family History Center. Marriage License for Nora E. Muss and Edwin Mallibien Stoll. The Church of Jesus Christ of Latter-day Saints. Jefferson County, Kentucky Marriage Records. Clerk of the County Court. Salt Lake City, UT, 1915. Film Number: 817767, Marriage License #136.

Family History Center. Marriage License for Stella E. Muss and David Frederick Duesing. The Church of Jesus Christ of Latter-day Saints. Clark County, Indiana Marriage Records. Clerk of the Circuit Court. Salt Lake City, UT, 1808-1951. Film Number: 1415878, Set #3, Marriage License #402.

Family History Center. Marriage License for Stella E. Muss Duesing and Joseph Alexander Hicks. The Church of Jesus Christ of Latter-day Saints. Floyd County, Indiana Marriage Records. Clerk of the Circuit Court. Salt Lake City, UT, 1819-1922. Film Number: 1411890, Section 2, Marriage License #304.

Google. Map of Bullitt County, Kentucky. Google Maps. Mountain View, CA, 2011.

Gregorchik, Kira Davis. Headstone for Stephen Edward Hannephin. Find a Grave. Saint Louis Cemetery. Louisville, KY, 2012. Memorial# 77892935.

Heaton, Debra. Headstone for Emory Ellis Briely and Betty Mae Cook. Find a Grave. Fairview Cemetery. Linton, IN, 2011.

Heaton, Debra. Headstone for Jane Ellen Briley. Find a Grave. Fairview Cemetery. Linton, IN, 2011.

Kenny & Julie. Headstone for Harel Lynn Carby, Sr. Find a Grave. Fort Sam Houston National Cemetery. San Antonio, TX, 2011. Memorial# 68183360.

Kentucky Yeoman Office, J.H. Harney. "Report of the adjutant general of the state of Kentucky." Frankfort, KY: public printer, 1866-1867.

Louisville Courier-Journal. Obituary 1 for Elizabeth "Bettie" Muss Applegate. Wednesday January 10 Issue. Louisville, KY, 1945.

Louisville Courier-Journal. Obituary 2 for Elizabeth "Bettie" Muss Applegate. Thursday January 11 Issue. Louisville, KY, 1945.

Louisville Courier-Journal. Obituary for Annabel "Anna" B. Stovall Applegate. Wednesday November 21 Issue. Louisville, KY, 1990. Section B, Page 4, Column 1.

Louisville Courier-Journal. Obituary for Charles Emory "Jack" Applegate. May 19 Issue. Louisville, KY, 1967. Section B, Page 12.

Louisville Courier-Journal. Obituary for Daisy E. Foster Muss. October 9 Issue. Louisville, KY, 1990. Section B, Page 4, Column 6.

Louisville Courier-Journal. Obituary for David Calvin Carby. Sunday June 19 Issue. Louisville, KY, 1949.

Louisville Courier-Journal. Obituary for David P. Doriot. Thursday September 19 Issue. Louisville, KY, 1957.

Louisville Courier-Journal. Obituary for James Wesley Applegate, Sr. Saturday June 23 Issue. Louisville, KY, 1979. Section C, Page 13, Column 2.

Louisville Courier-Journal. Obituary for Lillian "Lillie" May Merker Applegate. Saturday June 24 Issue. Louisville, KY, 1972. Section B, Page 15, Column 1.

Louisville Courier-Journal. Obituary for Martha "Mattie" Roberts Vaughn Jeffers Muss. March 27 Issue. Louisville, KY, 1947. Page 9, Column 8.

Louisville Courier-Journal. Obituary for Roy Walker Applegate. Saturday May 1 Issue. Louisville, KY, 1976. Section B, Page 9, Column 1.

Louisville Courier-Journal. Obituary for Sally Annis "Annis" Crabtree Muss. September 4 Issue. Louisville, KY, 1944. Page 13, Column 5.

Louisville Courier-Journal. Obituary for William Henry Armes, Sr. April 16 Issue. Louisville, KY, 1979. Section D, Page 7, Column 1.

Louisville Courier-Journal. Obituary for Zula Cook Applegate. Monday January 17 Issue. Louisville, KY, 1983. Section B, Page 5, Column 1.

Louisville Courier-Journal. Photos of those who died in the automobile accident. Sunday June 19 Issue. Louisville, KY, 1949. Page 1.

Louisville Courier-Journal. The convertible that was involved in the accident. Sunday June 19 Issue. Louisville, KY, 1949. Page 1.

Louisville Times. Obituary for Ellen "Ella" W. Hannephin Muss. Friday March 27 Issue. Louisville, KY, 1959. Page 13.

Louisville Times. Obituary for George W. Muss. Wednesday May 4 Issue. Louisville, KY, 1921. Page 19, Column 8.

Louisville Times. Obituary for Golda "Goldie" Naomi "Naomi" Muss Armes. Wednesday March 7 Issue. Louisville, KY, 1973. Section C, Page 11.

Louisville Times. Obituary for James Roy "Roy" Tylings Muss. Saturday December 30 Issue. Louisville, KY, 1961. Page 11.

Louisville Times. Obituary for John Earl Muss. Monday July 9 Issue. Louisville, KY, 1956. Page 12, Column 2.

Louisville Times. Obituary for Mary Emma Muss Doriot. Monday October 31 Issue. Louisville, KY, 1932. Page 14, Column 6.

Louisville Times. Obituary for Sarah "Sallie" Elizabeth Muss Snellen. Monday May 7 Issue. Louisville, KY, 1984. Section A, Page 7.

Louisville Times. Obituary for William Joseph "Joe" Muss. Monday August 12 Issue. Louisville, KY, 1974. Section C, Page 9.

Louisville Times. The convertible at the scene of the accident. Saturday June 18 Issue. Louisville, KY, 1949. Page 1.

Luitweiler, Eva. Headstone for William Henry Armes, Sr. and Golda "Goldie" Naomi Muss. Find a Grave. Knob Creek Union Church Cemetery. Cupio, KY, 2011. Memorial# 67598617 & 67598634.

Lyle Raymond Cook & Karla Denise Ezell Cook. William Malcolm Cook and Caroline F. Muss Family Photo Album. n.d.

McClure, Richard Grant. Headstone for Glenn David Muss. Find a Grave. Calvary Cemetery. Louisville, KY, 2012. Memorial# 69455700.

McInturff, David. Headstone for William Nathan Muss. Find a Grave. Arlington National Cemetery, Section 31 Plot 6148. Arlington, VA, 2012. Memorial# 49263184.

Missouri State Archives. Naturalization Record for John Muss. Clerk of the Saint Louis Court of Common Pleas, Saint Louis, MO. Volume R, Page 15, Reel C25813.

Montgomery County Records Center and Archives. "Archived Death Records." Dayton, OII, n.d.

Morris, Jeff. Headstone for Maude A. Mitchell. Find a Grave. Mitchell Hill Cemetery. Fairdale, KY, 2010. Memorial# 53991253.

National Archives and Records Administration. <u>Compiled Service Records of Volunteer Union Soldiers</u>. NARA. Washington, D.C., 1861-1865.

National Archives and Records Administration. <u>Passenger Lists of Vessels Arriving at New Orleans, Louisiana, 1820-1902</u>. NARA. <u>Microfilm publication M259. 93 rolls.</u> Washington, D.C., 1820-1902. Record Group 36.

New Albany Daily Ledger. <u>Obituary for Daniel "Dan" M. Harris</u>. <u>Tuesday, May 24 Issue</u>. New Albany, IN, 1921. Page 1, Column 4.

New Albany Daily Ledger. <u>Obituary for Mattie Harris</u>. <u>Friday, August 12 Issue</u>. New Albany, IN, 1910. Page 4, Column 2.

New Albany Evening Tribune. <u>Decree of Divorce for Daniel "Dan" M. Harris and Lida C. Flanigan</u>. <u>Tuesday, December 10 Issue</u>. New Albany, IN, 1912. Page 4, Column 2.

New Albany Evening Tribune. <u>Obituary for Hettie Rumsey Griggs Hicks</u>. <u>Friday April 14 Issue</u>. New Albany, IN, 1913. Page 4, Column 2.

New Albany Tribune. <u>Divorce for Samuel Holsworth Hicks and Nora V. Turner</u>. <u>Thursday May 19 Issue</u>. New Albany, IN, 1938. Page 1, Column 7.

New Albany Tribune. <u>Obituary 1 for Robert Lee Duesing Hicks</u>. <u>Monday December 12 Issue</u>. New Albany, IN, 1955. Page 3, Column 7.

New Albany Tribune. <u>Obituary 2 for Robert Lee Duesing Hicks</u>. <u>Tuesday December 13 Issue</u>. New Albany, IN, 1955. Page 3, Column 8.

New Albany Tribune. <u>Obituary for Edith May Harris Espin</u>. <u>Wednesday November 11 Issue</u>. New Albany, IN, 1959. Page 2, Column 1.

New Albany Tribune. <u>Obituary for Joseph Alexander Hicks</u>. <u>Monday October 14 Issue</u>. New Albany, IN, 1940. Page 1, Column 4.

New Albany Tribune. <u>Obituary for Stella E. Muss Duesing Hicks McAllister</u>. <u>Thursday January 6 Issue</u>. New Albany, IN, 1955. Page 3, Column 2.

New Albany Tribune. <u>World War II Draft for Robert Lee Duesing Hicks</u>. <u>Monday June 2 Issue</u>. New Albany, IN, 1941. Page 1, Column 7.

New Albany Weekly Ledger. <u>Obituary for Blucher Harris</u>. <u>Wednesday, September 27 Issue</u>. New Albany, IN, 1922. Page 2, Column 3.

New Albany Weekly Ledger. <u>Obituary for Charles Muss</u>. <u>Friday August 7 Issue</u>. New Albany, IN, 1931. Page 7, Column 3.

New Albany Weekly Tribune. Obituary 1 for Nellie Louise Hicks. <u>Friday July 23 Issue</u>. New Albany, IN, 1915. Page 4, Column 2.

North County Times. <u>Obituary for Pamela Blakemore</u>. <u>Friday February 24 Issue</u>. Escondido, CA, 2006.

Pawlik, Peter-Michael. <u>Von der Weser in die Welt; Die Geschichte der Segelschiffe von Weser und Lesum und iher Bauwerften 1770 bis 1893; Schriften des Deutschen Schiffahrtsmuseums, Band 33</u>. Vol. I. Hamburg: Kabel, 1993. III vols.

Public Press. <u>Obituary 2 for Nellie Louise Hicks</u>. <u>Tuesday July 27 Issue</u>. New Albany, IN, Page 4, Section C4.

Public Press. <u>Obituary for Stella Harris</u>. <u>Tuesday August 9 Issue</u>. New Albany, IN, 1910. Page 4, Column 3.

Ransdell, Eden. <u>Headstone for Lida C. Flanigan Harris Muss</u>. Find a Grave. <u>Milltown Cemetery</u>. Milltown, IN, 2010. Memorial# 49452853.

Ravenstein, Ludwig. <u>Atlas des Deutschen Reichs</u>. University of Wisconsin-Madison Libraries. <u>Online edition created in the Digital Production Facility of the University of Wisconsin-Madison Libraries</u>. 1998-1999.

Robinson, Craig. <u>Headstone for Michael Edward Ciresi and Clara Lee Carby Ciresi</u>. Find a Grave. <u>Riverside National Cemetery</u>. Riverside, CA, 2011. Memorial# 492319.

San Fernando Valley Sun. <u>Obituary for Orville Emmitt Carby, Jr.</u> <u>Thursday March 24 Issue</u>. San Fernando, CA, 1960.

Sorah, Jason R. <u>Headstone for John Muss</u>. Find a Grave. <u>Dayton National Cemetery</u>. Dayton, OH, 2011. Memorial# 2572644.

Sörvig, Frederik Martin. <u>Water-colour</u>. Peter-Michael Pawlik. <u>Von der Weser in die Welt; Die Geschichte der Segelschiffe von Weser und Lesum und ihrer Bauwerften 1770 bis 1893: Schriften des Deutschen Schiffahrtsmuseums, Band 33</u>. Hamburg: Kabel, 1862. 271.

Swelnis, Joe. <u>Headstone for Charles L. Applegate & Elizabeth "Bettie" Muss Applegate</u>. Find a Grave. <u>South Jefferson Cemetery</u>. Louisville, KY, 2011. Memorial# 70311500 & 70311474.

Swelnis, Joe. Headstone for Elizabeth "Bettie" Muss Applegate & Charles L Applegate. Find a Grave. South Jefferson Cemetery. Louisville, Kentucky, 2011. Memorial# 70311500 & 70311474.

Terre Haute Star. Obituary for Henry Wayne Cook. Friday September 10 Issue. Terre Haute, IN, 1954. Page 2.

Terre Haute Tribune. Obituary 1 for Ellen Arlena Cook Corzine. Thursday December 29 Issue. Terre Haute, IN, 1960. Page 2.

Terre Haute Tribune. Obituary 2 for Ellen Arlena Cook Corzine. Friday December 30 Issue. Terre Haute, IN, 1960. Page 28.

Terre Haute Tribune. Obituary for Betty Mae Cook Briley. Monday August 19 Issue. Terre Haute, IN, 1968. Page 2.

Terre Haute Tribune. Obituary for Beulah May Withem Cook. Tuesday July 7 Issue. Terre Haute, IN, 1953. Page 2.

Terre Haute Tribune. Obituary for Caroline "Carrie" F. Muss Cook. Tuesday January 5 Issue. Terre Haute, IN, 1937. Page 2.

Terre Haute Tribune. Obituary for George W. Cook. Monday September 13 Issue. Terre Haute, IN, 1965. Page 2.

Terre Haute Tribune. Obituary for Joseph P. Muss. Tuesday July 8 Issue. Terre Haute, IN, 1924. Page 2.

Terre Haute Tribune. Obituary for Myrtle Ruth Corey Cook. Thursday June 15 Issue. Terre Haute, IN, 1967. Page 8.

Terre Haute Tribune. Obituary for Seth Isaac Hart. Tuesday January 25 Issue. Terre Haute, IN, 1955. Page 2.

Terre Haute Tribune. Obituary for William Malcolm Cook. Monday November 11 Issue. Terre Haute, IN, 1940. Page 2.

The Courier-Journal. Coroner's Jury Charges Muss With Wife Murder. Friday June 26 Issue. Louisville, KY, 1914.

The Courier-Journal. Muss Asserts He Is Not Sorry He Killed Wife. Friday June 12 Issue. Louisville, KY, 1914.

The Courier-Journal. Obituary for Rebecca Jane Moore Muss. Thursday December 5 Issue. Louisville, KY, 1910. Page 7, Column 8.

The Daily Report. Obituary for Anna "Annie" Adress Muss Carby. Thursday, June 17 Edition. Ontario, CA, 1976. Page 4.

The Republican. Obituary for Nitis Louise Funk Cook Hart. Saturday May 29 Issue. Danville, IN, Page 8, Column 2.

The Tennessean. Obituary for Donald Edwin Stoll. Tuesday August 8 Issue. Nashville, TN, 2000.

The Tennessean. Obituary for Margaret Jean McCrone Stoll. Monday February 11 Issue. Nashville, TN, 1991.

The Valley News. Obituary for Orville Emmitt "Slim" Carby, Sr. Thursday, January 8 Edition. Temecula, CA, 1970.

U.S. Department of Veterans Affairs. "Dayton National Cemetery." Burial Location Request for John Muss. Washington, DC, n.d.

Glossary

n.d. ....No Date

MNU ....Maiden Name Unknown

SNU...................................Surname Unknown

Name Index

A

Forst
Henry J., *148*
Mary E., *148*

Forsyth
Dr. J. S., *35*

Foster
Charles, *17, 56*
Charles "Charley", *27*
Daisy E., *27, 30, 90, 92, 93, 94, 173*
James Jr., *26, 27, 28, 90, 93, 94*
James Sr., *27, 56*
Sarah A., *23, 26, 27,* 29, *52, 56, 93*
William Theodore, *27, 28, 52*

Francis
Elmer Nelson, *125*

Frasher
Earl K., *191*

Frump
Charles Willard, *125*
Edna Rosella, *125*
George Washington, *125*
Hazel B., *125*
John Charles, *125*
John Ray, *125*
Manola Moyne, *121, 124, 125*
Olive May, *125*

Fuller
W. B., *54*

Funk
Allen, *125*
Alvarado Erwin, *162*
Cassius M., *124*
Charles "Charley" Edgar, *162*
Cora, *125*
Daniel Vorhees, *121, 124*
Eunice, *125*
Harry E., *223*
Ida Jane, *125*
James Oscar, *157, 223*
James Thomas, *162*
John H., *125*
Kearn, *161*

Lewis Royer, *125*
Max L., *125*
Nitis Louise, *40, 121, 122, 123, 124, 125, 127*
Ralph Coy, *124*
Robert A., *162*
Roxana, *39, 158, 161, 162*
Samuel Edward, *162*
Virgil C., *124*
Weeden F., *162*
William Robert, *162*

G

Gailbreath
Mr., *79*

Gardner
Susan "Sue" Lee, *207*

Garey
Ms., *197*

Gatewood
John W., *157*

Gerber
William E. Jr., *176*

Glascoe
Humprey Gilbert "Gilbert", *183*

Glass
Theodore A., *171*
Viola J., *171, 172*

Glossup
Lavirle, *197*

Godbey
Rosa Ethel, *223*

Goldsmith
Bluford "Blue" L., *39*

Gooch
Florence, *27*

Goode
Robert Lee, *182*

Gowen
  Amanda "Manda" E., *79*

Graham
  William "Bill", *185*

Gralow
  Bruce Barr Jr., *204*

Grant
  Annie Mae, *176*

Green
  Ernest J., *104*
  Francis Pauline, *104*
  James Rubin, *104*
  John Dennis, *104*
  John T., *104*

Gregory
  Chester William, *195*
  Margaret "Margie" L., *103, 195, 196*

Griffin
  George, *85*
  Gilbert, *57*

Griffith
  Anna "Annie", *125*
  George Eaton, *176*
  Georgia Lee, *102, 176, 183*

Griggs
  Franklin "Frank" M., *141, 142*
  Hettie Rumsey, *141*

Gross
  Chloe Bell, *176*

Grubbs
  Lucy "Alice" Jane, *79*

Gunterman
  Myrta V., *223*

H

Haase
  Mary Jo, *203*

Mattie May, *58, 61*
Stella, *58, 62*

Harshfield
Cora, *56*
Laura, *155*

Hart
Barbara "Barbary" Lucinda, *123*
Beryl Ray, *126*
Dan Smiley, *126*
David "Davie", *101*
Elizabeth, *126*
Lillian G., *126*
Lorene E., *125*
Luella K., *126*
Mona M., *125*
Seth Isaac, *123, 124, 125, 126, 127*
William A., *123*

Hartman
William Joseph Sr., *205*

Hay
Oscar L., *52*

Heady
Darthula, *39*

Heath
William "Will" F., *156*

Hedges
Bettie S., *224*
Joseph "Joe", *158, 223, 224*
Robert L., *224*

Heggy
Richard "Rick" Homer, *195*

Helt
Joe, *192*

Henderson
Joseph "Joe" T., *100*
Matt B., *223*
Nancy C., *223*
Robert B., *157, 223*
Roy, *101*

Osborne
  Francis "Fannie", *139*

P

Palmer
  Carol M., *197*

Parris
  Lucy Ann, *27*

Patterson
  Kibby Felecia, *216*

Peiffer
  Alfred Melrose, *78*

Phillips
  Ida Nell, *196*

Phipps
  Constance Bernice, *184*

Pinkston
  Samuel "Squire" T., *156*

Pleasant
  John J., *190, 191*

Powers
  William H., *69*

Prather
  James Thomas, *80*

Q

Quick
  Essie Ellen, *47*

Quinn
  Lori, *184*

R

Railey
  Elizabeth, *87*

Ramsey
  Martha "Mattie" E., *162*
  Thomas J., *24, 25, 84, 85*

Ratterman
  G & H, *46*

Rawlings
  Margaret C., *57*

Ray
  Glenn Malcolm, *208*

Raymond
  Nannie Pearl "Pearl", *156*

Reeder
  Inez Leota, *207*

Riera
  William R., *187*

Roberts
  Alan D., *198*
  Boyd Alan, *103, 196, 197, 198*
  Elizabeth, *27*
  Mr., *197*

Robertson
  Gertrude V., *213*

Rochelle
  Thelma Louise, *193*

Roupe
  Dale, *186*

Roy
  Edward M., *158, 223*
  Oliver McKinley, *223*

Royce
  Walter C., *148*

Rumsey
  Hettie Griggs, *141, 147*

Rushall
  Diane Lorraine, *186*

S

Samuels
  Barbara C., *52*
  Jeanette, *28, 52*
  Mary Ann, *93*

Isaac D., *57*
John C., *57*
Korilla J., *57*
Margaret, *57*
Mary B., *156*
Nathan B., *57*
Richard, *56, 57*
William "Will" O., *154*

Slay
James Wesley, *195*

Small
Napoleon B., *27*

Smiley
Edith T., *125, 127*
Payson A., *125*

Smith
Edwin Vivian, *182*
Greg, *196*
William "Bill", *175*

Snaders
Malissa Jane, *85*

Snawder
Clementine, *157*
William "Willie", *157*

Snellen
Jefferson Maynard "Maynard", *104*
John W., *105, 199*
Pleasant, *156*
William M., *30, 104, 105*

Snowden
Mr., *199*
Robin Marie, *199*

Sparks
Sarah C., *27*

Spellman
G. C., *110*

Spencer
Daniel J., *185*
Kevin Anthony, *181*

Nora V., *144, 145*

Tydings
  Amelia S., *57*
  Dr. Richard L., *68*

Tyler
  Eliza "Lucy", *69*

U

Underwood
  Danny Travis, *198*

Utterback
  Corbin Daniel, *80*
  Ella, *80*
  Hezekiah, *80*
  James T., *80*
  John W., *80*
  Laura Anna, *80*
  Nimrod, *80*
  Susan, *76, 78, 79, 80*
  William, *80*

V

Vallandingham
  Garner Yancy, *182*

Vanaisdal
  Sarah Agnes, *39*

Vanhecke
  Amanda L., *176*
  Frank R. Jr., *176*
  Frank R. Sr., *176*
  Jason E., *176*
  Veronica, *176*

Vaughn
  Burk, *83*
  John L., *85*
  John Lewis, *81*
  Joseph "Joe" H., *17*
  Martha "Mattie" Roberts, *25, 30, 81, 82, 83, 84, 85, 86, 171*

Viers
  Sudie M., *30, 87*